THE NEW CULTURAL ATLAS OF

THE ISLAMIC WORLD

Edited by Sally MacEachern

THE NEW CULTURAL ATLAS OF
THE ISLAMIC WORLD

Edited by Sally MacEachern

Marshall Cavendish
Reference
New York

This edition first published in 2010 in the United States of America by Marshall Cavendish.

Marshall Cavendish
99 White Plains Road
Tarrytown, New York 10591-9001

Library of Congress Cataloging-in-Publication Data

Marshall Cavendish Corporation
  The new cultural atlas of the Islamic world.
      p. cm.
  Includes bibliographical references and index.
  ISBN 978-0-7614-7879-9 (alk. paper)
  1. Islamic countries--Civilization--Maps. 2. Islamic countries--History--Maps. 3. Islamic countries--Antiquities--Maps. I. Title.
  G1786.E6M3 2009
  911'.1767--dc22

                                        2009008602

Printed and bound in Singapore

Picture Credits

Front Cover: Corbis: Bruno Ehrs

Corbis: Riza Abbasi 54, Mihr ali 149, Yann Arthus-Bertrand 75, Betmann 152, Christie's Images 74, Michele Falzone 58, Chris Hellier 76, 78, Alir Jarekji, 161, Kazuyoshi Nomachi 52, Kerim Okten 44-45, Dagli Orti 115, Christine Osborne 144, Carl & Ann Purcell 178, Smithsonian Institution 175, The Gallery Collection 133, 162, Li Xiaoguo 102; **Getty Images:** AFP 158, Bridgeman 2, 15, 47, 62, 116, 168, Mike Copeland 130-131, Fred Dufour/AFP 57, Farjana Khan Godhuly/AFP 14-15, Wilfried Krecichwost 80, Harvey Lloyd 84-85, National Geographic 56, Chris Rennie/Robert Harding World Imagery 104, Time Life 63; **Shutterstock:** Ayazad 24-25, 171, Beanda Ahmad Hisham 154-155, javarman 177, Vladimir Melnik 9, 172-173, Luciano Mortula 68, Pascal Rateau 64, Konstantin Shishkin 107; **Topfoto:** Alinari 94, British Library/HIP 30, 72, 113, 123, Image Works 163, Stapleton/HIP 141, The Granger Colection 20-21, 22, 41, 43, 65, Topham 51, 67, World History Archive 176; **Werner Forman:** 34.

Artworks: Brown Reference Group.

For the Brown Reference Group Ltd:
Editorial Director: Lindsey Lowe
Senior Managing Editor: Tim Cooke
Editor: Sally MacEachern
Design Manager: David Poole
Designer: Kim Browne
Picture Manager: Sophie Mortimer
Production Manager: Alastair Gourlay
Indexer: Indexing Specialists (UK) Ltd.

Text adapted from the *Atlas of the Islamic World Since 1500*, revised edition, 1990, Checkmark Books (Facts On File), New York. Original text by Francis Robinson.

Contents

Timeline

	SAFAVID/IRAN	MUGHAL/SOUTH ASIA	OTTOMAN/WEST ASIA AND NORTH AFRICA
1500	1501–10 Shah Ismail conquers Iran and establishes a Shia state 1514 Iran defeated at Chaldiran: loss of Diyarbakir and Iraq 1524–33, 1579–88 Qizilbash tribes in power Uzbegs invade Khurasan ottomans invade Azarbaijan 1588–1629 Iran defeats Uzbegs and Ottomans, recaptures lost territory, and establishes strong central government Finest flowering of Iranian art New capital built at Isfahan *A young man. Safavid, 1630.*	1526 Babur victorious at Panipat and establishes Mughal rule in India 1556–1605 Akbar extends empire throughout northern India Policy of religious tolerance Arts flourish under imperial patronage 1569–85 New capital built at Fatehpur Sikri 1598 Capital moved to Agra *Taj Mahal. Mughal, 1648.*	1500–70 empire expands to east and south: Azarbaijan (1514), Syria and Palestine (1516), Egypt (1517); Hijaz, Yemen and Iraq by 1534 1520–66 Sulaiman the Magnificent advances into Europe: Belgrade (1521), Mohacs (1526), Vienna (1529), Greece (1 540s); and North Africa to Morocco (1551) and Malta (1565) 1571 defeated at Lepanto Arts flourish, especially ceramics and architecture Lznik pottery: 1490——15 blue and white; 1525–50 Damascus and Golden Hor ware; 1550–1700 Rhodian ware 1491–1588 Sinan, architect of Shehzade (1544–48), Sulaimaniye (1550–57) and Selimiye (1569–75) mosques *Sulaiman the Magnificent, 1520-66.*
1600	Weakening of the dynasty and its religious legitimacy	1624 Death of Sirhindi 1632–54 Taj Mahal built at Agra by Shah Jahan 1638– New capital built at Delhi (Shahjahanabad) 1658–1707 Awrangzeb captures Bijapur (1686) and Golkonda (1687): empire now at greatest extent, but arts cease to flourish and Marathas establish state in the Deccan	Crete taken (1669), Ukraine (1670s), Vienna attacked (1683) 1699 Ottomans surrender Hungary, Transylvania and Podolia
1700	1722 Mahmud of Qandahar takes Isfahan and destroys the empire 1736–48 Nadir Shah reestablishes Safavid rule and 1739 sacks Delhi Return to tribal rule after his death.	Weakening of Muslim power in primarily Hindu environment 1761 Delhi sacked by Ahmad Abdali of Afghanistan By 1800 Marathas rule subcontinent from Rajasthan to the Deccan, Sikhs contiol Punjab, and Gangetic plain in British hands	Weakening of central authority 1718 Ottomans surrender Serbia and Wallachia but regained in Austrian war of 1735–39 1740 Muhammad al-Wahhab campaigns for renewal in Arabia 1774–1812 Loss of Black Sea north coast. Crimea and Bessarabia to Russia 1798 French invade Egypt
1800	Continual pressure from Britain and Russia Growth of Western education	1803 Delhi falls to British Mujahidin and Faraizi movements preach reform 1818 British rule established throughout India 1857 Indian Mutiny: holy war declared against British 1877 Aligarh College founded to offer Western education	1802–05 Wahhabi revolt in Iraq, Syria and Arabia 1818 Muhammad Ali of Egypt checks Wahhabis and restores sultan Wahhabis retain influence in Arabia 1830 French invade Algeria; 1881 Tunisia 1869 Suez Canal opened 1882 British occupy Egypt ottomans move towards Western-style secular governmen
1900	1908 Anglo–Iranian Oil Company strikes oil 1921 Compulsory state education introduced 1935 University of Teheran founded Gradual Europeanization and secularization of society 1953 Western-led coup deposes Musaddeq 1978–79 Revolution led by Ayatullah Khomeini establishes an Islamic republic	1906 All-India Muslim League founded 1947 Formation of Muslim state of Pakistan; Indian independence 1971 Pakistani civil war ends in secession of Bangladesh	1908 Young Turks come to power By 1920 Ottomans confined to Anatolia 1920 French given mandates for Lebanon and Syria; British for Iraq, Transjordan and Palestine 1922 Ataturk expels Greeks 1923 sultanate abolished; 1924 caliphate abolished; European-style rule imposed 1925 Abd al-Aziz Ibn Saud conquers Hijaz and 1938 founds Saudi Arabia 1951 Libya independent under King Idris 1956 Tunisia independent under President Bourguiba Nasser nationalizes Suez Canal 1962 Algeria independent under President Ben Bella 1981 President Sadat assassinated

AFRICA	SOUTHEAST ASIA	CENTRAL ASIA AND CHINA
ew empires in Morocco and Niger Basin 506–43 Ahmad Gran challenges Christian Ethiopia n Upper Egypt Muslim Arabs conquer Nubia Iid-16th century-18th century Muslim sultanate of the Funj 570–1619 King Idris Aloma makes Kanem-Bornu a power in the central Sahara onghai empire of Gao weakened by antipathy between Muslims and followers of traditional religions Iorocco: strongly Islamic but weakened by succession struggles; cultural life dominated by maraboutic sufis	Muslim sultanates replace Hindu regimes in Sumatra and Java	Uzbegs threaten to dominate from Bukhara Muslim strength declines as trade along the Old Silk route falls into European hands Tatar khanates on the Asian border with Europe subdued by Russia
Friday mosque at Mopti, Mali	*Javanese dancer.*	*Yomud prayer rug (detail).*
680 First Fulani war culminates in establishment of Islamic state in Bondu	1608–37 Sultan Iskander Muda makes Aceb a focus for trade in the southern seas; also center of scholarship in SE Asia 1613–46 Sultan Agung controls almost all Java from Mataram Islamization indicated by spread of Malay language, stylization of batik patterns and greater modesty of women's dance 1631–70 Hasan al-Din extends Macassar empire, yielding to the Dutch in 1667 1641 Dutch conquer Malacca	1644 Manchu dynasty alienates Chinese Muslims Decline in arts except coinage and carpet weaving
Niger states lost to heathen Bambara Fulani extend Islamic influence in west 725 Second Fulani war establishes Muslim dynasty in Futa Jallon 776 Third Fulani war establishes Islam in Futa Toro	By 1800 Islamic sultanates on Java and Sumatra lose power to Dutch	Nomads subdued by Russian advance Attempt to assimilate Chinese Muslims to Confucianism 1758–60 China dominates Tarim Basin
Khalwatiya and Idrisiya lead reformist movements 1804 Usuman dan Fodio, supported by Fulani and Hausa, forms sultanate of Sokoto 1863–93 Tijani empire from Niger to Senegal 885–98 Mahdist state established in Sudan	803–37 Padri movement extends Islamic influence in Sumatra 1825–30 Reformist movement in Java boosts Islamization 1873–1910 Aceh war opposes Dutch expansion in north Sumatra Dutch authority now complete throughout archipelago	Naqshbandi sufis wage holy war against Russia and Chinese Manchus and preach reform "New Sect" encourages Muslim revival throughout China Russia imposes direct rule on Central Asia
900 Britain colonizes Nigeria (inc. Sokoto) 1912 French capture Morocco and the Sahara 1912 Italy conquers Libya European rule stimulates growth of Muslim institutions 1956 Morocco independent	1912 Formation of Islamic league 1938 Formation of Portal Islam Indonesia 1942–45 Japanese occupation strengthens Islam 1949 Indonesia independent	1917 Russian Revolution brings cultural disaster to Muslims

Introduction

The rise of Islam and the interaction of Muslims with other peoples of the Earth over the past 14 centuries is one of the great stories of world history. The purpose for life established by Islam is one of the main ways humans have given meaning to existence. These facts alone mean that Islam should command our attention. Today one-fifth of the world's population are Muslims who live almost entirely in its developing regions; the growing political and economic interdependence of global life means that movements amongthem have increasing repercussions on the world beyond. It is important, as never before,that the dynamics of Muslim history and the values of Muslim peoples should be widely comprehended.

One purpose of this Atlas is to provide a historical framework for today's Muslim world. It is particularly concerned to demonstrate how Islamic society has been maintained, how it has been transmitted from generation to generation, and how it has been spread throughout the world.

A second purpose has been to introduce the reader to the lives which Muslims live. Wherever possible, Muslims have spoken for themselves, so we hear how they call on God, or dream of the pleasures of the pilgrimage, or assert their way forward as against that of the West. Part Three, in particular, examines aspects of religious life, the artistic expressions of Islamic values, and the various types of Muslim society and their interactions with the modern world. Taking all parts together, readers should be able to acquire a clear idea of what Muslims believe and the manifold ways in which their faith molds their lives.

A third purpose has been to provide a basis for a broader vision of the islamic world. Established understandings of Islam have been to some considerable extent formed by the experience of the central Islamic lands. This book sets out to present in addition the often very different experience of the further Islamic lands, in southeast Asia, in Africa, and in Central Asia and China, where Islam has faced powerful cultures, sometimes on a less than equal footing. These parts of the Muslim world, where almost as many Muslims live as in the central Islamic lands, are relatively little studied. Knowledge of them adds both to our appreciation of the Muslim achievement and to our understanding of the many ways there are of being Muslim.

RULERS OF THE ISLAMIC WORLD

MOROCCO
Saadians
1511 Muhammad al-Mahdi (in Sus)
1517 Ahmad al-Araj (in Marrakesh till 1540)
1517 Muhammad al-Shaikh al-Mahdi (at first in Sus, later in Fez)
1557 Abd Allah al-Ghalib
1574 Muhammad al-Mutawakkil al-Maslukh
1576 Abdal-Malik
1578 Ahmad al-Mansur
1603–08 Muhammad al-Shaikh al-Mamun
1603–08 Abd Allah al-Wathiq (in Marrakesh)
1603–28 Zaidan an-Nasir (at first in Fez only)
sons of Ahmad in rivalry for the succession
1623 Abdal-Malik
1631 al-Walid
1636 Muhammad al-Asghar
1654–59 Ahmad'al-Abbas
in Marrakesh only

Filalis
1631 Muhammad I al-Sharif (in Tafilalt)
1635 Muhammad II
1664 al-Rashid
1672 Ismail al-Samin
1727 Ahmad al-Dhahabi
1729 Abd Allah (1735–45 power contested by various usurpers and pretenders)
1757 Muhammad III
1790 Yazid
1792 Hisham
1793 Sulaiman
1822 Abd al-Rahman
1859 Muhammad IV
1873 al-Hasanl
1895 Abdal-Aziz
1907 al-Hafiz
1912 Yusuf
1927 Muhammad V (first reign)
1953 Muhammad
1955 Muhammad V (second reign)
1962 al-Hasan II
1999 Muhammad VI

NIGERIA
Sokoto caliphate
1754 Usuman dan Fodio
1817 Muhammad Bello
1837 AbuBakrAtiku
1842 Ali
1859 Ahmad
1866 Ali
1867 Ahmad Rufai
1873 AbuBakr

1877 Muadh
1881 Umar
1891 Abd al-Rahman
1902 Muhammad Attahiru I
1903 Muhammad Attahiru II
1915 Muhammad Maiturare
1924 Muhammad
1931 Hassan
1938 AbuBakr

EGYPT
Muhammad Ali's line
1805 Muhammad Ali Pasha
1848 Ibrahim Pasha
1848 Abbas I Pasha
1854 Said Pasha
1863 Ismail (khedive from 1867)
1879 Tawfiq
1892 Abbas II Hilmi
1914 Husain Kamil (sultan)
1917 Ahmad Fuad I (king from 1922)
1936 Faruq
1952 Fuad II
1953 republic

Presidents
1953-54 Neguib
1956 Nasser
1970 Sadat
1981 Mubarak

OTTOMAN EMPIRE
Ottomans
1481 Bayazid I
1512 Selim I Yaviz ("the Grim")
1520 Sulaiman II Qanuni ("thelaw giver" or "the Magnificent")
1566 Selim II
1574 Murad lll
1594 Muhammad III
1603 Ahmad I
1617 Mustafa I (first reign)
1618 Uthman II
1622 Mustafa I (second reign)
1623 Murad IV 1640 Ibrahim
1648 Muhammad IV
1687 Sulaiman III
1691 Ahmad II
1695 Mustafa II
1703 Ahmad III
1730 Mahmud I
1754 Uthmanlll
1757 Mustafa III
1774 Abd al-Hamid I
1789 Selim III
1807 Mustafa IV
1808 Mahmud II
1839 Abd al-Majid I
1861 Abdal-al-Aziz
1876 Murad V
1876 Abd al-Hamid II
1909 Muhammad V Rashad

1918 Muhammad VI Wahid al-Din
1922-24 Abd al-Majid II (as caliph only)

TURKEY
1923 Mustafa Kemal (Ataturk)
1938 Ismet Inonu
1950 Celal Bayar
1961 General Gursel
1966 Senator Cevdet Sunay
1973 Senator Fahri Koroturk
1980 General Kenan Evren
1989 Turgut Özal
1993 Süleyman Demirel
2000 Ahmet Necdet Sezer

LEBANON
1920 French mandate
1926 republic

Presidents
1926 Charles Dabbas
1934 Habib Saad
1936 Emile Edde
1941 independent
1941 Alfred Naccache
1943 al-Khuri
1952 Camille Chamoun
1958 FaudChehab
1964 Charles Helou
1970 Sulaiman Franjiya
1976 Elias Sarkis
1982 Amin Gemayel
1989 René Moawad
      Elias Hrawi
1998 Émile Lahoud

SYRIA
1918 Faisal (son of Amir Husain) heads autonomous government in Damascus
1920 French mandate
1941 independent
1943 republic

Presidents
1943 Shukri al-Quwatli
1949 Hashim al-Atassi
1951 General Fawzi Selo
1953-54 General Shishakli
1955 Shukri al-Quwatli
1958 Nasser (United Arab Republic)
1961 NazimQudsi
1963 Major General Amin al-Hafiz
1966 Nural-Din Atassi
1970 Ahmad Khatib
1971 Hafez al-Assad
2000 Bashar al-Assad

HIJAZ
Hashimites
1908 Amir Husain (sharif of Mecca)

1916 takes the title of king
1924 Ali
1925 Hijaz conquered by Saudis

TRANSJORDAN
1920 British mandate

Hashimites
1921 Amir Abd Allah
1946 Abd Allah takes the title of king (of
Jordan from 1949)
1951 Talal
1952 Husain
1999 Abd Allah II

IRAQ
1920 British mandate

Hashimites
1921 Faisal I Ibn Husain
1933 Ghazi
1939 Faisal II
1958 republic

Presidents
1958 Major General Najib al-Rubai
1963 Field Marshal Abd al-Salam
Muhammad Arif
1966 Lt-General Abd al-Rahman
Muhammad Arif
1968 Major General Ahmad Hassan Bakr
1979 Saddam Husain al-Takriti
2003 U.S.-led occupation

YEMEN
Zaidi imams: Qasimid line
c.1592 al-Qasim al-Mansur
1620 Muhammad al-Muayyad I
1654 Ismail al-Mutawakkil
1676 Muhammad al-Muayyad II
1681 Muhammad al-Hadi
1686 Muhammad al-Mahdi
1716 al-Qasim al-Mutawakkil
1726 al-Husain al-Mansur (first reign)
1726 Muhammad al-Hadi al-Majid (?)
1728 al-Husain al-Mansur (second reign)
1747 al-Abbas al-Mahdi (?)
c.1776 Ali al-Mansur
1806 Ahmad al-Mahdi (?)
? Ali al-Mansur (second
reign ?)
1841 al-Qasim al-Mahdi
1845 Muhammad Yahya
1872 Ottoman occupation
1890 Hamid al-Din Yahya
1904 Yahya Mahmud al-Mutawakkil
1948 Saif al-Islam Ahmad
1962 Muhammad Badr
1962 republic

Presidents
1962 Colonel Abd Allah Sallal
1968 Abd al-Rahman al-Iriani
1974 constitution suspended
1977 Lt-Col Ahmad Ibn Husain al-Ghashmi
1978 Lt-Col Ali Abd Allah Saleh

1980 Ali Nasser Muhammad
1986 Haidar Abu Bakr al-Attas
1990 Ali Abd Allah Saleh

ARABIA
Saudis
1746 Muhammad b.Saud
1765 Abd al-Aziz
1803 Saud b. Abd al-Aziz
1814 Abd Allah I b. Saud
1818-22 Ottoman occupation
1823 Turki
1834 Faisal I (first reign)
1837 Khalid b. Saud
1841 Abd Allah II (as a vassal of
Muhammad Ali of Egypt)
1843 Faisal I (second reign)
1865 Abd Allah III b. Faisal (first reign)
1871 Saud b. Faisal
1874 Abd Allah III (second reign)
1887 conquest by Rashidis of Hail, Abd Allah
remains as governor of Riyadh til 1889
1889 Abd al-Rahman b. Faisal, vassal
governor
1891 Muhammad b. Faisal, vassal governor
1902 Abd al-Aziz II
1953 Saud
1964 Faisal II
1975 Khalid
1982 Fahd
2005 Abd Allah

OMAN AND ZANZIBAR
United Sultanate
1741 Ahmad b. Said
1783 Said b. Ahmad
?1786 Hamid b. Said
1792 Sultan b. Ahmad
1806 Salim b. Sultan
1806 Said b. Sultan (division of the sultanate
on Said's death)
Zanzibar
1856 Majid b. Said
1870 Barghash b. Said
1888 Khalifa b. Barghash
1890 Ali b. Said
1893 Hamid
1896 Hammud
1902 Ali b. Hammud
1911 Khalifa
1960 Abd Allah b. Khalifa
1963 Jamshid
1964 revolution and incorporation in the
Republic of Tanzania
Oman
1856 Thuwaini b. Said
1866 Satim b. Thuwaini
1868 Azzan b. Qais
1870 Turki b. Said
1888 Faisal b. Turki
1913 Taimur b. Faisal
1932 Said b. Taimur
1970 Qabus b. Said

IRAN
Safavids
1501 Ismail I
1524 Tahmasp I
1576 Ismail II
1578 Muhammad Khudabanda
1588 Abbas I
1629 Safil
1642 Abbas II
1666 Sulaiman I (Safi II)
1694 Sultan Husain I
1722 Tahmasp II
1732 Abbas III
1749 Sulaiman II
1750 Ismail III
1753 Husain II
1786 Muhammad
nominal rulers

Afsharids
1736 Nadir Shah
1747 Adil Shah
1748 Ibrahim
1748-95 Shah Rukh (in Khurasan)

Zands
1750 Muhammad Karim Khan
1779 Abul Fath
Muhammad Ali
conjointly
1779-81 Sadiq (in Shiraz)
1779-85 Ali Murad {in Isfahan)
1785 Jafar
1789-94 Lutf Ali

Qajars
1779 Agha Muhammad
1797 Fath Ali Shah
1834 Muhammad
1848 Nasir al-Din
1896 Muzaffar al-Din
1907 Muhammad Ali
1909-24 Ahmad

Pahlavis
1925 Riza Shah
1941 Muhammad Riza Shah
1979 Islamic republic

Presidents
1980 Abol Hassan Bani-Sadr
1981 Hojjatolislam Sayad Ali Khamenei
1989 Akbar Hashemi Rafsanjani
1997 Muhammad Khatami
2005 Mahmoud Ahmadinejad

INDIA
Mughal Emperors
1526 Babur
1530 Humayun (first reign)
1540-55 Suri sultans of Delhi
1555 Humayun (second reign)
1556 Akbarl I
1605 Jahangir
1627 DawarBaksh
1628 Shah Jahan I

1657 Murad Bakhsh (in Gujarat)
1657 Shah Shuja (in Bengal till 1660)
1658 Awrangzeb Alamgir I
1707 Azam Shah
1707 Kam Bakhsh (in the Deccan)
1707 Shah Alam I
1712 Azim al-Shan
1712 Muiz al-Din Jahandar
1713 Farrukh-siyar
1719 Shams al-Din Rafi al-Darajat
1719 Rafi al-Dawla Shah Jahan II
1719 Niku-siyar
1719 Nasir al-Din Muhammad
1748 Ahmad Shah Bahadur
1754 Aziz al-Din Alamgir II
1760 Shah Jahan III
1760 Shah Alam II (first reign)
1788 Bidar-bakht
1788 Shah Alam II (second reign)
1806 Muin al-Din Akbar II
1837 Siraj al-Din Bahadur Shah II
1858 under British crown
1947 dominion

Governors-general
1947 Earl Mountbatten of Burma
1948 Chakravarti Rajagopalachari
1950 republic

Presidents
1950 Rajendra Prasad
1962 Savepalli Radhakrishnan
1967 ZakirHusain
1969 Varanagrii Venkata Giri
1974 Fakhruddin Ali Ahmed
1977 Neelam Sanjiva Reddy
1982 Giani Zail Singh
1987 Ramaswamy Venkataraman
1992 Shankar Dayal Sharma
1997 Kocheril Raman Narayan
2002 A.P.J. Abdul Kalam
2007 Pratibha Patil

PAKISTAN
Governors-general
1947 Muhammad Ali Jinnah
1948 Khwaja Nazimuddin
1951 Ghulam Muhammad
1955 Major General Iskander Mirza
1956 Islamic republic

Presidents
1956 Major General Iskander Mirza
1958 Field Marshal Ayub Khan
1969 Major General Yahya Khan
1971 Zulfiqar Ali Bhutto
1973 Fazl Elahi Chaudhry
1978 General Zia ul-Haq
1988 Ghulam Ishaq Khan
1993 Farooq Leghari
1998 Muhammad Rafiq Tarar
2001 Pervez Musharraf
2008 Asif Ali Zardari

BANGLADESH
1971 republic

Presidents
1972 Abu Sayeed Chowdhury
1973 Mohammadullah
1975 Shaikh Mujibur Rahman
1975 Mushtaq Ahmad
1975 Abusadat Muhammad Sayem
1977 Major General Ziaur Rahman
1981 Abdus Sattar
1982 General Muhammad Hossain Ershad
1983 Hossain Mohammad Ershad
1990 Shahabuddin Ahmed
1991 Abdur Rhaman Biswas
1996 Shahabuddin Ahmed
2001 Badruddoza Chowdhury
2002 Jamiruddin Sircar
2002 Iajuddin Ahmed

AFGHANISTAN
Durranis
1747 Ahmad Shah Durrani
1773 Timur Shah
1793 Zaman Shah
1800 Mahmud Shah (first reign)
1803 Shah Shuja (first reign in
     Kabul, from 1800 ruler in
     Peshawar)
1809 Mahmud (second reign in
     Kabul till 1818, in Herat till
     1829)
1818 Ali Shah
1839 Shuja (second reign)
1842 Fath Jang

Barakzais
1819 Dost Muhammad
1863 Shir Ali (first reign)
1866 Afzal
1867 Shir Ali (second reign)
1879 Muhammad Yaqub Khan
1880 Abd al-Rahman Khan
1901 Habib Allah
1919 Aman Allah (Amanullah)
1929 Nadir Shah
1933 Muhammad Zahir Shah
1973 republic

Presidents (selected)
1973 Sardar Muhammad Daud
1978 Nur Muhammad Taraqqi
1979 Hafiz Allah Amin
1979 Babrak Karmal
1987 Mohammad Najibullah
1992 Burhanuddin Rabbani
1996 Mohammed Omar
2001 Hamid Karzai

THE CRIMEA
Girai Khans
1478 Mengli (third reign)
1514 Muhammad I
1523 Ghazi I
1524 Saadat I

1532 Islam I
1532 Sahib I
1551 Dawlat I
1577 Muhammad II
1584 Islam II
1588 Ghazi II (first reign)
1596 Fath I
1606 Ghazi II (second reign)
1608 Toqtamish
1608 Salamat I
1610 Muhammad III (first reign)
1610 Janbeg (first reign)
1623 Muhammad III (second reign)
1627 Janbeg (second reign)
1635 Inayat
1637 Bahadur I
1641 Muhammad IV (first reign)
1644 Islam III
1654 Muhammad IV (second reign)
1666 Adil
1671 Selim I (first reign)
1678 Murad
1683 Hajji II
1684 Selim I (second reign)
1691 Saadat II
1691 Safa
1692 Selim I (third reign)
1699 Dawlat II (first reign)
1702 Selim I (fourth reign)
1704 Ghazi III
1707 Qaplan I (first reign)
1708 Dawlat II (second reign)
1713 Qaplan I (second reign)
1716 Dawlat III
1717 Saadat III
1724 Mengli II (first reign)
1730 Qaplan I (third reign)
1736 Fath II
1737 Mengli II (second reign)
1740 Salamat II
1743 Selim II
1748 Arslan (first reign)
1756 Halim
1758 Qirim (first reign)
1764 Selim III (first reign)
1767 Arslan (second reign)
1767 Maqsud (first reign)
1768 Qirim (second reign)
1769 Dawlat IV (first reign)
1770 Qaplan II
1770 Selim III (second reign)
1771 Maqsud (second reign)
1772 Sahib II
1775 Dawlat IV (second reign)
1777 Shahin (first reign)
1783 Russian annexation of the Crimea
1784 Bahadur II
1785 Shahin (second reign)
as Russian vassals

CENTRAL ASIA
Samarqand (Shaibanids)
1500 Muhammad Shaibani
1510 Kochkunji
1530 Abu Said
1533 Ubaid Allah

1539 Abd Allah I
1540 Abdal-Latif
1551 Nuruz Ahmad
1555 Pir Muhammad I
1560 Iskandar

Bukhara (Shaibanids)
1583 Abd Allah II
1598 Abd al Mumin
1599 Pir Muhammad II

(Janids)
1599 Baqi Muhammad
1605 Wali Muhammad
1608 Imam Quli
1640 Nazir Muhammad
1647 Abd al-Aziz
1680 Subhan Quli
1702 Ubaid Allah
1705 Abul Faiz
1747 Abd al-Mumin
1751 Ubaid Allah II
1753 Muhammad Rahim
       (Mangit)
1758 Abul Ghazi

(Mangits)
1785 Mir Masum Shah Murad
1800 Haidar Tora
1826 Husain
1826 Umar
1827 Nasr-Allah
1860 Muzaffar al-Din
1868 Russian protectorate

Khiva
c. 1515 Ilbars I
c. 1525 Sultan Hajji
       Hasan Quli
       Sufyan
       Bujugha
       Avanak
       Kal
c. 1540 Akatai
1546 Dost
1558 Hajji Muhammad I
1602 Arab Muhammad I
1623 Isfandiyar
1643 Abul Ghazi I
1663 Anusha
c.1674 Muhammad Arank
1687 Ishaq Aqa Shah Niyaz
1702 Arab Muhammad II
       Hajji Muhammad II
1714 Yadighar
1714 Arank
1715 Shir Ghazi
c. 1730 Ilbars II
1740 annexation by Nadir Shah
1741 Tagir, Persian governor
1741 Abu Muhammad
1741 Abul Ghazi II
1745 Kaip
c. 1770 Abul Ghazi III
1804 Iltazar
1806 Muhammad Rahim

1825 Allah Quli
1842 Rahim Quli
1845 Muhammad Amin
1855 Abd Allah
1855 Qutlugh Muhammad
?1856 Saiyid Muhammad
1865 Saiyid Muhammad Rahim
1873 Russian protectorate

Khokand
c. 1700 Shah Rukh Beg
       Rahim
       Abd al-Qarim
       Erdeni
1770 Sulaiman
1770 Shah Rukh II
?1770 Narbuta
1800 Alim
1809 Muhammad Umar
1822 Muhammad Ali
1840 Shir Ali
1841 Murad
1845 Khudayar (first reign)
1857 Malla
1859 Shah Murad
1861 Khudayar (second reign)
1864 Saiyid Sultan
1871 Khudayar (third reign)
1875 Nasir al-Din
1876 annexed by Russia

INDONESIA
Sultans of Mataram
1575 Mas Ngabehi Suta Wijaya
       (Senapati)
1601 Panembahan Seda Krapyak
       (Raden Jolang)
1613 Sultan Agung (Mas Rangsang)
1649 Mangkurat I (Seda Tegal Arum)
1677 Mangkurat II (Kartasura)
1703 Mangkurat III
1708 Pakubuwana I (Puger)
1719 Mangkurat IV (Jawa)
1727 Pakubuwana II (Kombul)
1749 Pakabuwana III (Swarga)

Surakarta
1788 Pakubuwana IV (Bagus)
1820 Pakubuwana V (Sugih)
1823 Pakubuwana VI (Bangun)
1830 Pakubuwana VII (Purbaya)
1858 Pakubuwana VIII (Angabehi)
1861 Pakubuwana IX (Bangun Kadaton)
1893 Pakubuwana X (Wicaksana)
1939 PukubuwanaXI
1944 Pakabuwana XII

Jogjakarta
1755 Mangkubuwana 1 (Swarga)
1792-1810 Mangkubuwana II (Sepuh) (first
       reign)
1810-11 Mangkubuwana III (Raja) (first reign)
1811-12 Mangkubuwana II (second reign)
1812-14 Mangkubuwana III (second reign)
1814-22 Mangkubuwana IV (Seda Pesiyar)
1822-26 Mangkubuwana V (Menol) (first

reign)
1826-28 Mangkubuwana II
       (third reign)
1828-55 Mangkubuwana V
       (second reign)
1855 Mangkubuwana VI
1877 Mangkubuwana VII
       (Angabehi)
1921 Mangkubuwana VIII
1939 Mangkubuwana IX

Aceh
1496 Ali Maghayat Shah
1528 Salah al-Din Ibn Ali
1537 Ala al-Din al-Zahar Ibn Ali
1568 Husain
1575 Sultan Muda
1575 Sultan Sri Alam
1576 ZainalAbidin
1577 Ala al-Din of Perak
       (Mansur Shah)
?1589 Sultan Boyong
1596 Ala al-Din Riayat Shah
1604 Ali Riayat Shah
1607 Iskandar Muda (Meukuta Alam)
1636 Iskandar Thani
1641 Safiyat al-Din Taj al-Alam bint Iskandar
       Muda
1675 Naqiyat al-Din Nur al-Alam
1678 Zaqiyat al-Din Inayat Shah
1688 Kamalat Shah Zinat al-Din
1699 Badr al-Alam Sharif Haslim Jamal al-
       Din
1702 Perkara Alam Sharif Lamtui
1703 Jamal al-Alam Badr al-Munir
1726 Jauhan al-Alam Amir al-Din
1726 Shams al-Alam
1727 Ala al-Din Ahmad Shah
1735 Ala al-Din Johan Shah
1760 Mahmud Shah (first reign)
1764 Badr al-Din Johan Shah
1765 Mahmud Shah (second reign)
1773 Sulaiman Shah (Udahna Lela)
1773 Mahmud Shah (third reign)
1781 Ala al-Din Muhammad Shah
1795 Ala al-Din Jauhar al-Alam
       (1815-23 contested by Sharif Saif al-
       Alam)
1823 Muhammad Shah
1838 Sulaiman (1850-57 contested by Ali Ala
       al-Din Mansur Shah)
1857 Ali Ala al-Din Mansur Shah (Ibrahim)
1870 Mahmud Shah
1874 Muhammad Daud Shah
1874 Dutch occupation
1945-49 War of independence
1949 republic

Presidents
1950 Muhammad Ahmad Sukarno
1966 Presidium
1968 General Suharto
1998 Jusuf Habibe
1999 Abdurrahman Wahid
2001 Megawari Sukarnoputri
2004 Susilo Bambang Yudhoyono

16

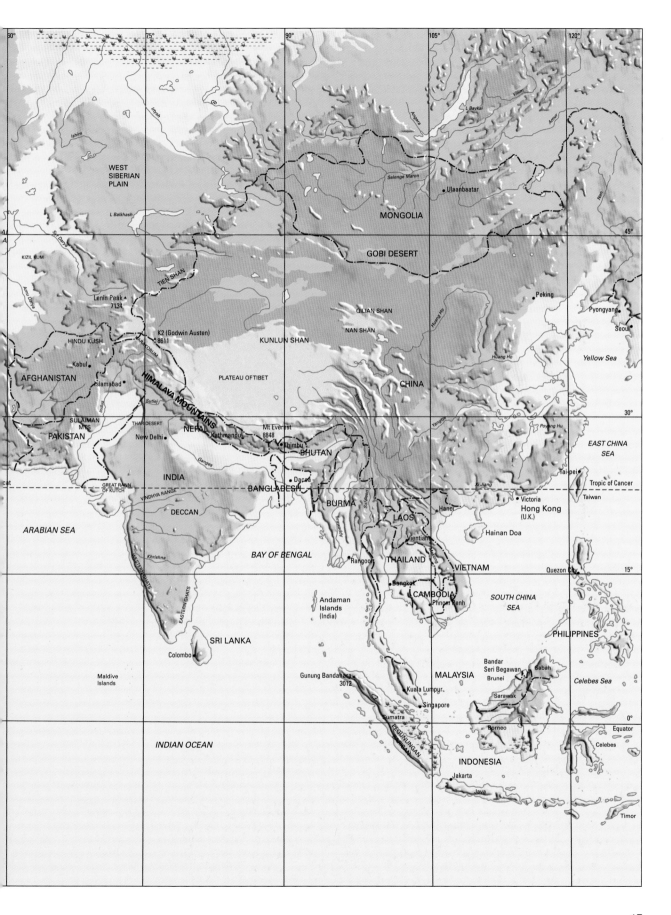

WEST SIBERIAN PLAIN

Ob

Ishim

L Balkhash

Syr Darya

KIZIL KUM

Amu Darya

TIEN SHAN

Lenin Peak ▲ 7134

HINDU KUSH

KARAKORUM

K2 (Godwin Austen) 8611

Kabul •

Islamabad •

AFGHANISTAN

SULAIMAN MTS

PAKISTAN

Indus

HIMALAYA MOUNTAINS

Sutlej

THAR DESERT

New Delhi •

Ganges

GREAT RANN OF KUTCH

cat

VINDHYA RANGE

INDIA

DECCAN

Khrishna

WESTERN GHATS

EASTERN GHATS

ARABIAN SEA

Maldive Islands

Colombo •

SRI LANKA

INDIAN OCEAN

Irtysh

Angara

L Baykal

Vilim

Amur

Selenge Maron

• Ulaanbaatar

MONGOLIA

GOBI DESERT

QILIAN SHAN

NAN SHAN

Huang Ho

KUNLUN SHAN

PLATEAU OF TIBET

Huang Ho

Mekong

Yangtze

CHINA

Nen

• Peking

Pyongyang •

Seoul •

Yellow Sea

Poyang Hu

EAST CHINA SEA

Ki Jiang

Tai-pei

Tropic of Cancer

Taiwan

NEPAL

Kathmandu

Mt Everest 8848

• Thimbu

BHUTAN

• Dacca

BANGLADESH

BURMA

Irrawaddy

Salween

• Hanoi

• Victoria

Hong Kong (U.K.)

Hainan Doa

LAOS

Mekong

• Vientiane

THAILAND

VIETNAM

Quezon City

Andaman Islands (India)

• Rangoon

• Bangkok

CAMBODIA

Phnom Penh

SOUTH CHINA SEA

PHILIPPINES

Celebes Sea

BAY OF BENGAL

Gunung Bandahara 3012

MALAYSIA

Bandar Seri Begawan

Brunei

Sabah

Sarawak

Kuala Lumpur •

• Singapore

Sumatra

PEGUNUNGAN BARISAN

Borneo

Celebes

Equator

INDONESIA

• Jakarta

Java

Timor

17

Western Attitudes to Islam

◀ *(pages 14–15) Muslims pray toward Mecca, a ritual that should be repeated five times a day.*

◀ *(previous pages) This map shows the physical geography of the Islamic world that stretches across Asia and into Africa.*

▶ *Invading French troops desecrated and plundered the Grand Mosque in Cairo, but Henry Lévy's 1875 painting glorified Napoleon's triumphant entrance.*

For much of the past 1300 years Europeans have regarded Islam as a menace. Devout Christians have felt challenged by a faith which acknowledged one God as creator of the universe but denied the doctrine of the Trinity; which accepted that Christ was a prophet and was born of a virgin but denied that he was divine or that he was crucified; which believed in a day of judgment and heaven and hell, but appeared to make sex the chief of heaven's rewards; which regarded the Christian Bible as the word of God but gave supreme authority to a book which seemed in great part to deny its teachings. Christian states have felt threatened by the success of Muslim power which penetrated to the heart of France in the 8th century, probed central Europe in the 16th and 17th centuries, and for nearly a thousand years patrolled the southern and eastern flanks of Christendom. Even in the 18th and 19th centuries, when the tables were turned and European power was spread throughout the world, Muslims were still seen to be a danger, this time to the security of European empire. Facts such as these have fashioned European attitudes to the Islamic world, fostering in many an antagonism and an unwillingness to sympathize with the Islamic vision of life and of how it should be lived; while the distinctive civilization which has been formed by this vision has been valued less for itself than as a foil against which European identity could be discerned and the European achievement measured.

From the beginning, European attitudes were fundamentally hostile. Early Europeans, cut off from the main centers of Muslim civilization by the Byzantine empire, built a vague and fantastic picture of Islam from Byzantine sources: it was a heresy derived from Christian teachings; the Quran had been borne to the people on the horns of a white bull; the Prophet was a sorcerer whose success owed much to his proclaimed revelation of divine approval for sexual license. From the beginning of the 12th century and the time of the First Crusade, however, a rather more serious appreciation developed, marked by the translation of the Quran into Latin by the English scholar, Robert of Ketton, in 1143. In the 13th and 14th centuries Europeans came to emphasize two elements of Islam. The first was the extent to which the Quran could be made to corroborate the Gospel. The second was an attack on the status of Muhammad as a prophet. How could a man who performed no miracles and who, according to Christian legend, lied and wallowed in debauch, be a prophet of God? And two particular aspects of his message were singled out as targets for Christian polemic: the support Islam was believed to give to the use of force (although Christians too waged holy wars), and the sexual freedom Muslims were supposed to enjoy in this life combined with the sensual ecstasy they were promised in the next.

From the 18th century onward, however, within Europe, Christian revelation was losing its comprehensive hold, and although the old Christian prejudices still survived, the change enabled Europeans increasingly to perceive other ways of understanding the world and even to sympathize with them. Simultaneously, the attitude of European powers to those of the Muslim world evolved from a real fear of the Ottoman threat to

confident equality as not just the Ottoman but the Safavid and the Mughal empires too declined. By the end of the 18th century Europeans were secure in their relations with Muslim powers, a change symbolized by the French invasion and occupation of Egypt in 1798, and the British conquest of Mysore, the last hostile Indian Muslim stronghold, in 1799. This confidence grew throughout the 19th century as the Russians and the Dutch joined the British and the French in bringing Muslim peoples under their control, until by the treaty of San Remo in 1920 three-quarters of the Muslim world was under European sway. As Europeans liberated themselves from the medieval Christian vision, met more Muslims, and came to know their civilization better, a deeper understanding of Islam became possible.

Nevertheless, seizing the opportunities made available by empire, Christian missionaries moved among Muslim peoples as never before; some slipped all too readily into the traditional association of Islam with sex and violence. Indeed, the terms "Muslim" and "fanatic" became almost synonymous for Europeans confronting Muslim resistance in places as far apart as Algeria, India, and Indonesia, particularly during the great European expansion of the 19th century.

There was no greater contrast to the attitude of Christian antagonism than the assumption by Napoleon, child of the Enlightenment, of a Muslim persona; he manipulated Muslim institutions as part of his imperial purpose in Egypt. "I respect God, his Prophet, and the Quran," he declared on landing in 1798, and then proceeded to act the Muslim ruler, honoring the Prophet, beginning his letters to Muslim potentates with the Islamic *basmala*, and winning the religious and social leaders to his side.

Undoubtedly there was also a tinge of Romanticism in Napoleon's attitude to Islam. In courting an Islamic identity he was striving to reach beyond the classical limits of 18th-century civilization just as his advance to Egypt challenged those of the European power system. In doing so he was exploring the possibilities of the Islamic world as a richly laid table at which the European imagination could feed. For a century or so European appetites had been whetted by the growing number of travelers' tales, and especially by the *Arabian Nights*, first translated by Galland in 1704. This

offered that sumptuous array of caliphs, viziers, slaves, genies, lamps, and fabulous happenings which has furnished much of the store of words and images Europeans use to embrace the Islamic world. For some this world now became an exotic realm in which they could explore new possibilities, as did Mozart in the *Abduction from the Seraglio* or Goethe in his *West-Easterly Diwan*; but it also became a world in which Europeans traveled in search of themselves, wearing outlandish dress—great has been the love of flowing robes among the British from Lady Hester Stanhope, who pitched her tent amid thousands of Bedouin, to T. E. Lawrence, who never seemed to get over the excitement of Arabs, camels, and war in the desert. But whether these Europeans journeyed in person or only in the imagination, they were concerned more to impose their vision on this world than to savor its reality. A new barrier of the imagination was being created to replace part of the old one of prejudice.

A further attitude which both fed off the others and helped shore them up was the profound sense of superiority which grew together with European empire. In India in the mid–1800s, Macaulay asserted that "by

▼ *The harem and its delights sparked the imagination of 19th-century painters such as Renoir who painted this Algerian odalisque in 1870, nine years before he visited Algiers.*

universal confession there are no books," of Muslim, or Hindu, learning, "which deserve to be compared with our own." Europeans were sure that they were both different from and better than Muslims.

Side by side with these broadening attitudes there developed the scholarly study of the faith and of Islamic societies. This began with more accurate translations of the Quran: that of Maracci into Latin in 1698 and of Sale into English in 1734. Sale's Quran also featured a preface in which he both spoke of Muslim achievements with admiration and used Muslim sources to write their history. Toward the end of the 18th century, large numbers of texts, both literary and religious, began to be translated into European languages. During the 19th century study continued to broaden as students of the science of religion, biblical criticism, and comparative philology, brought Islam and the languages Muslims spoke within their purview. At the beginning of the 20th century, the study of Islam emerged as an independent discipline. Since World War II, Islamic studies have steadily expanded as the subject has grown in the United States and as scholars have begun to apply the insights of the social sciences, particularly anthropology. Consequently, Islamic studies have gained new dimensions, in part because the anthropologist has extended the search for knowledge from the antique and citied communities of the central Islamic lands to tribes and villages in Africa and south and southeast Asia, and in part because by being able to see the many compromises Islam has made and is making with local cultures, we have come to learn of the many different ways there are of being Muslim.

As we would expect, the scholarly study of Islam reflected the attitudes of the society in which it was pursued. Confidence in the superiority of Western civilization, and of Western ways of looking at things over the Islamic, has been instinct in much Western scholarship. There is a tendency to produce studies which seem more concerned with debates going on among Western intellectuals than with an imaginative understanding of Muslim societies. It appears, moreover, particularly difficult for scholars raised in a fundamentally agnostic and materialistic environment to understand the power of faith. This may explain why some of the best and most sensitive research has been done by devout Christians. Although traditional sources of hostility to Islam derived from the medieval Christian polemic still flourish in secular form, it is devout Christians who seem to come closest to understanding Islam. The old objection which focused on the enjoyment of sex and sensuality has become a new objection to the position of women. The concern about violence has become disapproval of the inhumane punishments and bloodthirsty politics of some Muslim societies. The fear of Muslim power, which gave way after the expansion of the West to a sense of superiority, rises again as oil brings Muslims the ability to influence Western life and a new assertiveness brings them the will to do so. Moreover, if Westerners are no longer perturbed by the thought of Muhammad's imposture, they are worried by what now seems heresy in their eyes: the desire of many Muslims to subordinate the life of their society and the workings of the modern state to the holy law. Indeed, a disapproval of Islam, which sometimes amounts to outright hostility, seems ingrained in the secular culture of the West. Christians on the other hand have found a new affinity with those who also worship one God.

◄ Arthur Rackham's illustrations for **The Arabian Nights** *were based on Western perceptions and his imagination rather than any actual experience.*

The First Nine Centuries

The faith of Islam began around 610 CE
when Muhammad (born 570 CE), son of Abd
Allah, a Meccan merchant given to religious
contemplation, had a vision. While he was
asleep in his solitary cave on Mount Hira
some miles from the city, the Angel Gabriel
came to him and said: "Read." Muhammad
hesitated and the angel clasped him tightly
till Muhammad asked, "What shall I read?"
Then the angel said: "Read in the name of
thy Lord who creates—creates man from a
clot. Read and thy Lord is most Generous,
who taught by the pen, taught man what he
knew not." This was the first of many
messages from God which Muhammad was to
receive. They form the Quran, which in
Arabic means "reading" or "recitation."
Inspired by these messages Muhammad
preached to the people of Mecca, telling them
to give up the idols they worshiped and to
submit to the one and indivisible God.
Muhammad found few followers and provoked
much hostility. So, when in 622 he and his
supporters were invited to the oasis town of
Medina some 210 miles (340 km) northeast of
Mecca, they went.

That the emigration to Medina was the
decisive moment in Muhammad's mission was
recognized by the first generation of Muslims
who made 622 CE the first year of the Islamic
era. In Medina Muhammad wielded political
and military as well as religious authority. By
the time Muhammad died on June 8, 632, he
had given the nomads of this obscure corner
of the ancient world a faith in one God and a
book of revelations; he had also by means of
warfare and alliance led the expansion of his
community from Medina until it formed the
state which dominated western Arabia.

Muslims believe that Muhammad was the
last of God's prophets. He is seen as
completing the work begun by the great
Hebrew prophets, Abraham, Moses, and
Christ, in showing the way to a true
monotheism. Muhammad called the faith he
preached Islam, meaning "submitting" to
God; Muslims were those who submitted, and
the community of Muslims were those who
accepted God's final revelation to humankind
through Muhammad. In this community there
was no distinction between the religious and
the secular spheres; all things were subject to
God's will as revealed in the Quran. The
function of the leader of the community after
Muhammad, the caliph or successor, was to
administer God's will.

Fired by their new faith the Muslims
exploded out of western Arabia. By 634 the
rest of Arabia was conquered and they were
advancing into Palestine. Eight years later
they had defeated the great Byzantine and
Sassanian empires which lay to the north and
had taken control of Syria, Iraq, western Iran,
and Egypt. By the death of the third caliph,
Uthman, in 656, Muslim armies had
advanced through Cyrenaica in the west, the
Caucasus in the north, and to the Oxus and
the Hindu Kush in the east. By 712 they had
reached Tashkent and begun to secure
Central Asia. In 751 they defeated the
Chinese forces at the battle of the Talas
River. In the west they finished their
conquest of North Africa in 709 and
advanced through Spain into France, where
their expansion was finally halted by the
Franks at Poitiers in 732. By the mid–8th
century the caliphs ruled from Damascus a
vast empire stretching from the Indus valley

and Tashkent in the east to the Atlas mountains and the Pyrenees in the west.

During the first 120 years the Muslim community endured three great civil wars. A continuing element in the strife was the opposition of the party of the Prophet's cousin and son-in-law, Ali, that is the *Shia*

(party) of Ali, often just known as the Shias, to those who occupied the caliphate. They believed that rightful leadership belonged with the descendants of the Prophet. Their opposition came in the open during the reign of the third caliph, Uthman, and war broke out when Uthman was assassinated and Ali

▼ *The first nine centuries of Islamic history were a period of almost continuous expansion until about 1500.*

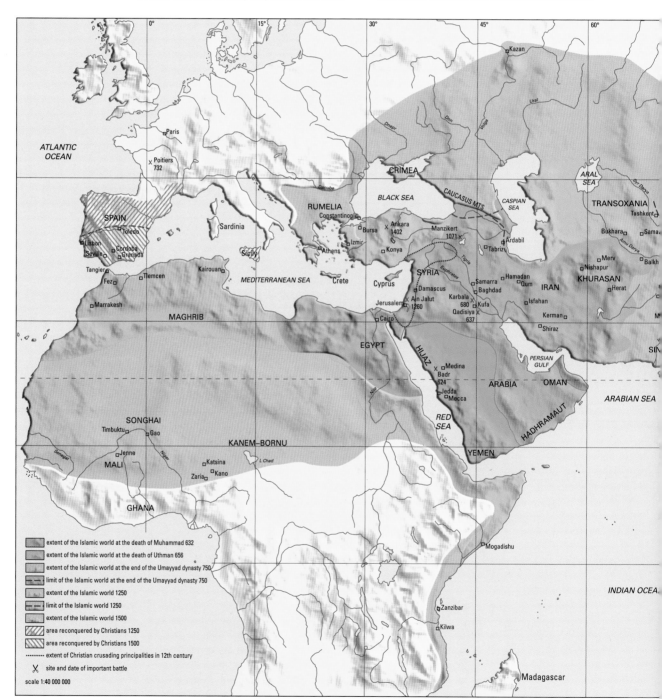

ATLANTIC OCEAN

Paris

× Poitiers 732

SPAIN
Toledo
Lisbon
Seville Cordoba Granada

Tangier
Fez
Tlemcen
Marrakesh

MAGHRIB

Sardinia

MEDITERRANEAN SEA

Sicily

Kairouan

Crete

CRIMEA

BLACK SEA

RUMELIA
Constantinople
Bursa × Ankara
1402
Izmir
Athens
Konya

CAUCASUS MTS

Manzikert
1071 ×
Ardabil
Tabriz

CASPIAN SEA

ARAL SEA

TRANSOXANIA
Tashkent

Bukhara Sama
Amu Darya

Merv
Nishapur
Qum

KHURASAN
Herat

Cyprus
SYRIA
Damascus
Jerusalem × Ain Jalut
1260
Cairo

Samarra Hamadan
Baghdad
Karbala
680 Kufa
Qadisiya ×
637

IRAN
Isfahan

Kerman

Shiraz

Balkh

EGYPT

HIJAZ

× Medina
Badr
624
Jedda
Mecca

RED SEA

ARABIA

PERSIAN GULF

OMAN

HADHRAMAUT

YEMEN

SIN

ARABIAN SEA

SONGHAI
Timbuktu Gao

KANEM–BORNU

Jenne
MALI
Katsina
Zaria Kano

L Chad

GHANA

Mogadishu

Zanzibar

Kilwa

INDIAN OCEA

Madagascar

☐ extent of the Islamic world at the death of Muhammad 632
☐ extent of the Islamic world at the death of Uthman 656
☐ extent of the Islamic world at the end of the Umayyad dynasty 750
–·– limit of the Islamic world at the end of the Umayyad dynasty 750
☐ extent of the Islamic world 1250
–·– limit of the Islamic world 1250
·–·– extent of the Islamic world 1500
▨ area reconquered by Christians 1250
▨ area reconquered by Christians 1500
········ extent of Christian crusading principalities in 12th century
× site and date of important battle
scale 1:40 000 000

succeeded to the caliphate in compromising circumstances. It ended only after Ali himself was assassinated in 661 and his eldest son resigned his claims to the office. Shia opposition, however, did not end here; indeed it was stimulated further by the fact that the caliphate, originally an elected office and always so ideally, now became the dynastic possession of the Umaiyads, an aristocratic Meccan clan. In 680 Husain, the son of Ali, led a revolt against the Umaiyad caliph Yazid and was massacred with most of his small force at Karbala. Immediately there was a fresh surge of Shia resistance which lasted until 692. In the long run it transformed the party into a religious sect whose distinctive belief was to replace the caliph with an imam from whom they received in each generation the original light of Muhammad's revelation and whose most hallowed rites mourned the slaughter of the purest sources of that light at Karbala. Thus the Shias continued to oppose the Umaiyad caliphate and fought a third civil war which ended in the destruction of the dynasty in 750 and the enthronement of the descendants of the Prophet's uncle, al-Abbas, in their stead.

The establishment of the Abbasid caliphate marked the end of the first phase of Muslim expansion. A great civilization was created. The Arabs brought to it Muhammad's revelation and the study of the traditions relating to the Prophet's life, philology, and the law. These interacted with the deep-rooted cultures and civilizations the Arabs ruled, slowly fashioning a Muslim life. The conquered peoples met and mingled as never before in the great *Pax Islamica* carved out by Arab

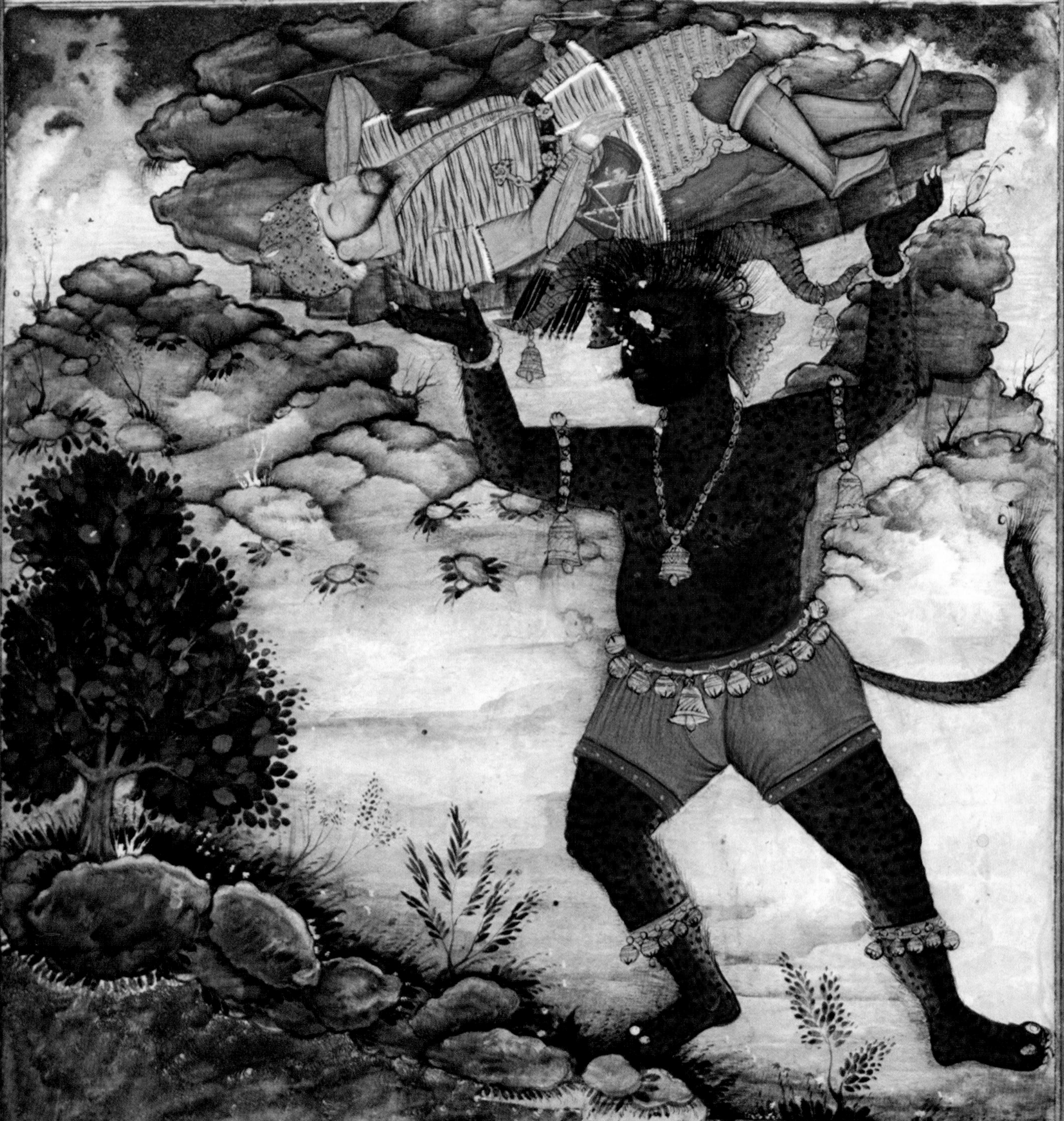

arms. Trade grew, towns burgeoned, and Baghdad, the Abbasid capital founded in 762, was a major entrepôt larger than its Greek and Sassanian predecessors. The great mosques of Samarra in Iraq, Kairouan in Tunisia, and Ahmad Ibn Tulun in Cairo stand witness to the power and confidence of the new civilization. The tales of the *Thousand and One Nights*, which are drawn from Egypt, India, China, Greece, and elsewhere, reveal the far-flung horizons of the Baghdad of Caliph Harun al-Rashid (786–809) and the magnificence of its life.

Religious studies multiplied in towns from Samarqand to Spain, and the pursuit of knowledge broadened to embrace history, literature, Greek medicine and Greek mathematics, which was developed to include algebra and trigonometry, and geography. At the same time the Muslim master science, the law, was given decisive form. Based on the Quran and the traditions, four great codes were produced, legislating for all aspects of human life. Arabic was the language of the law and of religious culture wherever Muslim communities grew up, and so by and large it was to remain.

Although Arab culture continued to grow as a unifying force throughout the Muslim world, the power of the caliphate declined. The Abbasids, in fact, never ruled the Muslim world as the Umaiyads had done; their very accession had in 756 CE led to the establishment of an independent emirate in Spain by a fleeing Umaiyad prince. In the late 8th and 9th centuries other independent regimes were established: the Idrisids, Aghlabids, and Tulunids in the Maghrib and Egypt, the Tahirids, Saffarids, and Samanids in the eastern lands. These dynasties, while effectively independent, recognized the Abbasid caliph as the head of all Islam. In

the 10th century, however, this supremacy was challenged by Shia Fatimids, rising first in Tunisia and later in Egypt, which they conquered in 969 and where they established their own caliphate which at its height ruled much of North Africa, Syria, and south and west Arabia. In self-protection the Spanish Umaiyads promptly declared their own caliphate at Cordoba, and for a time there were three caliphs in the Muslim world. The legitimacy of the Abbasid caliphs was the most widely recognized, although from the mid-10th century they were no more than puppets of the Buyids, a family of Shia brigands who carved out a state in Mesopotamia and the Iranian highlands.

The 9th and 10th centuries saw the rise of independent Persian kingdoms in the eastern lands of the Abbasid caliphate. These courts, particularly that of the Samanids (819–1005), became patrons of a new evolving Persian culture. Persians had played a distinguished part in the flowering of Muslim literature in Arabic, as they continued to do in the religious sciences. But they also preserved their own pre-Islamic language, which, padded now with Arabic loan words and written in the Arabic script, rose to become the second language of Islam, dominant in the Muslim land empires of Asia, the medium of polite culture, and in its literary wealth both a source of education and a model of excellence.

The nomad invasions

By the end of the 10th century, Islam bounded a world which was rich in trade, brilliant in intellectual endeavor, considerable in artistic achievement, but which had lost the political unity and the military strength which marked its early years. For the next five centuries its

◄ *The* Shahnama *is the longest poem ever written by a single author. Abu'l-Qasim Hasan Firdausi's epic work narrates the history of Iran from the dawn of time to the early 7th century. This 17th-century miniature depicts the hero Rustam being hurled into the sea by the demon Akvan.*

heartlands were to suffer invasions of nomads. In 977 a Turkish soldier of fortune seized control of Ghazna in the Samanid dominions and established a dynasty which in 17 great campaigns from 1000 to 1030 conquered north India. In the middle of the 11th century Turkish tribesmen (converted by the Samanids a century before), known as Seljuqs, quickly brought most of western Asia beneath their control and carried the flag of Islam into Asia Minor. In Africa, Arab tribes were destroying centers of civilization on the continent's northern shore, while in the far west Berber nomads were carrying Islam into the Senegal and Niger basins. By 1100 Turks controlled the caliphate but shared power in the Islamic community with the Fatimids of Egypt.

The Turks brought fresh blood and new energy to Islam. They freed the Abbasids from their Buyid thralldom and created the universal sultanate. Henceforth the caliph bestowed legitimacy on the effective holders of power as he did when he crowned the first Seljuq sultan in 1058, while it was now the sultan's duty to impose his authority on the Islamic community, defending it against attacks from outside and denials of God's word within. In the east the Ghaznavid Turks firmly established Muslim power in northern India, effectively beginning the expansion in the subcontinent where Islamic civilization was to flower most abundantly. In the west the Seljuq invasion of Asia Minor began the process which was to make it the modern land of the Turks and the base from which the greatest Islamic empire of the past 600 years would expand into southeast Europe.

The great Seljuq victory over the forces of Byzantine Christendom at Manzikert in 1071 led to the preaching of the First Crusade some 25 years later, and a stream of Frankish crusaders over the following 200 years. The crusading activities in Palestine, though they bulk large in Western memory, were no more than a minor irritant to the Muslims, and in the long run, more than anything else, important for the boost they gave to Muslim–Christian trade in the Mediterranean and the deterioration which they brought to the conditions of Christians under Muslim rule. Outside Palestine, however, the Muslims suffered some permanent defeats. In 1091 the Normans completed the reconquest of Sicily, in 1147 Lisbon was recaptured by the Second Crusade, and by 1212 the Spanish Christians had reconquered most of Spain, leaving just a small enclave at Granada.

The Mongols were the last great nomadic invasion of the settled world. The first wave was led by Gengis Khan who between 1220 and 1225 brought Transoxania, Khurasan, and the Caucasus beneath his control. The second wave left Central Asia under the command of his grandson Hulagu in 1255. By 1258 Baghdad had been sacked and the last Abbasid caliph and his family destroyed, trampled to death beneath carpets. By 1260 most of the Muslim world, except Egypt, Arabia, Syria, and the lands to the west, acknowledged the supremacy of the pagan Mongol. These areas survived the Mongol scourge more by luck than by anything else; it was only the chance of the Great Khan Mongke's death in 1259 which turned Hulagu's eyes eastward and left the Egyptian Mamluks only a fraction of his army to defeat at Ain Jalut, near Nazareth, in 1260. This victory enabled the Mamluks to reestablish the caliphate in Cairo until the Ottoman conquest in 1517. For a while Muslims under Mongol suzerainty were ruled from the Mongol capital in Beijing (Peking), but by 1258 they were divided between three great

Mongol states. When these states declined and Mongol prestige sank, it was restored by Timur Lang, the lame, better known in English as Tamerlaine, who commanded the last great wave of invaders from the steppes of Central Asia. Between 1370 and 1405 he won a vast empire which stretched from Tashkent to Mesopotamia, and he went one better than his forbears by conquering Delhi and frightening Cairo into submission.

By the beginning of the 14th century the Mongols had accepted Islam and their Khans patronized Islamic learning, the arts, and sciences. In Tabriz Rashid al-Din the world historian flourished; in Tamerlaine's Samarqand Saad al-Din Taftazani wrote books which were to be at the heart of Islamic learning to the present day; Nasir al-Din Tusi and Ulugh Beg fostered astronomy; Saadi, Hafiz, and Jami brought Persian poetry to its highest pitch; miniature painting, fertilized by Chinese influences, blossomed to bring forth its finest fruit in the work of Bihzad at the court of Herat; architecture reached new heights as the Mongols rebuilt some at least of the cities they had destroyed. The Persian culture developed and spread so widely that it become the dominant culture of the eastern Islamic world. Finally the Mongols were Turkicized as they had been Islamized, and the political dominance of the Turkish peoples from Asia Minor to northern India was confirmed.

The widening Islamic world

As Islam fought its great contest with the Mongols, it was also expanding on the margins. The growth of trade played a leading role in its spread along the shores of the Indian Ocean and in sub-Saharan Africa. Muslim communities were established on the east coast of Africa, on India's southwestern shore and in the ports of China. By 1500 Islam was established around the coasts of the Malay peninsula and the northern coasts

▼ *This map shows the regions in which the various Sunni schools of law were dominant c. 1500. All schools except the Hanbali regarded each other as equally orthodox.*

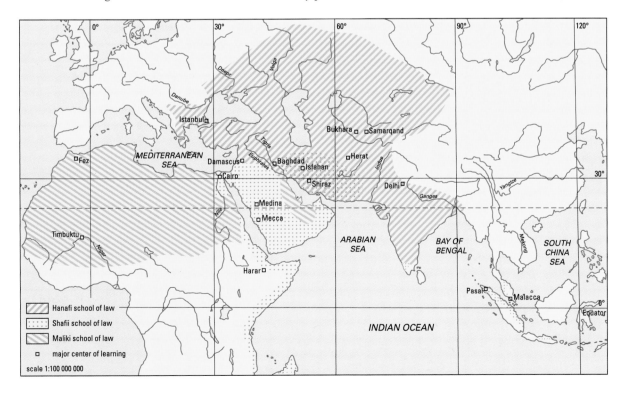

	Hanafi school of law
	Shafii school of law
	Maliki school of law
□	major center of learning

scale 1:100 000 000

of Sumatra and Java and was pressing into the Moluccas and the southern Philippines. In Africa south of the Sahara Muslim traders exchanged gold and slaves from the Guinea coast for handicrafts and salt from the north. Great states grew in the western Sudan: Ghana, Mali, and Songhai. Great cities such as Gao, Jenne, and Timbuktu also grew, where traders from many lands mingled with scholars and with poets.

Elsewhere expansion owed more to arms than to trade. In India the Turkish Khaljis and Tughluqs extended the sway of the Delhi sultanate to the south for a time, and when the tide of conquest receded, there emerged successor states in most of which Muslims ruled predominantly Hindu populations. In Asia Minor the Ottoman Turks established a small *ghazi*, or holy warrior, principality on the borders between Christendom and Islam. in the mid-13th century. By the mid-14th century it had conquered northwestern Asia Minor and entered Rumelia. The Ottomans took the Christian bastion of Constantinople in 1453, annexed Greece and Herzegovina, and began to exercise their sway over Bosnia and the states of the northern Black Sea shore. In China the Mongol Yuan dynasty (1279–1368) imported Muslims as civil servants; these helped to form Muslim communities throughout the land.

By 1500 all hope of political unity in the Islamic world had long since passed. Two main centers of power stood out: Egypt, where the Mamluk sultanate of Turks and Circassians still fostered high Arab culture, and the Ottoman empire, which now bridged the Bosphorus and was to claim to be the universal Islamic monarchy. Elsewhere power was divided among many sultans. Moreover the dispersion of political power was coming to be matched by cultural

diversification. Two great high cultures divided the Muslims: the Arab in Egypt, Africa, and among the traders of the southern seas, and the Persian which had spread in the great land empires created by the Turkish peoples. And as Islam continued to expand, increasing numbers joined the faith in Africa, in India, or in southeast Asia, whose prime means of cultural or religious expression owed little or nothing to Arab or Persian forms. Nevertheless matters of central importance were shared: the Quran, the traditions, and the law, and the skills needed to make them a social force, which meant a mastery of Arabic.

Islamic life: the law

The Quran was the first and the most profound guide to the living of Muslim life. It is divided into 114 chapters, called *suras*, arranged according to length. It is not known if the Quran was written down in full in Muhammad's lifetime and it is generally thought to have been compiled a few years after his death. For a while there were several versions but by the end of the Umaiyad caliphate the text had been established in all but a few details.

The Quran, Muslims believe, is the word of God; it explains all that man needs to know to live a normal and spiritual life. God is all-powerful. He created man who is ever in danger of incurring his wrath. Forgiveness cannot be won by merit; it flows only from God's grace, although a man may make himself worthy of forgiveness by a life devoted to God's service. Man, submitting to God, must follow the right path if he hopes to reach paradise. Should he turn from this path he will surely suffer on the day of judgment.

Quran means "recitation"; Muslims recite it whenever they pray. Indeed, Muslims

◀ A 17th-century Ottoman pulpit tile decorated with a stylized plan of the Kaaba, the sanctuary in the great mosque at Mecca.

▼ **Ulama** *were always ready to travel to learn. These maps show the travels of six figures: the scholars al-Ghazzali and Ibn al-Arabi; al-Taftazani, who worked at the court in Samarqand; the historian Ibn Khaldun; al-Asqalani, who brought the study of Hadith to its height; and al-Jurjani, whose works are still studied.*

worship by means of it, and in affirming it they renew the event of revelation. As Islam expanded, its message was brought to peoples who knew no Arabic, yet because the Quran was held to be untranslatable, no translations were made. Many came to affirm their faith in a language they did not understand, yet which gave voice to the very words of God. Others learned Arabic, which remained the lingua franca of Muslim scholarship, and so the Quran contributed to the unity of the community.

The second source of guidance were the *Hadiths*, the traditions relating to the life of Muhammad who is believed to have been divinely inspired in all that he said and did. In the early years, these were handed down by word of mouth. But then, as sects and rivalries sprang up, *Hadiths* began to be manufactured to support partisan interests. Scholars then began to study them to distinguish the genuine from the forged. By the end of the third century of the Islamic era, six great critical collections had been

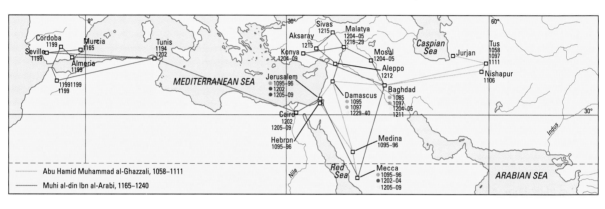

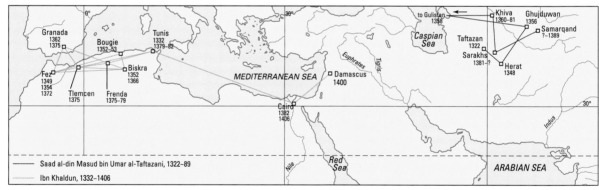

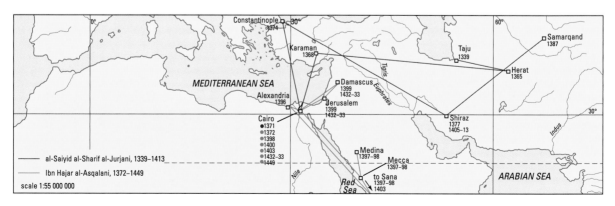

scale 1:55 000 000

compiled, two of which, those of Muslim and Bukhari, had acquired special authority.

The law is usually referred to as the *Sharia*, meaning originally in Arabic "the path leading to the water," that is, the way to the source of life. It grew from the attempts of early Muslims, as they confronted immediate social and political problems, to derive systematic codes of Muslim behavior from the Quran and the *Hadiths*.. During the Muslim community's first 200 years four main schools of legal interpretation developed (see map on p. 33): the Hanafi school, which grew up in the Abbasid capital of Baghdad and which is said to have been founded by Abu Hanifa (died 767); the Maliki school, which grew out of the practice of the Medinan judge Malik Bin Anas (died 795); the Shafii school, developed by a disciple of Malik, al-Shafii (died 820); and the Hanbalite school, founded by Ahmad Ibn Hanbal (died 855) in Baghdad. The first three schools all had differences of emphasis and technique, but recognized each other's systems as equally orthodox. The Hanbalite school developed as a reaction against what it felt to be the speculative innovations of the earlier established schools. Although recognized as the fourth orthodox school by the other three, Hanbalites were less willing to return the compliment.

Scholars treated the Quran as containing the general principles by which all matters should be regulated, and where the Quran was unclear they sought clarification from the *Hadiths*. The foundations of the *Sharia*, then, were the clear and unambiguous commands and prohibitions to be found in these sources. When points of law arose on which the Quran or the *Hadiths* offered no firm guidance, most scholars turned to *qiyas*, which meant arguing by analogy and applying to the new problem the principles underlying a decision which had already been reached on a comparable problem. As the years passed, scholars increasingly came to agree on points of law, and the principle of *ijma*, or consensus of the community, came into play. If the community embodied in its legal experts came to agree on a point, that agreement gained the authority of revelation itself and the development of new ideas on the subject was forbidden. Steadily more and more of the law was underpinned by *ijma*, and the right of *ijtihad*, or individual interpretation, became confined to the decreasing area on which no general agreement had been reached. By the mid-10th century most Muslim scholars had declared the "gate of *ijtihad*" finally shut. Henceforth, if a man questioned the interpretation supported by *ijma*, he committed *bida*, which is as near as Islam came to the Christian idea of heresy.

The *Sharia* grew slowly during the first three Islamic centuries into a unified system and in the process drew on much customary practice which had become embodied in the *Hadiths*.. But most Muslims since then have believed that it flowed from revelation and was the embodiment of the Divine Will: it could not be changed, and man was limited to development within the divine framework.

The *Sharia* embraces all human activities, defining both man's relations with God and his relations with his fellow men. In the first role it prescribes what a man should believe and how by ritual acts he should express his belief; in the second it covers those areas which in Western codes would come under the heading of civil, commercial, penal, private law, and so on. No formal legal code was ever created, the *Sharia* being more a discussion of how Muslims ought to behave.

Human actions are classified on a five-point scale: obligatory, meritorious, indifferent, reprehensible, forbidden. The object of the *Sharia* was to show man what he must do to live righteously in this world and prepare himself for the next.

It would be a mistake to imagine that this comprehensive system has ever been enforced in its entirety. It was impossible to enforce a system which included moral obligations as well as hard-and-fast rules. Moreover, few rulers could afford to allow the interpreters of the law of God to be completely out of their control. Nor could they afford to antagonize their partially Islamized peoples by trying at one stroke to abolish social and legal traditions which owed nothing to Islam. The *Sharia* had to

▼ *The map shows the spread of the main traditions of sufi teaching c. 1500 and marks the shrines of the founding saints of the leading orders.*

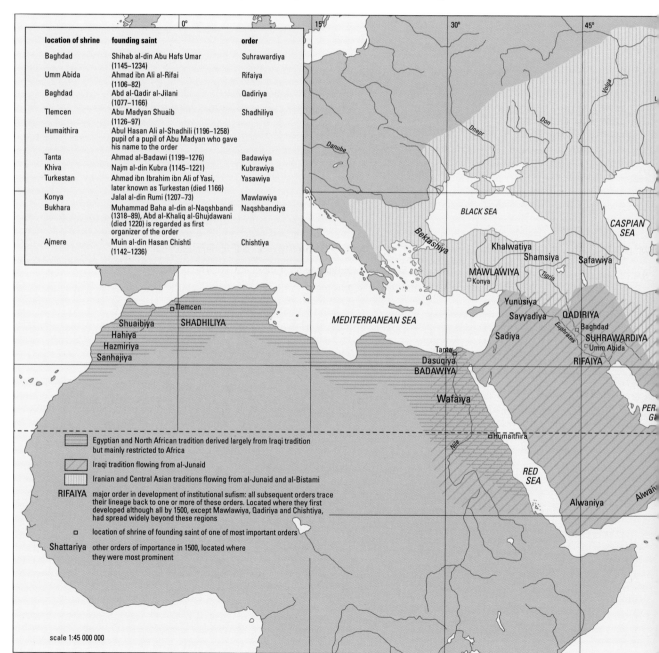

location of shrine	founding saint	order
Baghdad	Shihab al-din Abu Hafs Umar (1145–1234)	Suhrawardiya
Umm Abida	Ahmad ibn Ali al-Rifai (1106–82)	Rifaiya
Baghdad	Abd al-Qadir al-Jilani (1077–1166)	Qadiriya
Tlemcen	Abu Madyan Shuaib (1126–97)	Shadhiliya
Humaithira	Abul Hasan Ali al-Shadhili (1196–1258) pupil of a pupil of Abu Madyan who gave his name to the order	
Tanta	Ahmad al-Badawi (1199–1276)	Badawiya
Khiva	Najm al-din Kubra (1145–1221)	Kubrawiya
Turkestan	Ahmad ibn Ibrahim ibn Ali of Yasi, later known as Turkestan (died 1166)	Yasawiya
Konya	Jalal al-din Rumi (1207–73)	Mawlawiya
Bukhara	Muhammad Baha al-din al-Naqshbandi (1318–89), Abd al-Khaliq al-Ghujdawani (died 1220) is regarded as first organizer of the order	Naqshbandiya
Ajmere	Muin al-din Hasan Chishti (1142–1236)	Chishtiya

Egyptian and North African tradition derived largely from Iraqi tradition but mainly restricted to Africa

Iraqi tradition flowing from al-Junaid

Iranian and Central Asian traditions flowing from al-Junaid and al-Bistami

RIFAIYA major order in development of institutional sufism: all subsequent orders trace their lineage back to one or more of these orders. Located where they first developed although all by 1500, except Mawlawiya, Qadiriya and Chishtiya, had spread widely beyond these regions

☐ location of shrine of founding saint of one of most important orders

Shattariya other orders of importance in 1500, located where they were most prominent

scale 1:45 000 000

coexist with other laws, but it remained a potent ideal. All who accepted Islam, accepted in principle its authority and the fact that it should supplant other laws.

Islamic life: mysticism

Whereas the *Sharia* dictates the formal relations of the Muslim toward God and his fellow men, mysticism, or sufism, cultivates

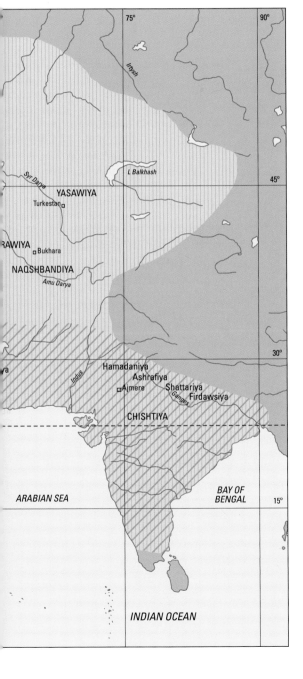

the inner attitude with which the believer performs his outward obligations.

Although instinct in the Quran and the *Hadith*, sufism grew as a distinct strand of Muslim devotion. The term "sufi" is probably derived from the Arabic *suf*, meaning wool, which referred to the simple woolen clothes worn by the mystics in contrast to the rich apparel of the worldly.

In the beginning the basis of sufi feeling was fear of God and of judgment, but by the second Islamic century the doctrine of love had become prominent. "Love of God hath so absorbed me," declared the woman saint Rabia (died 801), "that neither love nor hate of any other thing remains in my heart." By the third Islamic century Sufis had begun to develop the doctrine of the "inner way" or the spiritual journey toward God. The mystic was first a seeker, then a traveler, and then an initiate. He progressed along the way through processes of self-abnegation and enhanced awareness of God. The nearer he came to God, the more God spoke with his lips, controlled his limbs and moved the desires of his heart, until he reached the final stage when self was annihilated and totally absorbed in God.

Sufi claims to achieve knowledge of God through direct personal experience brought them into conflict with the *ulama* (plural of the Arabic *alim*, learned man), men learned in the Islamic sciences. The *ulama* were uneasy about the growing popular support for the sufi way, and feared for their role as protectors of the faith and sole arbiters of Islamic doctrine. They tried to silence the sufis, but repression could not prevent the continued growth of a movement which was deeply rooted in the Quran and which satisfied the religious hunger of many ordinary men and women.

MYSTICAL KNOWLEDGE

There is no chain in the transmission of mystical knowledge from the Prophet as firm as that for the transmission of the reliable Hadiths. This list names some of the leading mystics who lie between the Prophet and the emergence of the early mystic traditions.

Muhammad Ibn Abd Allah (d. 632)	**Hasan of Basra (d. 728)**
Ali Ibn Abu Talib (d. 661)	**Jafar al-Sadiq (d. 756)**
Abu Dharr al-Ghifari (d. 653)	**Abd al-Wahid Ibn Zaid (d. 793)**
al-Husain (d. 680)	**Rabia al-Adawiya of Basra (d. 801)**

One strand of the chain continued with Maruf al-Karkhi (d. 815), Sari al-Saqati (d. 867) and Abul Qasim Ibn Muhammad Ibn al-Junaid (d. 910), leading to the emergence of the Iraqi tradition (which emphasized sobriety). The other strand continued with Abu Ali al-Sindi (?) and Bayezid Bistami (d. 874) leading to the emergence of the Khurasanian tradition (which emphasized mystical intoxication). Note that there is no intention to indicate any direct line of transmission from the Prophet beyond Rabia al-Adawiya of Basra.

That the division between the two sides did not become unbridgeable is largely due to one man, the greatest figure in medieval Islam, indeed the most influential Muslim after Muhammad, al-Ghazzali (died 1111). Al-Ghazzali, as he reveals in his autobiography *The Deliverer from Error*, traveled long in search of God. Finding that the hyper-rationalism of the theologians could not satisfy the longings of his soul, he eventually "turned with set purpose to the method of mysticism...." He combined scholastic and mystical systems of ideas and found a place for an emotional religious life within Islam. What had been diverging paths were now linked, though distinct—moreover, the two paths came together in one man.

After al-Ghazzali sufism spread rapidly. In many areas so great was the sufis' appeal, and such was the support that they received from secular rulers, that there was little the *ulama* could do to limit their influence.

▶ The spiritual and mystic powers of sufi holy men were thought to give them the ability to bring about miracles, such as crossing a river on a prayer mat.

At the same time new elements, which were quite alien to early Islamic ideas, became fixed in sufi thought. One of the more important was the veneration of the sufi shaikh (*pir* in Persian), or master, by his disciples in his lifetime, which led to the worship of the shaikh after he died. Such practices challenged the central tenet of Islam, the Muslim's belief in the unity of God. Nevertheless they spread widely and with them spread another potentially dangerous doctrine, the belief in the *qutb*, the pole of the world, who with his saintly followers governs the earth. Most noted of all the sufi *qutbs* was Mawlana Jalal al-Din Rumi (died 1273), whose long religious poem, the *Mathnawi*, is the supreme work of Persian sufism, sometimes referred to as the Persian Quran.

A second new element was the spread of pantheistic thought. This was elaborated most effectively by the Spanish sufi scholar Ibn al-Arabi (died 1240 at Damascus), who in his master work, *The Meccan Revelations*, argued that all phenomena are manifestations of a single being which is one with God and produced a mystical interpretation of Islamic doctrine which he claimed had been revealed to him as the "seal of the saints." These pretensions which challenged the status of the Prophet were too preposterous to be taken seriously, but the doctrine of the "unity of being" was another matter; the wide popularity it gained threatened the *Sharia*.

To many *ulama* Ibn al-Arabi was hardly a Muslim, and from time to time his works have been proscribed, but they were extremely influential, especially in the Persian and Turkish areas of the eastern Islamic world. The doctrine of the "unity of being" had obvious uses when Islam was establishing itself among large numbers of

قضا را من و پیری از فاریاب رسیدیم در خاک مغرب به آب

مرا کشتی ارم بود برداشتند یکی کشتی و درویش ننشستند

سیاهان اندند کشتی خود دو که آن خدا ناخدا ترس بود

مرا کریه آمد زمستی خرفت برآن کریه درویش خندیدو

مخور غصه رای من ای ارجمند مرا پس آرد که گشتی رد

بگسترد سجاده بر روی آب خیالست نداشتم باجواب

زدم هوشیم دین آنشب بحفت بکه با بدان من کن دکفت

عجب ماندی ای باز خنده رای تا کشتی آورد و مار خدای

۱۶۹

▶ *Jal al-Din Rumi, the greatest mystic poet of Islam, invented the whirling dance of his Mawlawiya order to symbolize, so it is said, the search for his lost Beloved—a wandering sufi called Sham al-Din.*

shamanistic, Hindu, and animist peoples, as it made possible the compromises essential if the faith was to spread rapidly in regions with no traditions of ethical monotheism. The doctrine, however, also benefited from being embodied in the brilliant flowering of Persian poetry from 1200 to 1500. It was there in the odes of Hafiz who, following Ibn al-Arabi, uses the language of human love to express spiritual communion with God. It is most completely expressed in the *Mathnawi* of Rumi and the mystical poetry of Jami, men whose art placed Arabi's esoteric doctrine on the lips of all who used the second language of the Islamic world.

By 1500 most Muslims approached God as sufis. The *Sharia* had in no way managed to keep up with the rapid spread of sufi influence. Indeed, often being associated with the state and with aristocratic and intellectual education, the *Sharia* was at a disadvantage as it sought to shape the lives of the masses in the classical Islamic mold. Through sufism many popular religious observances had entered Islam. There was singing, dancing and mystic feats such as the eating of glass and walking on fire. Belief in the miracle-working power of saints was widespread and their tombs were places of worship. As sufi thought came to be dominated by the belief that God was immanent rather than transcendent so the body of Islam tended to reflect more the beliefs and structure of the societies it embraced than those enshrined in the *Sharia*.

Transmission of Islamic culture

Central to the historical development of Islam were the *ulama* and the sufis who preserved and transmitted the shaping forces of law and mysticism down the ages. The first

ulama were the religious specialists of the early Islamic era, the reciters of the Quran and the memorizers of the Hadiths. By 1500, their duties included the administration of mosques, schools, hospitals, and orphanages, in which functions they might control great corporate wealth. But their first task remained the preservation and transmission of the *Sharia*. As scholars they defended the orthodox understanding of the *Sharia*, as *qadis* they administered it on behalf of the state, as *muftis* they expounded it on behalf of the community for whom they issued *fatwas* (legal decisions) free of charge; they warned the people of their obligations under it in their sermons, and instructed Muslims of all ages in it in their schools.

The *ulama* taught in their homes or in the compounds of mosques and shrines. They also taught in madrasas, schools, which sprang up across the Islamic world in the 11th century. They taught Arabic grammar and literature, the *Hadiths*, the law, Quran commentary, and theology. Philosophic and scientific disciplines were barred.

Education was learning how things ought to be in the light of divine revelation. There was much rote learning, indeed some texts were written in rhyme to help memorization. Classical texts tended to gain in authority; as time passed, few new texts were written.

When a teacher finished teaching a book he gave his pupil an *ijaza*, or certificate, permitting him to teach the book which listed the teacher's teacher and followed the chain of transmission back to the original writer of the book. The pupil knew that he was now a carrier of part of the central traditions of his faith. His respect and gratitude for his teacher were boundless.

From the beginning, *ulama* had traveled great distances to sit at the feet of famous

▶ *The Mevlevi are sufis famous for the whirling dance they perform as an act of dhikr, or remembrance of God.*

teachers (see maps on p. 36), and the Islamic world was crisscrossed by a network of pupil–teacher loyalties, which formed the basis of a worldwide community of Islamic feeling and learning far stronger than the courts which sprang up within its frame.

The sufis developed an equally clear and all-embracing system for the transmission of mystical knowledge. From the 9th century disciples began to gather around outstanding spiritual personalities in hope of learning their *tariqat*, or "way" of approaching God. The shaikh or master normally had an established pattern of devotional practice called *dhikr* in which adepts often sought ecstatic religious experience by chanting, by dancing or by listening to music. Once a disciple had placed himself in the hands of a shaikh, he had to obey him at all costs, even if it meant going against the *Sharia*.

By the 12th and 13th centuries, most sufis traced their particular "way" back to a founding saint from whom their "way" took its name, and then from him through one or more of the great mystics of the early Abbasid period to a companion of the Prophet, usually Ali. Thus the spiritual training which the Prophet had given his followers was seen to have been handed down to the present through a series of holy men. The shrine of the founding saint was the focal point for the followers of a particular "way" or order. Hundreds of sufi orders grew up. The map on pages 38–39 indicates some of the more important which had become established by 1500. Their differences stemmed in part from the extent to which they were organized but primarily from variations in their rituals and ways of remembering God, and the extent to which they followed the *Sharia* closely or tolerated deviations from it.

The 16th and 17th Centuries

▶ By the middle of the 15th century artillery had become the dominant factor in siege warfare. Here Sulaiman the Magnificent besieges the Habsburg capital of Vienna in 1529.

In the century after 1500 Muslim power reached its peak. From West Africa, where new empires rose in Morocco and the Niger Basin, to Central Asia, where an energetic Uzbeg house threatened to dominate from Bukhara, to southeast Asia, where the first Muslim sultanates were coming to replace Hindu regimes in Sumatra and Java, Muslims were becoming more powerful; they did not see the growing activities of the Europeans, whether those of the Russians in Asia or the Portuguese in the southern seas, as a major threat. Most powerful by far were the Safavid, Mughal, and Ottoman empires which came to straddle the central Islamic lands. Here strong political institutions and centralized bureaucratic systems replaced the tribal confederations, the shortlived sultanates, and the weak regimes which had emerged as the Mongol tide receded. There was a flowering of the arts as rulers of genius spent the wealth raised by their efficient state machines. There was also a new threat to the cosmopolitanism of Muslim life and culture, which stemmed in part from the great boost the Safavids gave to Shiism by making it the official faith of their empire, but in the main from the very strength of the new regimes which enabled them to foster distinctive cultural worlds.

It is hard to be sure about the new sources of strength which made these three great empires possible. Their dynasties had deeply rooted power bases reaching back to the 14th century: the Ottomans already ruled much territory, the Safavids led a powerful sufi order, while the blood of Tamerlaine flowed in the veins of the Mughals. They may also have benefited from a new interest in agriculture: much attention was paid to irrigation works in Safavid Iran while Western visitors to the Ottoman empire often remarked on the new prosperity which had been brought to former Christian lands. Probably what was most important, as in contemporary Europe, was the emergence of gunpowder as the dominant force in war. By 1450 artillery was as crucial in siege warfare as it was soon to become in open battle; only 50 years later the handgun gained a similar importance. In general only a powerful ruler could pay for the growing rate of technological innovation that the increasing use of gunpowder involved, and having done so he had a decisive advantage both against subjects who wished to assert their independence from behind walled forts and against the nomads who in previous centuries had poured in from the steppes.

All three empires had some roots in the vision of world empire created by the Mongols and the political institutions they had developed. Indeed, these empires were the culmination of what has been termed the "military patronage state." Typical of this form of government was the absorption of all state functions into a royal military household in which bureaucrats, and sometimes *ulama* responsible as *qadis* for the administration of the holy law, would be ranked in the same way as the military elite. The royal household regarded all economic and cultural resources as its own, and assumed with equal ease the right to take control of the private endowments off which *ulama* lived or to resettle large segments of the population to suit its purpose. Dynastic law ran side by side with the holy law and the customary law. In fact a carefully defined sphere had usually been found for the holy

law which did not conflict with these other more flexible legal traditions, and the idea had formed that any ruler who enforced the holy law within these limits was a legitimate caliph. Nevertheless, should dynasties pay too scant a respect to the holy law, there were always some among the pious who would use the opportunity to attempt to carve out a wider role for God's law in the lives of mortal men, than royal power allowed.

The Safavid Empire

The first Safavids were sufi shaikhs whose disciples provided the platform on which they established themselves as rulers of Iran. The

Safavid order was founded by Safi al-Din (1252/3–1334) whose ancestors had during three centuries acquired a reputation for piety in the Azarbaijani mountain town of Ardabil. Safi al-Din was the spiritual successor of Shaikh Zahid of Gilan and his achievement was to turn a local sufi order into one with disciples throughout eastern Anatolia, Syria, Iran, the Caucasus, and even among the Mongol nobility. During the 15th century the order became a revolutionary movement as its beliefs grew more Shiite and acquired political importance as the Safavid shaikhs commanded their disciples to fight for these beliefs—Safavid soldiers were dubbed Qizilbash (Redheads) by the Turks on account of their distinctive red turbans with 12 folds commemorating the 12 Shiite imams. Between 1459 and 1494 three heads of the order died violently, but in 1501 the 14-year-old Shah Ismail was able to defeat the Turkoman rulers of northern Iran at Sharur and have himself proclaimed Shah Ismail I (1501–24) in Tabriz.

▼ *Shah Ismail took just nine years to extend Safavid territory to its greatest extent. His heirs fought to defend those gains. This map shows the Safavid empire in the 16th and 17th centuries.*

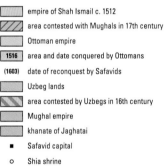

	empire of Shah Ismail c. 1512
	area contested with Mughals in 17th century
	Ottoman empire
1516	area and date conquered by Ottomans
(1603)	date of reconquest by Safavids
	Uzbeg lands
	area contested by Uzbegs in 16th century
	Mughal empire
	khanate of Jaghatai
■	Safavid capital
○	Shia shrine

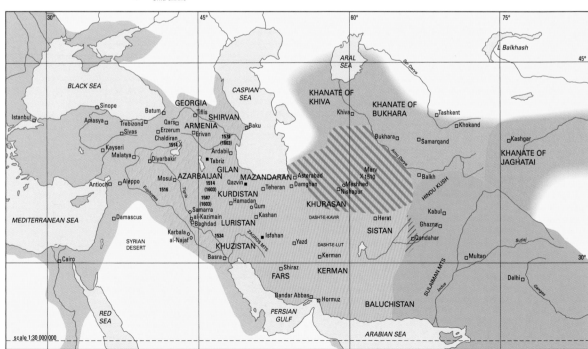

In 1501 Ismail ruled only Azarbaijan; by 1510, after conquering the remainder of Iran and the eastern Fertile Crescent, he had achieved what were to be the furthest limits of Safavid dominion. But immediately he was confronted by the danger of having to fight on two fronts. In the east he was up against the Uzbegs. As soon as he had met that threat, the Ottomans were on the march in the west. This conflict was always likely because the very emergence of the Safavid Shia state and the activities of its militant supporters in eastern Anatolia threatened the Ottoman empire. The outcome was the crushing defeat of the Safavids at Chaldiran (1514) and the loss of Diyarbakir and the Shia sacred cities in Iraq.

The failure at Chaldiran brought into the open the problem which was to dog the Safavids for the rest of the century, the competition for power with the Qizilbash. Before Chaldiran the Qizilbash regarded Shah Ismail not just as the head of their order and their spiritual director but as a manifestation of God himself. Now the spell was broken; the Qizilbash reverted to being tribal leaders in need of discipline. For two periods (1524–33, 1579–88) the Qizilbash were in complete control; for much of the period in between, however, Ismail's son, Shah Tahmasp (1524–76), ruled with some effect by holding the ring between the Turkoman Qizilbash and the Persians, the main groupings in the state. Tahmasp has had a bad press; nevertheless his achievement should be measured by the fact that he brought the Safavid state through five Uzbeg invasions of Khurasan and four Ottoman invasions of Azarbaijan.

Safavid fortunes were rescued and then brought to their peak by Tahmasp's grandson, Shah Abbas the Great (1588–1629). Coming to the throne aged 17, his first move was to rein in the Qizilbash and to place the state on a new basis. He turned to the large numbers of Georgian, Circassian, and Armenian prisoners of war and their descendants who had become Muslims and had been Persianized. These he formed into a personal force, known as the "slaves of the royal household." They were then made to supplant the Qizilbash tribal levies in the field, to oust the Qizilbash chiefs from the major offices of government, and to act as a counterweight to the tribal forces in the state. Loyalty to the Shah was now the key to advancement. By 1598 Abbas felt able to go on the offensive against the empire's old enemies to whom he had been forced to surrender territory at the beginning of his reign. By 1606 he had administered decisive defeats to both the Uzbegs and the Ottomans, recaptured much lost territory, and reduced the threat of attack from east and west.

Shah Abbas brought peace and fostered industry, and he patronized one of the finest flowerings of the Persian artistic genius. He compares well with his contemporaries, Akbar of India and Elizabeth of England. But his greatest achievement was the fashioning of a state which was strong enough to carry it through nearly a century of weak rule. The price was a rapid increase in crown lands to pay for the hugely expanded royal household, which in the long run weakened the empire. For a time, however, it solved the problem of establishing strong institutions of central government in a largely tribal society.

Shiism and the Safavid state

Shah Ismail's most important act on taking power was to declare that the official religion of the Safavid state would be Twelver (Ithna Ashari) Shiism. Shiism, it will be recalled, began as a movement of political opposition to the early caliphs, which justified itself by claiming that the only legitimate successors of Muhammad were the descendants of his cousin and son-in-law Ali. The belief developed that, along with the exoteric interpretation of the Quran, there was a secret interpretation which had been transmitted from Muhammad to Ali and from Ali to his heir; hence the only authoritative source of guidance were those successors of Ali to whom this secret knowledge had been transmitted, and who had thus been designated imam, or leader of the community. Gradually the imams were raised to a superhuman status which was expressed in the belief that they were incarnations of Divine Light which had descended to them through the prophets from Adam. It followed that they were infallible and without sin. The Twelvers, the most important Shia sect, recognized twelve imams, the last being Muhammad al-Muntazar, who disappeared down a well, or so it is said, around the year 873 and whose return is expected. There were many other Shia sects, of whom the most important were the Zaidis, dominant in the Yemen, who recognized only the first four imams and ascribed to them no supernatural attributes, and the Ismailis, who recognized the first seven imams and were represented by the Qarmatian revolutionary movement which flourished in eastern Arabia in the 10th century, the Fatamid caliphs who ruled Egypt from 969 to 1171, and the infamous order of Assassins.

The Shias are most clearly distinguished from the orthodox or Sunni community by where they locate religious authority. For Sunnis it lies in the consensus of the community which underpins the holy law; for Shias it lies in the infallible imams, belief in

whom is the third article of the Shia creed after God and his Prophet. Sunnis have all the guidance they are going to receive in the Quran, the traditions, and the holy law: ideally they must strive to live according to a pattern of perfection formed finally in the middle of the 10th century. Shias, on the other hand, through their imams and those who claim to represent them, have the possibility of a renewed source of guidance in succeeding generations. Shah Ismail and his heirs presented themselves as incarnations of the Twelfth Imam Later in the development of the Safavid state Shia *ulama* were to claim to be *mujtahids*, men with the right in the absence of the Imam to establish rulings in holy law, something which Sunni *ulama* no longer considered possible. So Shiism offered much greater opportunity for legal development and adaptation to changing circumstances. The Shias also evolved markedly different emphases in their rites. If Sunni religious energy is absorbed in the remembrance of God, that of the Shias is absorbed to a great extent in the remembrance of the martyrdom of Husain in particular and of the imams in general, all of whom are supposed to have been murdered by Sunnis. Muharram is the month of mourning, and 10 Muharram (Ashura), the day on which Husain was killed at Karbala, is the high point of the religious year, celebrated by processions bearing models of Husain's tomb, self-flagellation in repentance for disloyalty to the house of Ali, the retelling of the story of Karbala in a state of high emotion, and the cursing of the Sunnis. As one would expect, pilgrimage to Karbala and the tombs of the other imams has come to be as important as pilgrimage to Mecca.

Twelver Shiism was the rock on which the early Safavid state was built. It was a

▶ *This Mughal painting of the emperor Jahangir (right) and Shah Abbas (left) is making a political point. The image suggests peace and harmony, but Jahangir is in the dominant position, with the halo centered on his head.*

▲ Evening prayers at the shrine of the Eighth Imam, Imam Riza, at Meshhed, one of the most sacred Shia sites in Iran and a focus of pilgrimage.

theocratic state, Shah Ismail being the Twelfth Imam made flesh. His family further bolstered their claim for respect by asserting a spurious descent from the Seventh Imam, Musa al-Kazim. There were, moreover, aspects of Iranian belief and of Shiism which contributed to the process. From at least the 13th century Iranian sufis had expressed a strong loyalty to Ali, while Shias had long claimed that Husain married the daughter of Yazdigird III, the last Sassanian king, thus linking the house of Ali to the deeply rooted Iranian monarchical tradition. On coming to power Ismail set about imposing Shiism on what was, outwardly, a predominantly Sunni population. He threatened force and the people succumbed; Sunni *ulama* resisted and were faced with the alternatives of flight or death. Being a Shia now became the test of loyalty to the state. After a similar fashion the loyalties of the Safavi sufi order cemented the early state machine; Shah Ismail was the perfect sufi master, and the Qizilbash, who filled the principal offices, were his disciples. Thus people and government were united in a common religious devotion to their king.

The Safavid shahs claimed throughout the 16th and 17th centuries that they were incarnations of the Twelfth Imam, but the value of this claim as a source of authority began to weaken even in Shah Ismail's reign. We have seen how the Qizilbash lost faith in Ismail's spiritual leadership after the defeat of Chaldiran. Then around the same time the theocratic quality of the regime was further diminished by the separation of religious and political powers as a distinction came to be made between the state religious institution and the state bureaucracy. This was the first hint of the crucial change which was to take place in the relations between the *ulama* and the state in the coming 200 years. At the beginning the *ulama* were an instrument of state power. Large numbers had had to be imported from Syria and Bahrain as there were few Shia *ulama* in Iran; consequently they owed everything—endowments, functions, titles—to the state. Moreover, although it is unlikely that they would have endorsed Safavid claims to be imams incarnate, they do seem to have been willing to accept a theory of the divine right of kings, based on the concept that the shah was the shadow of God (*zill-allah*) on earth. Furthermore, *ulama* did not begin openly to question this theory until the time of Shah Abbas, when Mulla Ahmad Ardabili told the shah that he did not rule by divine right but held his power as a trust on behalf of the imam and that it was for the *ulama* to decide whether that trust was being honored or not. After the death of Shah Abbas the *ulama* challenged the legitimacy of royal government more vigorously by asserting that the only proper representative of the Imam was a learned and competent *mujtahid*. They were now bidding to take control of the Shia people whom the Safavids had created.

Thus the Safavids laid the basis of the modern Iranian state, roughly marking out its borders, establishing a monarchical ideal, and through Twelver Shiism giving it a sharply defined identity. On the other hand, by being harnessed to the most powerful state form of the time, Twelver Shiism also had great opportunity for growth and development. Hitherto the faith of a minority, it now acquired forms through which it could embrace a whole people. Institutions grew strong on state patronage in lands and taxes; theology and jurisprudence were further refined; while from its interplay with the Safavid state there emerged doctrines which threatened the legitimacy of all future Iranian government which was not in the hands of the mujtahids. The outcome was a great Shia edifice erected in the midst of the international Sunni community. Fruitful interaction did still happen, but significant cultural, political, and intellectual barriers had been raised.

The blossoming of Iranian art

The Safavids presided over the finest flowering of Iranian art. Like the princes of Renaissance Europe they were often artists themselves. Shah Ismail was a poet and Shah Tahmasp a painter, but most important they were great patrons, men of highly refined taste who fostered the gifts of talented men and developed close relationships with them; Shah Abbas would hold the candle while his favorite calligrapher, Ali Riza, was at work. Miniature painting was the field in which the fruits of patronage were first and most brilliantly revealed. After defeating the Uzbegs Shah Ismail carried back with him Bihzad, the master painter who brought the high refinement of the Herat school to combine with that of Tabriz. Later Bihzad was appointed director of the royal library, which was not so much a library as we would understand the term as a workshop in which all the arts of making a book were practiced. Here, under the expert patronage of Shah Tahmasp, Safavid painting was brought to its peak in a jeweled style of taut perfection, and breathtaking harmony of color and rhythm in design, which was used to illustrate great works of Iranian literature like Firdawsi's *Shahnama* and Jami's *Haft Awrang*. By the time of Shah Abbas manuscript illustration was giving way to single page painting, and the depiction of a legendary past to the idealized portrayal of beautiful people in coy

embrace or offering wine with youthful charm. By the mid-17th century new trends had emerged of blatant eroticism and a concern for harsh reality. There had been a marked transition which doubtless owed something to the freshening air of secularism in a society once dominated by a triumphant theocracy. Certainly there was decadence as the marvelously controlled set-pieces of early Safavid art gave way to svelte youths sniffing languidly at flowers, and masterly technique to a coarsening of skill, yet there was also the opening vista of a whole new way of seeing life as artists came to paint the real world about them.

As far as other arts are concerned, the elaborate and ornate Safavid poetry did not match that of Saadi, Hafiz, and Jami, although it is not now considered to be as inferior as it was formerly. Metalwork was excellent, though not quite approaching the standard of the Seljuq and Mongol periods. On the other hand, carpets, textiles, and ceramics reached unprecedented heights of perfection. Leading painters from the royal workshops often had a hand in design, and all benefited from royal encouragement, most especially from Shah Abbas who was determined to make the nation's artistic talents serve the export trade. He raised the cottage industry of carpet weaving into a national industry with factories in different parts of the country. Textile factories wove an amazing range of silks, brocades, damasks, velvets, and the like of unrivaled quality, color, and design, and so considerable was the enterprise that in Isfahan alone employment was available for 25,000 people. Potteries also produced a wide range of colors, styles, and glazes, and to improve Iran's chances in the European market 300 Chinese potters were imported to impart their

skills. The supreme achievement of the Safavid potters, however, was the tiles they fired to decorate the great buildings of their time. Such was their mastery over mineral pigments and glazing that the tiles still gleam in the torrid Iranian sun as brightly as they did 400 years ago.

Safavid painting

We can enter the world of the Safavids most readily by looking at their paintings. Primarily, these were designed to illustrate manuscripts or to fill albums collected by connoisseurs. The early Safavids were bibliophiles. Heirs to a world in which men lived mainly in tents, they disdained cumbersome possessions. It is easy to understand the popularity of the portable book and to sense how the miniature world of dazzling color and delicacy, which so often featured gardens decked with flowers and cooled by streams, appealed to men who lived ruggedly in a barren landscape.

The Safavids developed the brilliant artistic traditions fostered by the descendants of Tamerlaine at Herat. When Shah Ismail captured the city in 1510 he carried Bihzad, the leading painter, back to Tabriz. His son, Shah Tahmasp, spent most of his early years in Herat, where he studied painting to the extent that he was able to follow his artists' work as closely as if it was his own. He numbered leading painters among his bosom companions, although this did not prevent him from cutting off the nose of the painter who ran off with his favorite pageboy.

Young painters had to learn the essential social graces from literature to etiquette; they had to master the preparation of the basic tools of the craft from making brushes out of kitten or baby squirrel hairs to grading and

◀ This miniature painting of a bird and a scene of lovers with an attendant is by Riza Abbasi. The script border is made up of verses from an epic poem.

pulverizing pigments. There was constant practice at drawing trees and dragons, horses and warriors; there was the slow attuning of the eye to the properties of each color both separately and together with others. In time the apprentice might be allowed to color in a minor part of a master's work. If he showed outstanding talent, the odds were that he would eventually be employed in the royal library. The products of the royal library in Tabriz brought the art of the book to perfection.

The greatest product of the royal library was a *Shahnama* of Firdawasi, commissioned by Shah Ismail for his son Tahmasp. Most of the outstanding court painters of the time contributed, and the scale of the project can be appreciated from the fact that it contained 250 miniatures, whereas no extant contemporary manuscript contains more than 14.

Isfahan: City of Shah Abbas

Nothing represented the artistic achievement and the prosperity of the Safavid period as fittingly as Isfahan. In this town, 5,250 feet (1,600 m) above sea level on the central Iranian plateau and girdled by mountains, Shah Abbas established his capital and planned a great city worthy to be the focus of his empire; he was assisted by a veritable Iranian Leonardo da Vinci, Shaikh Baha al-Din Muhammad Amili, an eminent theologian, philosopher, Quran commentator, jurisprudent, astronomer, teacher, poet, and engineer, the very exemplar of his age.

The outcome was one of the world's most beautiful cities, and also one of the largest of its time, 23 miles (38 km) in circumference and boasting 162 mosques, 48 madrasas, 1801 caravanserais, and 273 public baths, with water, trees, and parks everywhere and housing about one million people. There were many "spacious caravanserais, very fine bazaars and canals and streets lined with plane trees," according to one French visitor; "from whatever direction one looks at the city it looks like a wood."

There were two main features, the Chahar Bagh, a magnificent avenue 2½ miles (4 km) long lined by gardens and court residences, and the Maidan, a rectangle 55 yards (507 m) long and 173 yards (158 m) wide, around which Shah Abbas raised two tiers of shops whose progress was broken only by the principal buildings, the unpretentious Ali Qapu palace—the shahs did not build to set themselves apart from their people—the beautiful Lutf Allah mosque, and the majestic royal mosque. These houses of prayer were masterpieces of Iranian architecture, although the greatest masterpiece of all was the vision which created the city.

The Maidan was the focus of the city's life, both a marketplace and a sportsfield. Here the shah might play polo or just mingle with his people.

There was also the great bazaar covering 11½ square miles (30 sq km), which was, according to one visitor, "the surprisingest piece of Greatness in Honour of Commerce the world can boast of." This bazaar, moreover, led into the huge central maidan carrying the theme of commerce into the heart of the new royal city.

"The beauty of Isfahan steals on the mind unawares," recorded the English scholar and traveler, Robert Byron, in 1934: "You drive about, under avenues of white tree-trunks and canopies of shining twigs; past domes or turquoise and spring yellow in a sky of liquid violet-blue; along the river patched with twisting shoals, catching that blue in its muddy silver, and lined with feathery groves

▼ *The bazaar is still the focus of Isfahan's commercial trade. Here Iranian women shop for gifts a few days before the Persian new year.*

where the sap calls, across bridges of pale toffee brick, tier on tier of arches breaking into piled pavilions; overlooked by lilac mountains, by the Kuh-i-Sufi shaped like Punch's hump and by other ranges receding to a line of snowy surf; and before you know how, Isfahan has become indelible, has insinuated its image into that gallery of places which everyone privately treasures."

The Mughal Empire

The empire of the Mughals, unlike that of the Safavids, was founded in a society where Islam was less deeply rooted; indeed, where the majority of the people were Hindus. The Mughals, moreover, not only brought beneath their sway the classical centers of Hindu civilization in the north, like Benares and Ajudhia, but almost all the subcontinent in which the Hindus lived. Their response to the challenge of ruling a still vital civilization of unbelievers was to leave indelible marks on their achievement.

Babur (1483–1530), the founder of the Mughal empire, had good qualifications for such a task, being descended through his father from Tamerlane and through his mother from Gengis Khan. He spent his youth trying to recapture Samarqand as a prelude to rebuilding his ancestor's vast empire, but by the time he was 30 he had done no more than establish a realm in Afghanistan based on Kabul, Qandahar, and Badakshan. Despairing of success in his homeland, he turned his gaze toward India, which was divided among many rulers. In the south there was the Hindu Vijayanagar empire and a string of Muslim commercial principalities down the southwest coast. In the center there was a covey of small Muslim sultanates. In the north there were two significant powers, the warrior Rajput

princes of Rajasthan and the Lodi Afghans who ruled the Indo-Gangetic heartland from the banks of the Indus to the borders of Bengal. Babur saw many divisions and little stability and seized his opportunity, defeating the Lodi army in 1526 at the hotly disputed field of Panipat, where his Turkish artillery were decisive.

Babur, a man of sensibility, taste, and humor whose memoirs glitter with intelligence, brought the Mongol vision of empire to India. But, as he died in 1530, he did not enjoy it for long. He was succeeded by Humayun, his able though wayward son, who held sway for a shaky 10 years after which he was overthrown by his vassal, Sher Khan Sur, who ruled Bihar, and he was forced to take refuge at the court of the Safavid Shah Tahmasp. The Suris quickly took a firm grip, reforming land revenue assessments and creating a vigorous centralized bureaucracy. It seemed that the Mughal era was no sooner begun than ended. Only a lingering claim to Indian empire remained.

Humayun, however, was able to restore Mughal fortunes. The Suri dynasty succumbed to faction, and Humayun, helped by Shah Tahmasp, regained his patrimony in 1555. Within six months he was dead; he fell down his library stairs, which was an appropriate end for a man of learning and culture. Nevertheless, the period of Mughal greatness now began. In 1556 Humayun's son Akbar, most gifted of the remarkable Mughal line, succeeded at the age of 14. Within 10 years he began to absorb the petty regimes on his borders. By 1569 all Rajputana was subdued, except Mewar whose proud prince was still a fugitive in the jungle, or so the legend goes, when Akbar died; by 1572 he had overrun fertile Gujarat

◀ *The Imam Mosque is one of the glories of Isfahan, famed for its seven-color mosaic tiles and calligraphic inscriptions.*

▶ *This map illustrates the expansion of Mughal rule from 1526 to the beginning of the 18th century, when it reached its greatest extent.*

and by 1576 Bengal, richest province of the north; then followed Kashmir (1586), Orissa (1592), Baluchistan (1595), and a little later the Deccan kingdoms of Berar and Khandesh. By Akbar's death in 1605 his empire stretched from the Hindu Kush to the Bay of Bengal, and from the Himalayas to the Arabian Sea and the center of the Deccan plateau. There remained two unstable frontiers: that in the northwest which Jahangir (1605–27) and Shah Jahan (1627–58) contested with the Safavids and which was preserved with the loss of Qandahar (1649) into the 18th century, and that in the south, where the Mughals slowly advanced at the expense of the Muslim sultanates of the Deccan. When Awrangzeb (1658–1707) captured Bijapur (1686) and Golkonda (1687), he expanded the empire to its greatest extent, although by this time it was being weakened by internal rebellions.

Akbar created the administrative and political system which brought the empire strength and durability. Following a pattern sketched by the Suris, he built a government machine which took royal power right down to the villages where officials collected the revenue. Central to the success of the Mughals was their generally fair and accurate system of revenue assessment. Admittedly they demanded a high rate, normally one-third of the annual produce, although this was not unusual in agrarian empires. On the other hand, peasants had revenue remitted in bad years, were allowed to keep the profits of good years, and were encouraged by the system to bring more land into cultivation. Much of this achievement was due to the contribution of Akbar's revenue minister, the Hindu Todar Mai. The proceeds filled the imperial treasury, paid for the dynasty's great building projects, and supported the imperial service, which lay at the heart of the government machine. This service, the forerunner of the British Indian Civil Service, was organized as one great military household answerable to the emperor alone. The officers, called *mansabdars*, holders of commands, were arranged in 33 grades from a commander of 10 to a commander of 5000. They did not inherit their positions, progressing only by imperial favor; they were the pool of talent from which the emperor drew his civil and military officers. Two points should be noted about them in Akbar's time: first that they were mainly foreigners, only about one-third being born in India, and second that, although they were assigned the revenues of specific lands and were encouraged to visit them, they were actually paid by the royal treasury.

The whole framework of Akbar's government depended on Hindu cooperation. Half of the *mansabdars* born in India were Hindus and their faith did not prevent them from rising high in what was a career open to talent. Most of the lesser officials, those who were in fact responsible for day-to-day administration, were also Hindus, as they were later to be under the British. The dependence on Hindus in the administration was mirrored in politics in relations with the Rajput chiefs who had been the Mughals' major Hindu competitors for power in northern India. Once defeated, they were drawn into the service of the empire as military commanders, provincial governors, and counselors of the emperor. They were allowed to rule their own chiefdoms and shared the same privileges at court as Muslim nobles. Indeed, their partnership in empire reached into the royal bed; Akbar married a princess from Jaipur, and so the mother of his heir, Jahangir, was a Hindu.

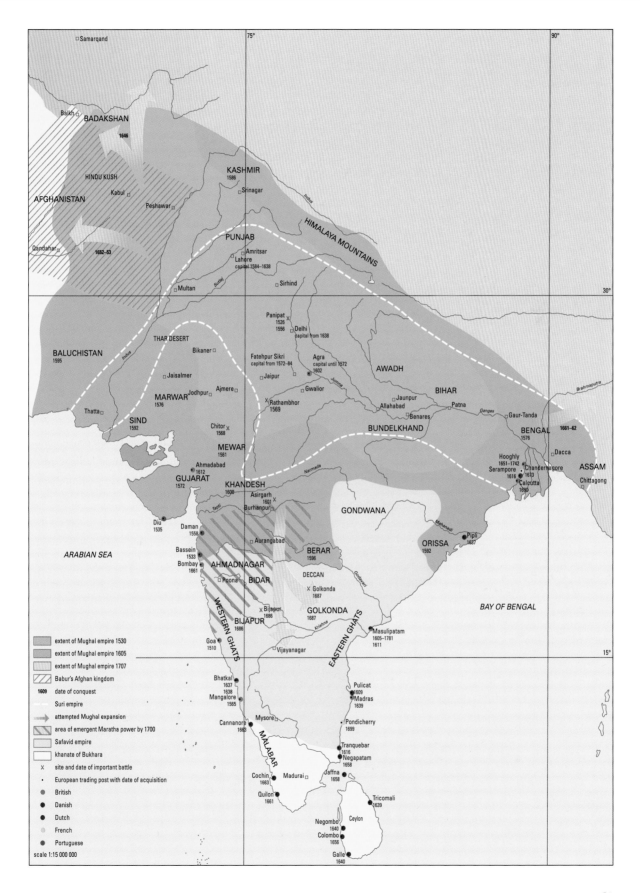

□Samarqand

75°   90°

Balkh□
BADAKSHAN
1646

HINDU KUSH
KASHMIR
1586

Kabul□   □Srinagar

AFGHANISTAN   Peshawar□

PUNJAB   HIMALAYA MOUNTAINS

Qandahar□   **1652–53**   □Amritsar
                        □Lahore
                        capital 1584–1638

□Multan   Sutlej   □Sirhind   30°

BALUCHISTAN
1595   THAR DESERT   Panipat
                                 1526
                                 1556   Delhi
                    □Bikaner   capital from 1638

                              Fatehpur Sikri   Agra   AWADH
                              capital from 1572–84 capital until 1572
                    □Jaisalmer   □Jaipur 1602   BIHAR
                                                 □Gwalior
           □Jaisalmer   Jaunpur   Patna
MARWAR Jodhpur□ Ajmere□   X Rathambhor   Allahabad□
1576   1569   □Benares   □Gaur-Tanda
Thatta□   Brahmaputra
        SIND   Jumna   BENGAL   **1661–62**
        1592   Chitor X   BUNDELKHAND   **1576**
                          1568   □Dacca
                MEWAR   ASSAM
                1561   □Chittagong
                     Ahmadabad□   Narmada
                         1612
           GUJARAT   KHANDESH   Hooghly
           1572   1600   1651–1742
                       Asirgarh   Serampore Chandernagore
                        1601 X   1616 1673
                    Burhanpur   Calcutta
Diu□   GONDWANA   1690
1535   Mahanadi
    Daman□
     1558   Aurangabad□   ORISSA   Pipli
ARABIAN SEA   Bassein□   BERAR   **1592**   1637
               1533   Tapti   **1596**
            Bombay□
             1661   AHMADNAGAR   □Poona   DECCAN
                                  BIDAR   Godavari
                                         X Golkonda
                                           1687
                        X Bijapur   GOLKONDA   BAY OF BENGAL
            BIJAPUR   1686   1687
             1686   Krishna   EASTERN GHATS
         Goa□
         1510   WESTERN GHATS   □Vijayanagar   15°
                                               Masulipatam
                                               1605–1781
                                               1611
              Bhatkal
               1637
               1638   Pulicat
        Mangalore   1609
          1565   Madras
                            1639
              Mysore□ Pondicherry
    Cannanore   1699
      1663
       MALABAR   Tranquebar
                  1616
                 Negapatam
                  1658
         Cochin□ Madurai□   Jaffna
          1663   1658
            Quilon
             1661   Tricomali
                             1639
                    Negombo   Ceylon
                     1640
                    Colombo
                     1656
                       Galle
                       1640

Legend:

	extent of Mughal empire 1530
	extent of Mughal empire 1605
	extent of Mughal empire 1707
	Babur's Afghan kingdom
1609	date of conquest
	Suri empire
	attempted Mughal expansion
	area of emergent Maratha power by 1700
	Safavid empire
	khanate of Bukhara
x	site and date of important battle
•	European trading post with date of acquisition
●	British
●	Danish
●	Dutch
○	French
●	Portuguese

scale 1:15 000 000

The pious strive to defend Islam

The natural accompaniment of such reliance on Hindus was the policy of religious toleration which Akbar adopted, as had other Muslim rulers of Hindu peoples before. Soon after his reign began he abolished first the tax on Hindu pilgrims, and then the *jizya*, the tax levied by holy law on unbelievers in Muslim territory. He took steps to avoid giving offense to other faiths, replacing the Islamic lunar calendar with the solar calendar and forbidding Muslims to kill or eat the cow which Hindus revered. Concerned that no penalties should attach to any particular religion, he set aside the death penalty prescribed by the holy law for apostasy, and financed the places of worship of all faiths. That he valued justice and human dignity above the provisions of any particular faith was demonstrated by his opposition to the Muslim practice of slavery

no less than to the high-caste Hindu practice of burning a widow along with her dead husband. Obviously such a liberal policy required firm control of the Muslim religious establishment. Like the early Safavids, Akbar strove to make the *ulama* dependent on the state and resumed many of their grants. He demanded that they attend court if they wished to benefit from royal funds. Intolerance was forbidden. When in the 1570s the official leaders of the *ulama* tried to persecute Akbar's freethinking friends, the family of Abul Fazl, they were disgraced.

Akbar's public religious tolerance was matched by a private religious eclecticism. He sought all kinds of religious knowledge with extraordinary zeal. At first he was devoted to sufi saints, traveling almost every year to the shrine of Muin al-Din Chishti at Ajmere and ensuring that two of his sons were born at the house of Shaikh Salim

▲ *This 17th century miniature painting depicts the Mughal emperor Akbar astride an elephant.*

◄ *Emperor Babur, founder of the Mughal dynasty, strove for over 30 years to win an empire that would match the achievements of his ancestors.*

▲ *Shaikh Salim Chishti promised the childless Akbar that he would have three sons. When his prophecy came true, Akbar decided to build a new capital city at Fatehpur Sikri, where the Sufi saint lived.*

Chishti at Fatehpur Sikri. Then, in the mid-1570s, he seems to have had a mystical experience which led to whole days and nights being spent in prayer; encouraged by the rationalist Abul Fazl, he opened a "House of Worship." Here he presided over religious discussions in which Sunni *ulama*, sufis, Hindus, Zoroastrians, Jews, Jains, and Jesuits from Goa all participated. The *ulama* did not acquit themselves well, calling each other "fools and heretics" until they became, as the historian Budauni recorded, "very Jews and Egyptians for hatred of each other." In 1582 Akbar founded the "Divine Faith" (*Din-i-Ilahi*) which was his own eclectic cult, much influenced by Zoroastrianism and focused on himself.

Akbar's public policy was continued by Jahangir and Shah Jahan; and his tolerant and syncretic approach to Islam in India culminated in Shah Jahan's favorite son,

Dara Shikoh (1615–59). This prince, who was to be executed for apostasy by his younger brother Awrangzeb, began as a sufi of the Qadri order, writing irreproachable mystical works which were much influenced by Jami. Then he sought the company of Hindu mystics, translated their scriptures, and came to build a structure of syncretic thought in which he identified the essence of Hinduism with the essence of Islam. Not surprisingly, behind much of his thinking lay the pantheistic sufism of Ibn al-Arabi, long influential in India. His aim, however, was less to move from Islam toward Hinduism than to find the ground they shared. But in the process he demonstrated the great danger in the combination of sufi and Hindu pantheism, how in fact they might combine to undermine Islamic orthodoxy.

The pious felt bound to resist such developments. They were led by followers of the Naqshbandi order, and their resistance gained momentum after Khwaja Baqi-billah came to India in the last years of Akbar's reign. One of his disciples, Abd al-Haqq of Delhi (1551–1642), laid down the lines of a learned counter-offensive, especially in the study of the traditions. Even more important was Baqi-billah's favorite disciple, Shaikh Ahmad Sirhindi, who through sufism itself redirected Muslim attention to the Quran, the traditions, and the holy law. He refuted the pantheists and upheld the transcendence of God and the need for man to be guided by his revelation. Few followed Sirhindi at the time, and when he presumed on Jahangir's succession to delight in the death of Akbar and to urge the new emperor to mold the state on the basis of the holy law, he was made to cool his heels in prison.

The tide began to turn when Awrangzeb came to the throne. He was friendly with *ulama* and with followers of Sirhindi, and had an orthodox temperament. As his reign unfolded, he slowly withdrew from the eclectic rule of his forebears into a distinctly communal style. Religious disabilities were imposed on Hindus; many temples were destroyed after 1669; and from 1679 the *jizya* was levied again. The emphasis on the emperor as the ruler of a multi-confessional society was cut down. He attended fewer Hindu festivals and gave up making the dawn appearance to the people on a balcony. He also strove to cast Indian society into an orthodox mold, reintroducing the lunar calendar, discouraging the study of pantheistic thought, enforcing the holy law in a whole range of matters, and commissioning the compilation of a comprehensive digest of Hanafi jurisprudence, the *Fatawa-i Alamgiri*, on the basis of which the empire would become an Islamic theocracy.

With the reign of Awrangzeb following on closely behind the work of Abd al-Haqq and Ahmad Sirhindi, a new strand developed in Indian Islam. In subsequent centuries members of the Mujaddidi branch of the Naqshbandi order, which Sirhindi founded, were to extend this strand not just through India but throughout much of the Islamic world. It was to be an extraordinary source of vitality both before and during the European onslaught.

▼ *Art flourished under the Mughals. This detail from a 16th-century painting depicts Noah's ark, threatened, according to Muslim tradition, by Iblis, the devil.*

▶ *Emperor Shah Jahan enthroned in his durbar, or audience chamber. During his reign literature, art and calligraphy flourished, but architecture was his passion.*

Cultural expression of synthesis

Mughal art expressed both the power of the empire and the compromises on which it was based. The arts flourished under all the emperors to the end of the 17th century except Awrangzeb, under whom patronage ran dry and inspiration withered. One typical area was music, where a syncretic tradition which dated back to the 13th century was sustained by men like Faqir Allah, whose analysis of the principles of musical composition, *Rag Darpan* (1666), was derived in part from Sanskrit sources. Another was language. The court spoke Persian, but in the interaction between the court and the world in which it moved the new Urdu language was growing up—a northern Indian dialect in grammar but largely Persian in vocabulary, an expressive tongue which was to become the favorite language of Indo-Muslim civilization.

Akbar was the founder of Mughal painting. In exile in Kabul he and his father had both taken lessons from two leading Safavid court painters, Mir Saiyid Ali and Abdus Samad, who were persuaded to join them in India when they reconquered the empire. Akbar placed them in charge of the royal studios in which over a hundred painters, mainly Hindus from Gujarat, Rajasthan, and Kashmir, learned to blend the formal and richly jeweled style inherited from Bihzad to their own lively and colorful traditions.

When Akbar died, there were 24,000 illustrated manuscripts in his library. Although he could not read, he loved to have others read to him. Reflecting, no doubt, the emperor's restless curiosity, the range of subjects painted, as compared with the productions of Safavid artists, broadened significantly. The Persian literary classics favored by the Iranian and Central Asian courts were still illustrated, and into this category falls the first great project of the royal studio, the famed *Hamzanama*, which contains 1400 paintings on cloth. But Hindu epics like the *Ramayana* and the *Mahabharata* were also illustrated, as were the great sagas of the Mughal house, the *Timurnama*, the *Baburnama*, and the *Akbarnama*, the last being an unparalleled pictorial record of the reign.

Jahangir was, if anything, an even more enthusiastic patron than his father and took pride in his connoisseurship, claiming to be able to recognize at a glance the work of artists alive and dead. In his time Mughal painting achieved its widest range of mood and most distinctive forms.

Architecture expresses even better than painting both the marriage of Islamic and Indian modes and the vaunting power of the empire. Nowhere is synthesis more clearly achieved than in Akbar's temporary capital of Fatehpur Sikri, a few miles from Agra, which has been preserved almost intact to the present day. Built between 1569 and 1585, its architecture combines the Muslim tradition of arches, domes, and spacious courts with the Hindu tradition of flat stone beams, ornate decoration, and solidity. Power flows from the work of Shah Jahan, builder of builders, who restored the imperial capital to Delhi and constructed yet another city at this ancient focus of Indian government: Shahjahanabad. Around it ran a great red sandstone wall; on a plinth at the center stood the largest congregational mosque in India; overlooking the river Jumna stood a vast palace fortress, the Red Fort, in which the visitor who penetrated to its heart found superb white marble pavilions decorated with gold and precious stones. Shah Jahan would have been esteemed for these buildings and

others elsewhere, but then he also raised at Agra a wondrous masterpiece, the incomparable Taj Mahal, built to hold the body of Mumtaz Mahal, the queen he loved, and defying, as a contemporary chronicler so aptly said, "an ocean of descriptions." Here to synthesis and power was added perfection.

Mughal Moods

The Mughals, like the Safavids, were great bibliophiles. They went one better, however, than their Iranian contemporaries. They not only collected books and commissioned illustrated editions, they also wrote them. We have already noted Babur's memoirs, one of the world's great autobiographies. Jahangir also wrote memoirs which are less well known, although remarkable for the picture they give of court life as well as of the emperor's consuming interest in painting and in the world about him.

Painting sets out most clearly, along with architecture, the synthesis between Islamic culture and Hindu India on which the Mughal empire rested. So Akbar's studios not only illustrated Turkish, Arabic, and Persian classics, they also produced editions of the Hindu epics, the *Ramayana* and the *Mahabharata*. If the first masters in the studios were leading Safavid painters, the 150 or so painters' names that are known are those of Hindus, mainly from western India. In such hands the formal style of Iran and Central Asia, with its mosaics of brilliant color, was given an increasingly distinctive Indian impress, of life, humanity, more literal depiction of human and animal forms, and new color preferences, for dark greens, olives, and grays.

The art reached its height under Jahangir. "As regards myself," he confided in his memoirs, "my liking for painting and my practice in judging it have arrived at such a point that when any work is brought before me... I say on the spur of the moment that it is the work of such and such a man. And if there be a picture containing many portraits, and each face be the work of a different master, I can discover which face is the work of each of them. If any other person has put in the eye and the eyebrow of a face, I can perceive whose work the original face is, and who has painted the eye and the eyebrows."

Garden Tombs

"These are the Gardens of Eden," declared the inscription over the gateway of Akbar's garden tomb at Sikandra; "enter them to dwell therein eternally." The word "paradise" is simply a transliteration of the old Persian word *pairidaeza*, meaning a walled garden, which traveled through Greek and Latin into English. The Mughals brought the vision alive on earth by burying their celebrated dead in garden tombs. The mausoleum was the focal point of a walled garden which was designed, as was the building itself, to represent basic cosmological ideas. It also asserted the power of the dynasty, not least in the scale of the architecture. The four greatest tombs, those of Humayun, Akbar, Jahangir, and Shah Jahan, rank with the Pyramids as the world's finest funerary monuments. "I have never seen the vision lovelier," the English novelist E. M. Forster wrote of Shah Jahan's Taj Mahal. "I went up the left hand further minaret and saw all the magnificent buildings glowing beneath me and all the country steaming beneath a dim red and grey sky, and just as I thought nothing could be more beautiful a muezzin with a most glorious voice gave the evening call to prayer from a Mosque: 'There is no God but God.'"

◀ *The Taj Mahal (1632–54) at Agra is the supreme example of a garden tomb— a mausoleum that was the focal point of a walled garden.*

The Ottoman Empire

In 1500 the Ottoman state was rapidly becoming one of the most powerful in the world, and the next 70 years were to see a tremendous expansive thrust. The greatest area of expansion was to the east and south. Azarbaijan was conquered in 1514, Syria and Palestine in 1516, Egypt in 1517. The holy cities of Mecca and Medina soon followed, and later the Yemen, and the very important province of Iraq in 1534. The Ottomans were drawn to the south by the need to ward off the Portuguese who were threatening Muslim trade and pilgrimage routes. Initially they had tried to meet the problem by propping up the Mamluk regime in Egypt, but soon found it inept and so annexed that wealthy province to the empire. The Ottomans were drawn to the east by the rise of the Safavids, whose militant Shiism threatened their hold on the tribes of eastern Anatolia. The victory of Selim I (reigned 1512–20) over Shah Ismail at Chaldiran removed the threat to the Ottoman heartland. Nevertheless, for the next two centuries the empire was much absorbed in long and debilitating wars with the Safavids over religion, trade, and territory.

The traditional direction of expansion was to the northwest. It was mainly in this direction that, right from the foundation of the holy warrior state by Osman I (reigned 1281–1324) in northwestern Anatolia, the Ottomans had striven to subject infidel territory to Muslim rule and the holy law. After Selim I's great victories in the east and south, his successor, Sulaiman the Magnificent (reigned 1520–66), began his reign with a major victory, capturing Belgrade, the southern stronghold of the Hungarians, in 1521. This was followed by the destruction of the Hungarian army at Mohacs in 1526 and the siege of the Habsburg capital of Vienna in 1529, which was lifted just as the city was about to capitulate only because Sulaiman's army wanted to get home before winter set in. For a while the Ottomans accepted the Hungarians as vassals, but by the 1540s they had taken formal control of a vast swathe of territory whose frontier stretched in a great crescent which extended from Trieste to within sight of the walls of Vienna and east to the Crimea.

The Ottomans advanced in no less marked fashion in the Mediterranean. From the late 15th century they had controlled the Black Sea, an achievement which followed from the command of the Bosphorus won by the conquest of Constantinople. Now they took control of the Aegean, expelling the Knights of St. John from Rhodes in 1522 and the Venetians from their outposts on the Aegean mainland by the 1540s. At the same time, using Moorish pirates as proxy forces to begin with, they annexed the North African

ATLANTIC OCEAN

FRANCE

Paris

Madrid

SPAIN

Algiers

ALGERIA
1519
Tlemcen

Fez

MOROCCO

SAHARA

0°

Ottoman lands 1512

conquests of Selim I 1512–20

conquests of Sulaiman the Magificent 1520–

conquests of 1566–1683

area temporarily held by Ottomans, later reconquered by Safavids

Spalato   Venetian possession

1578   date of conquest

(1603)   date of loss

✕   site and date of important battle

scale 1:28 000 000

coast as far as Morocco and then defended it against Habsburg counter-attacks, an overall strategy which sometimes benefited from French aid. The star of this Mediterranean expansion was Khairuddin, known as Barbarossa to the Christians, who rose from being a pirate based on

Tunis in 1502 to become grand admiral of the Ottoman fleet in 1533. This expansion reached its peak as twice, in 1551 and in 1565, the Ottomans attempted to seize Malta, the key to the western Mediterranean. After the second attempt failed, they annexed Cyprus in 1570 and concentrated on

▼ *The map shows the expansion of the Ottoman empire from a small crusading state in 1512 to the most powerful state in the western world in 1683.*

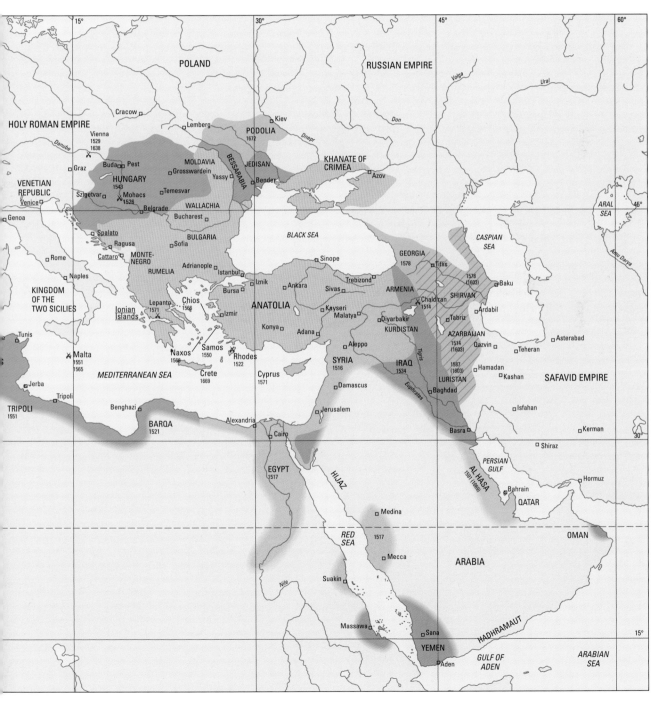

consolidating their hold on the eastern Mediterranean, a hold which was only temporarily shaken by their overwhelming defeat at Lepanto in 1571.

By the reign of Selim II (1566–74), known to his subjects as "Selim the Yellow" and to Europeans as "Selim the Sot," the great expansion was drawing to a close. For the next hundred years the Ottomans defended the frontiers they had or recaptured territory they had lost. Then there was a brief flurry of further expansion: Crete was taken in 1669, the Ukraine in the 1670s, and in 1683 the Ottoman army was once more beneath the walls of Vienna, but it was beaten back.

Under Sulaiman the Magnificent society was divided into the large mass of subjects, Muslim and non-Muslim, who produced the wealth which supported society's other class, the military, who manned the state apparatus. A late 17th-century Ottoman chronicler, Mustafa Naima, saw the relationship between the two as a "cycle of equity": 1. there could be no rule or state without the military; 2. maintaining the military required wealth; 3. wealth was raised from the subjects; 4. the subjects could only prosper through justice; 5. without rule and state there could be no justice.

To be a member of the ruling military class a man had to be a Muslim, in heart and soul, be loyal to the sultan, and follow all the complex culture which formed the Ottoman way. Men who did not possess these attributes were considered part of the subject class, whatever their fathers may have been. In Sulaiman's time the class was recruited in part from the old Turkoman families who had ruled much of Anatolia after the decline of the Seljuqs, many of whom were granted *timars* or lands in exchange for which they performed government service, and in part

from slaves who emerged from a system of recruitment and training known as the *devshirme*, meaning to collect or assemble. This was a levy on the sultan's Christian subjects which became a firmly established practice in the mid-15th century. At regular intervals agents did a sweep through the provinces selecting Christian youths fit for the sultan's service. The most gifted, about 10 percent of the levy, were sent to the palace school, where they learned to read and write Arabic, Persian, and Ottoman Turkish; they were converted to Islam and were instructed in the religious sciences; they learned to wrestle, shoot, and ride; and finally they were trained for a particular branch of the administration. The remainder of the levy were sent to work for Turkish farmers in Anatolia, where they too were converted to Islam, became physically hardened, and absorbed the Ottoman way of life so that they were fitted for their destiny, which was usually to serve in the elite corps of the army. All alike had no connections with established Ottoman society except through the sultan. Understandably, sultans came increasingly to appreciate the value of a well-indoctrinated and completely loyal body of slaves, and from the reign of Mehmet II (1444–46, 1451–81) they came to play an increasingly large part in the state service. By the time of Sulaiman the Magnificent they dominated the service, having to a large extent displaced the old Turkoman aristocracy from the key positions. Indeed, they had come to play a part in the state which resembled that of the "slaves of the royal household" in the Safavid state under Shah Abbas the Great.

The state service divided into four functional sections. At the head there was the palace, containing the harem which was

◀ Sulaiman the Magnificent was not only an outstanding military commander but also an enlightened ruler who oversaw some of the great Ottoman achievements in the law, art, literature, and architecture.

HARIA
NVS
BARE
RVSS

at times very influential, and those who served the sultan both within the palace and in his relations with the outside world. Then there was the bureaucracy, which embraced the Imperial Council, the central organ of Ottoman administration headed by the grand vizier, and the Imperial Treasury which controlled finance. Next were the armed forces, the most important part of which was the slave army, the standing army of the sultan, in which the Janissary infantry, a highly trained force numbering 30,000 men, were the elite corps. Finally there was the learned institution, which was staffed by *ulama* who enforced the Sharia and transmitted their Islamic knowledge to the next generation, and which was the one area of the state's activities in which members of the Ottoman families in touch with society continued to predominate.

The focal point of the system was the sultan. He was the master of the ruling class, while they were his slaves and their lives and property were at his disposal; even members of the old Turkoman families had to accept slave status, which legally no free-born Muslim could do, if they wanted to enter the state service. On the other hand, the sultan was the protector of the ruled whose traditions and religions, Muslim and non-Muslim, as well as whose lives and property he made it his business to safeguard. In theory he had absolute power over all men but in fact the sultan was often as much a tool of as master of the complex administrative structure, which showed itself well able to function whether he was active in government, or retired, as sultans did increasingly from the late 16th century onward, to the delights of the harem.

◄ *A 16th-century portrait of the brilliant admiral Khairuddin, known as Barbarossa (red beard) to Christians, who dominated the Mediterranean for years.*

▼ *The magnificent Sulaimaniye mosque complex (built 1550–57) in Istanbul, Turkey.*

This powerful system was one of the strongest pre-modern forms of government. The basic framework of administration was able to sustain the empire as a great power into the mid-19th century. Yet it is clear that at this very time the Ottoman advance grinds to a halt, remains stationary for a hundred years or more, bar the hiccup of the late 17th century, and then begins the long retreat which culminates in the total collapse of World War I (1914–18).

One explanation for this decline sees the key problem in the military system. There, was a single grand army in which the sultan had to be present and it operated from Istanbul, where the great state bureaucracy was centered. Vienna and Mosul were as far as it could reach in a campaigning year, and more distant provinces could not be held against serious opposition. The army, however, depended on victorious campaigns and new territory for its morale and its rewards, so once victories and annexations decreased, the army deteriorated, and the state system which was founded upon it decayed.

In addition, rival powers, especially in Europe, were growing stronger, which made further expansion increasingly difficult. Economic developments in the world at large, moreover, were undermining the empire as a base. Ottoman policy had always been one of self-sufficiency, the different areas of the empire being developed to complement each other, but it was quite unable to resist the high demand for raw materials stimulated in Europe by vast inputs of silver from the New World, the economic growth which followed, and the general rise of European capitalism and European-

▼ *The Baghdad Kiosk is part of the huge palace complex of Topkapı Saray, at Istanbul, the palace of the Ottoman sultans from the 15th to the end of the 19th century.*

dominated trade. Ottoman merchants could not compete with European prices for raw materials. Then, adding insult to injury, raw materials returned as cheap finished goods which undercut the products of the Ottoman craft industries. The problems were exacerbated by a doubling of the population in the 16th century. Prices quadrupled in the 200 years after 1570, which tended to make land more valuable as a source of investment than as the basis on which the *timar* holders could realize their obligations to the state as soldiers or as administrators.

The limitations of the military system and the external economic pressures might not have been so damaging had there not been a weakening at the heart of the state's strength, the administrative system. Discipline slackened. Corruption set in and competence was undermined as offices began to be sold. At the same time the sultans' grip of the system loosened, in part because the freak of heredity that brought to the Ottoman line a succession of rulers of genius down to the mid-16th century came to an end, and in part because the slaves themselves worked to prevent the emergence of a strong monarch. No longer did the sultan come forward as the victor in a military contest among the claimants to the succession but as the consequence of a political contest between slave factions allied to family interests within the harem, all of which wanted the elevation of a pliable ruler. In these circumstances it was the grand vizier rather than the sultan who was usually the strong man in the state. Further signs of the slackening discipline appeared in the early 17th century as the *devshirme* was abandoned and the character of the slave household changed. From being a regularly recruited, socially isolated elite corps in which promotion was by merit, it became a privileged hereditary group concerned to hasten the progress of their sons through bribery. This indiscipline at the center was transmitted to the provinces, as is revealed by the many rebellions which broke out in the 16th and early 17th centuries, sometimes under the leadership of the displaced Turkoman aristocracy.

That the halting of the Ottoman advance flowed in large part from the weakening of central government is suggested by the brief resurgence of the Koprulu vizierate. Mehmed Koprulu was appointed grand vizier (1656–61) at a time of great crisis; many rebels were defying the government in eastern Anatolia, and the Venetians had just destroyed the fleet at the mouth of the Dardanelles. Reputedly one of the last members of the slave household to be recruited through the *devshirme*, he used an almost arbitrary terror to remove the abuses which had infected the system. His son, Ahmed (vizier 1661–76), followed his example, although he did not spill so much blood, and so did his foster-son, Kara Mustafa (vizier 1676–83). The result was to restore both military efficiency and military power, and to enable the Ottomans once again to threaten the Habsburg capital.

The pious and the state

The Ottoman *ulama* were in harmony with the Ottoman state, unlike the *ulama* of Safavid Iran, who worked themselves free of state control to challenge the legitimacy of royal government, and the *ulama* of Mughal India, some of whom attacked the state's compromises with Hinduism. This is due in part to the missionary fervor of the early Ottoman holy warrior principality: it bred a sense of communal solidarity and responsibility which influenced the

development of Ottoman culture and the
Ottoman state down the ages. The gradual
growth of the Ottoman empire also helps to
account for the difference: it slowly
established an identity of interests with the
ulama and with sufis hallowed by custom.

By the time of Selim I the Hanafi form of
the *Sharia* had become the law of the
Ottoman empire, although it did not apply in
the Maghrib, where the Maliki form was
dominant, or in Egypt and the holy cities of
Mecca and Medina, where the Shafii form
was dominant. Concern for orthodoxy was
brutally emphasized by large-scale
massacres of Shias. Under Sulaiman the
Magnificent the principles on which the
Sharia was accommodated within the state
were elaborated; hence he was known to the
Ottomans as the "Lawgiver." The work was
done by Khoja Chelebi (1490–1574),
renowned as the greatest legal mind of the
empire, and Shaikh al-Islam (head of the
religious institution) from 1545 to his death.
In practice there were two large areas of
orthodox Muslim life in which the *Sharia* did
not run. One was in matters relating to state
organization and administration, where the
Sharia offered no more than principles,
leaving much room for interpretation. Here
the sultan, acting on precedent, made
regulations, which was regarded as a
legitimate proceeding by most *ulama*, who
nevertheless found their role restricted to
ensuring that the new regulations were
consistent with the *Sharia*. The second area
was at the local level, where a myriad
Muslim villages, guilds, and town quarters
had their own internal means of government
and of reconciling strife. But still the *Sharia*
and the values it generated furnished the
criteria by which action was judged, and in
the Ottoman empire the holy law was more

fully carried into effect than in any other
major state in Islamic history.

As the *Sharia* was at the center of the
state, so were its guardians, the *ulama*. They
had great prestige. By the time of Sulaiman
the Magnificent there was an extended
hierarchy of learning. Budding *ulama* began
by attending elementary mosque schools,
which gave the rudiments of religious
instruction, and went on to work their way
up through four grades of madrasas. There
they were given a very thorough training in
the Islamic sciences, until they reached the
topmost grade, that of the *semaniye*
madrasas, which were built in the mid-16th
century adjoining the Sulaimaniye mosque
in Istanbul. Students who failed to complete
the full curriculum either entered the
bureaucracy or became minor *qadis*; those
who completed the full course often became
teachers, again beginning in the elementary
mosque schools and working their way up
through the system by merit. Teachers were
allowed to apply for posts as *qadis*, and the
higher they had risen in the madrasa
hierarchy, the more senior the posts for which
they might apply. Only teachers in the
advanced and *semaniye* madrasas might
become *qadis* of major cities like Damascus,
Cairo, or Jerusalem, while only teachers in
the *semaniye* madrasas might become Shaikh
al-Islam. Royal authority was felt throughout
the system. In administering the law, *qadis*
had to obey the edicts of the sultan;
meanwhile the opinions of *muftis* had merely
to be "respected." Posts were filled by the
sultan and the grand vizier on the advice of
the Shaikh al-Islam, and they were held at
the sultan's pleasure.

It is remarkable that the *ulama* should
have seemed to succumb so completely to
the authority of the state. They were ordered,

graded, and controlled as nowhere else in the Islamic world. Evidently they were satisfied that the state supported the *Sharia* so strongly and that their authority was so great that there was in practice no conflict.

The mark of the integration of the *Sharia* with the workings of the state was the position of religious minorities. Sufis who went too far were persecuted, and so were Shias, although those in the Shia stronghold of Iraq were not troubled. The Coptic, Greek, Armenian, Syrian Christian, and Jewish communities, who were *dhimmis* and therefore tolerated minorities according to the *Sharia*, were allowed to organize into separate communities, or *millets*, under their own religious leaders and subject to discriminatory taxation. Initially, Christians provided contingents for the army and participated in the guilds. By the 17th century, however, their contingents were no longer welcome, while the guilds were splitting into Christian and Muslim sections. The growing barriers between Muslim and non-Muslim presaged weakness as Ottoman Muslims turned inward to the Islamic community and Ottoman Christians came increasingly to look to the Christian West.

Cultural face of the Sharia state

Ottoman culture seems significantly different from that of its contemporaries. There is, for instance, little of the glitter of Safavid Iran or the vibrant humanity of Mughal India. The ruling elite who made their way up through the state madrasas and palace schools were much concerned with the needs of government, mindful of the restrictions of the *Sharia*, and reflected a world in which order and hierarchy were strong.

Poetry flourished as it did in most Muslim societies. Ottoman science was given a major

boost by the opening of the *semaniye* madrasas adjoining the Sulaimaniye mosque, which produced outstanding work in mathematics, astronomy, and medicine. Geographical writing was stimulated by the expansion of the empire on land and sea, and historical writing stemmed from the desire to record it. Biography, which to a large extent meant recording the lives of the transmitters of Islamic culture, flourished as never before, the encyclopedist, Katib Chelebi (1609–57), producing a masterwork, which drew together the achievement of Islamic culture in Arabic, Persian, and Turkish, and described the lives of those who had contributed to it. Euliya Chelebi (1614–82) spent 40 years journeying in the Ottoman dominions and in Europe, and then devoted the last three years of his life to marshaling his impressions in a *Book of Travels* in 10 volumes.

Ottoman painting has been less highly regarded than that of the Safavid and Mughal courts, but few would deny that there were artists of great originality and expressive power. The early classical style betrayed signs of Persian influence, but as the style developed it acquired its own distinctive quality. At its height court painting reflected distinctive features of the Ottoman state: the sense of order revealed in paintings of the army, the importance of hierarchy displayed in those of the court, and the administrative competence suggested by the concern for the accurate depiction of detail.

The 16th century was also a period of high achievement in carpets, textiles, and ceramics. Iznik, the old Byzantine Nicaea, was the center of ceramic production where craftsmen adopted underglaze painting and developed the capacity to produce seven different colors in this form (deep blue, green, lilac, aubergine, white, black, and a

◀ Looking across the waters of the Golden Horn in Istanbul to the 1,500-year-old cathedral of St Sophia on top of the opposite hill. Under Ottoman rule the church was converted into a mosque with the addition of minarets.

▶ *These plans and sections illustrate Sinan's attempts to surpass the magnificent cathedral of St Sophia, shown here, in Istanbul.*

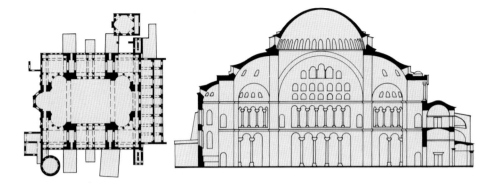

bright coral red) which was an unparalleled technical achievement. At the same time they produced a host of rich but naturalistic designs based on plum and cherry blossom, hyacinths, carnations, peonies, but most of all tulips; 41 different tulip designs are to be seen, for instance, in the tiles of the mosque of Rustam Pasha in Istanbul. Iznik pottery reveals the rapid development of technical skills from 1490 to 1525, when decoration was simply blue and white, to a second phase (1525–50) when more shades of blue and a sage green appear, and then a third phase (1550–1700), when the full range of color and design is employed. By this time, however, the prime effort of the Iznik potters had been directed to tiles, where their most glorious achievement was in the decoration of great buildings such as the mausoleum of Sulaiman, the private rooms of the Topkapi palace, or the mosque of Sultan Ahmed, the interior of which is covered by 20,000 tiles in 70 different designs.

Architecture, which reached its height at the zenith of imperial power in the 16th century, best symbolizes the Ottoman spirit. Over this achievement one man presided: Sinan (1491–1588), royal architect for 50 years, whose genius was matched by a personality which enabled him to turn his post into a powerful office of state. He designed more than 300 buildings, fountains and tombs, caravanserais and kiosks, baths and bridges, madrasas, and mosques, scattered throughout the empire. His three greatest buildings are the Shehzade mosque and the Sulaimaniye mosque, built in Istanbul, and the Selimiye mosque, at Edirne.

The Buildings of Sinan

Sinan Pasha expressed in his buildings the discipline, might, splendor, and devotion to Islam which marked the empire. He became royal architect in 1538 and held the post for 50

▶ *In his early design, the Shehzade, built 1544–48, Sinan rearranged the four half-domes so that they buttressed the main dome.*

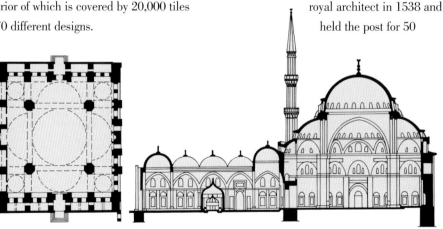

◄ *The Sulaimaniye, built 1550–57, has almost the same proportions as those of St Sophia but Sinan emphasized its breadth.*

years, with the official title of "Architect of the Abode of Felicity," or the Topkapi palace. Topkapi is not a palace at all in the European sense, but a series of pavilions, courts, gardens, reception halls, treasuries, baths, kitchens, and so on, built down the centuries according to the needs of ceremony and practicality. There was no master plan. Almost every part of the palace should be considered as a separate monument, often a separate work of art.

Sinan's most notable work in Istanbul commemorates his great contemporaries. There are the tombs of Sulaiman the Magnificent, of his much-loved Russian queen, Roxelana, and of the brilliant admiral, Khairuddin. There are the mosques of the grand viziers, Sokullu Mehmed Pasha and Rustam Pasha, and that of the Princess Mihrimah who was married to Rustam Pasha. Most notable, however, are the two mosque complexes he built for Sulaiman the Magnificent in Istanbul and the one for Selim II at Edirne.

Sinan was both irked and inspired by the 1000-year-old cathedral church of St. Sophia in Istanbul. He felt that it was an affront to Islam that the emperor Justinian's architects had been able to span with a dome a greater area than Ottoman architects had been able to achieve. He determined to do better. The three great mosque complexes, the Shehzade, the Sulaimaniye' and the Selimiye, mark major stages in his approach to the problem. With the span of the dome of the Selimiye he succeeded. Islam could not have triumphed with a more magnificent building.

► *(following pages) Originally built as a church by the Byzantine emperor Justinian, St Sophia was converted to a mosque in the mid-15th century. Its architecture became the model for mosques throughout the Ottoman empire.*

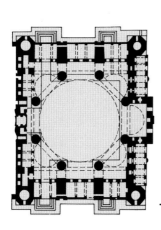

◄ *In the Selimiye, built 1569–75, Sinan succeeeded not only in spanning a wider area than St Sophia but also in creating a perfect Islamic space.*

Further Islamic Lands

We now turn to lands beyond the control of the great Muslim empires, to southeast Asia, to Africa, and to Central Asia and China, where in 1500, North Africa and Central Asia apart, large numbers of Muslims had appeared but recently. They tended to have a firm foothold in particular areas rather than in the region as a whole. They were often a minority and faced great and powerful cultures like the Confucian in China or the Hindu-Buddhist in Java. They had, moreover, no overwhelming military predominance. Islam was not borne into these regions by military might; instead it slowly seeped in, mingling with local cultures and drawing people to the worship of the one God.

Commerce had carried Islam to these lands. Muslim traders, making good use of the fortunate geographical position of the

Islamic heartlands, came in the years before 1500 to control much of the international traffic along the trade routes of the world: the routes of the southern seas which linked the east coast of Africa, the Red Sea, and the Gulf to the rich ports of India, of southeast Asia, and of China; the routes across the Sahara, and especially from the wealthy cities of the Magrib, into the western Sudan and the Niger Basin; and the great Asian land route, the Old Silk route, from the eastern Mediterranean, through Iran, Turkestan, and along the Tarim Basin into China. These arteries of world economy formed natural channels along which Islamic influences flowed; as Muslims came to dominate key areas of the system, their non-Muslim trading partners often came to embrace Islam as well, in part because

▼ This map shows the long-distance trade routes across the Islamic world c. 1500. Islam spread along these commercial arteries.

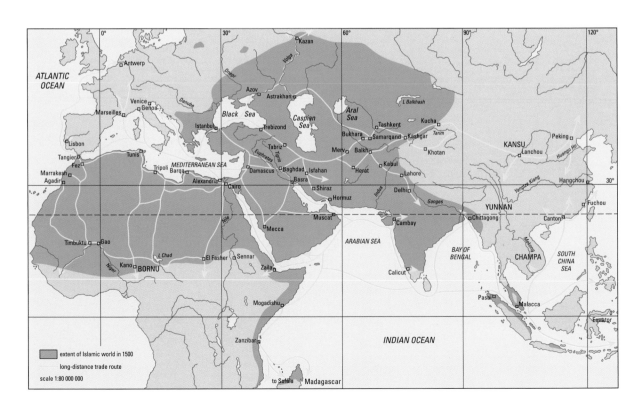

business was so much smoother if men shared a common culture and a common law, although we should not forget the openness of trading communities to new ideas and new experience. After 1500, where Islam had already gained a foothold, traders provided the channel along which cultural reinforcements flowed to enable consolidation to take place. When trade declined, as it did in China, the Muslim foothold in the Confucian world came under threat. Where Islam had yet to penetrate, as in the east of the Indonesian archipelago or in the lands of the upper Niger, traders continued to perform their pioneering role.

The actual work of spreading the faith is usually attributed to saints and sufis. According to Javanese tradition Islam was introduced to the island by nine saints, while in the Upper Volta region of West Africa its arrival is normally traced back to wandering holy men. Some of these founders were very possibly involved in trade themselves; many, however, would merely have accompanied traders on their boats and in their caravans, hoping to render religious services to their fellow travelers and to the communities with which they traded. Doubtless some of these sufis were also deeply learned in the Islamic sciences, but it would have been unwise for them to insist on a strict application of the *Sharia*. The power to support such a stand was unlikely to be forthcoming; moreover, the conflict between the demands of the holy law and local religious practice was likely to be too great. Instead, they shared their knowledge of religious experience with mystics of other faiths. They helped propitiate the supernatural forces which hemmed in and seemed ever to threaten the lives of common folk. They interpreted dreams, brought rain, healed the sick, and

made the barren fruitful. They mediated between rulers and ruled, natives and newcomers, weak and strong. By accommodating themselves to local needs and customs, they gradually built a position from which to begin the long, slow process of Islamization, by which the people were gradually drawn into an Islamic cultural milieu and brought to conform to the *Sharia*. Rapid conversion was rare. Sufis intent on gaining acceptance in new areas did not present Islam in all its exclusiveness and its demands for unqualified commitment; and for most individuals who were potential converts the cost of conversion, of breaking away from their society, and of achieving a total reorientation of the soul, were generally too great to bear. The normal process was one of gradual adhesion in which, for instance, individuals might begin to include visits to saints' tombs among their established religious practices or communities might, like the Bedouin Arabs of the Prophet's time, come nominally to accept Islam after their chiefs or kings had been converted. Islamic and pre-Islamic practices mingled freely in the religious activities of the people, who sometimes came to believe that their particular mixture was the "true" Islam.

Such was the character of the first main stage in Islamization, in which Islam displayed flexibility and sympathy as it interacted with non-Islamic cultures. The second main stage followed as the new Muslims now began to interact with the culture and tradition of the older Islamic lands, traveling to sit at the feet of learned *ulama* in Mecca or Medina or Cairo, or welcoming them in their midst as models of behavior; such processes could lead eventually to reform movements aimed at removing pre-Islamic practices.

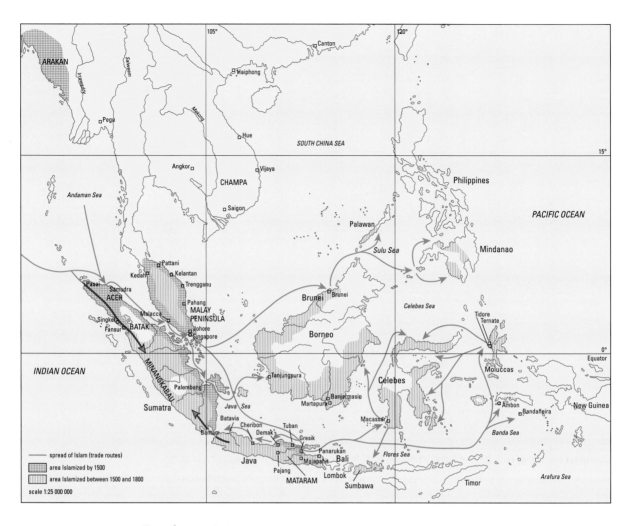

▲ *In 1500 Islam had a footing on a few coastlines; by 1800 it had spread through much of island southeast Asia and had established itself in the Javan hinterland.*

Southeast Asia

In 1500 Muslims were established in many parts of Southeast Asia. They dwelt in many small trading communities down the Burmese coast, and especially in Arakan whose kings were subject to the sultan of Bengal. There was a distinct community of Muslim Chams in Indo-China who had but recently been conquered by the Vietnamese. Moving south to island Southeast Asia we find important Muslim states at the western gateway to the archipelago: Pasai in northern Sumatra, which had been the first Muslim stronghold in the region, and Malacca on Malaya's southern shore, which in the 15th century had come to dominate the straits. From Malacca Muslims had gained a footing along the northerly trade route which ran by northwest Borneo to the Sulu islands and the southern Philippines. They had also spread their influence down the southerly trade route which ran along Java's northern shore and southern Borneo till it reached the Moluccan spice islands of Ternate and Ambon. In some places the Muslims were just a community of foreigners, in others they had brought natives and rulers to share in their beliefs. They had, however, rarely been established for long enough to make a serious impression on the hinterland, although they do seem to have gained a foothold at the Hindu–Buddhist court of the Javan kingdom of Majapahit.

The 16th century began badly for Islam. Malacca was captured by the Portuguese in

1511 and Pasai in 1521. Within three years, however, the new state of Aceh drove the Portuguese out of northern Sumatra and devoted much of the following century to trying to drive them out of the Malay peninsula, on occasion with Ottoman help. Aceh became the new Muslim stronghold, attracting Muslim traders from Malacca and controlling the east and west coasts of Sumatra. The height of prosperity was reached under Sultan Iskander Muda (reigned 1608–37), when Aceh became a focus for all those who traded in the southern seas: Europeans, Indians, and Chinese alike. Religious learning was patronized, great buildings were raised, and Islam was brought to much of Sumatra, including Minangkabau. But soon afterward Aceh declined. The closing of Japan, the Manchu conquest of China, the rise of Macassar to the east, and the Dutch conquest of Malacca in 1641 stemmed the life-giving flow of trade. Yet the state remained relatively strong to the end of the century, important enough to receive a Meccan embassy and able to refuse the demands of an English one.

Macassar replaced Aceh as the standard-bearer of Islam against the European interloper. On September 22, 1605, the prince of Tallo embraced Islam, and on November 19, 1607, the first Friday prayer was held. From now on the Macassarese, noted for their devotion to the faith, fought the Dutch as Christians and as their rivals for control of the spice trade. Their greatest leader was Hasan al-Din (reigned 1631–70) whose empire at its height stretched from Borneo to New Guinea and from Lombok to the southern Philippines. Only after long and bitter fighting did he in 1667 accept Dutch terms which destroyed Macassar's dominance in the trade and politics of the region.

While Aceh and Macassar were advancing Muslim interests along the coasts, Muslims were also making gains inland, notably in Java, the richest and most populous island of the region. Demak, prominent among the Chinese-Javanese Muslim lordships of the northern coast, first spread westward, absorbing Cheribon and carrying Islam into south Sumatra; it then advanced eastward, destroyed the remnants of ancient Majapahit in 1527, and only failed in 1546 before the last bulwark of Hinduism in east Java. At the same time sufis became increasingly active throughout the island; many of them taught a pantheistic mysticism which found a happy home among the numerous Javanese who were still Hindu. Some sufis associated with Muslim rulers, but most kept their distance from earthly powers, gathering disciples around them and dwelling in separate communities. They helped in the rise of Demak, Shaikh Ibn Mawlana of Pasai, for instance, leading the campaign to convert pagan west Java into the Muslim state of Bantam. But after Demak declined, these sufis, whose spiritual authority also brought temporal power, came forward as the arbiters of the island's politics. Prominent among them were: the holy men of Kudus who ruled the old Demak heartland till 1588, the holy men of Giri whose disciples carried Islam to the east of the archipelago and whose fame reached as far as China, and the holy men of Adi Langu whose most eminent representative, Sunan Kali Jaga, became spiritual patron of the empire of Mataram.

The rise of Mataram marked a new stage in the expansion of Islam on Java. For the first time Muslim power was based not on the coastline but at the traditional center of Javanese government in the hinterland. At the height of its power under Sultan Agung (reigned 1613–46) Mataram controlled almost all Java except the enclave where the Dutch held out at Batavia. Sultan Agung's regime had a decidedly Muslim face: he introduced the Islamic calendar, visited the graves of saints, and received the title of sultan from Mecca. Like many Muslim princes he found himself opposed by the guardians of the faith. How far the struggles which followed were either part of the traditional tension between the ports of the northern shore and the rice-growing hinterland, or part of the endemic tension between spiritual and temporal authority in Islam, we cannot know. What is clear, however, is that he and his successors came so much into conflict with the powerful holy men, who led revolts and strove to influence the succession, that from the late 17th century they were forced to rely on Dutch aid to preserve their authority. The price was the steady surrender to the Europeans of their territory, which by the late 18th century had been pared down to south central Java.

As a political force the holy men were subdued yet survived. Usually called *Kiyayi*, they lived in special Muslim holy villages whose peoples followed their example, or established themselves outside village communities in small settlements where they would pass on their knowledge of the Quran, the traditions, the law, and mysticism.

In Aceh the learned served the state which made much of scholars and religious

▼ *This map shows the sultanates of the Malacca straits and Java in the 16th and 17th centuries. Note the centers of the Javanese holy men.*

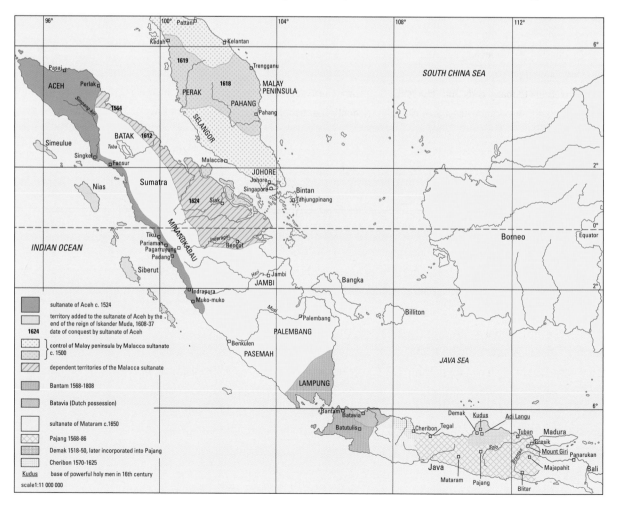

learning. In the 17th century Aceh was the foremost center of scholarship in the archipelago. Here *ulama* and books came from India and Arabia, while the Acehnese made the pilgrimage to Mecca and studied under the leading *ulama* of the Hijaz, the Yemen, and the Gulf, while emissaries went to the Mughal and Ottoman courts.

In Mataram, where Islam struggled with the ancient Hindu–Buddhist traditions, most Javanese had probably become Muslims by the end of the 18th century. At the heart of the struggle between the two great religious traditions lay the problem of bringing an utterly transcendent God to a people who assumed that he existed in everything. When sufis adapted their approach to the world which they wished to transform, they came dangerously close to pre-Islamic beliefs. If some came to comprehend the prospect of the God, others, possibly most, continued their devotions to many gods and demigods alongside their observance of Islamic rites.

In Aceh fewer such ambiguities flourished. Here the great issues of the day lay less between an Islamic and a Hindu-Buddhist pantheism than between two schools of *ulama* struggling to advance their careers. In the early 17th century Aceh seems to have been dominated by a school of heterodox sufis and admirers of Ibn al-Arabi, some of whose writings still exist. Hamza of Fansur (died c. 1600) was the leading light and his pupil and successor Shams al-Din of Pasau was a favorite of Sultan Iskander Muda. Then, just after the sultan's death in 1637, a learned Indian, Nur al-Din al-Raniri, arrived, attacked Shams al-Din's views, burned his books, and persecuted his disciples. Their differences amounted to no more than disagreement over how strictly Ibn al-Arabi's work should be interpreted, yet so close were

the connections of Aceh with the intellectual centers of Islam and so great was the interest aroused by the divisions among its *ulama* that by 1640 echoes of this dispute had reached Medina, where one of the leading figures of the day, Ibrahim al-Kurani, wrote a magisterial work to resolve it.

The 300 years after 1500 form a crucial phase in the progress of Islam in Southeast Asia. No progress was made in Burma or in Indo-China, where international trade was sluggish. In the Philippines, from 1570, the Muslims were kept penned into southern Mindanao by a successful Spanish occupation. In the rest of island Southeast Asia, on the other hand, great progress was made. Although no significant Muslim power survived to the late 18th century and the Dutch East India Company came to occupy the greater part of Java, the Dutch had acquired no overwhelming political predominance, while commercially they were declining. People did not take to European culture and few embraced Christianity. On the contrary, it was the Dutch who had gone far toward molding their ways to the world in which they moved. The significant influences from the West remained those which came via Muslim mouths and Muslim pens, those borne by Nur al-Din al-Raniri or Abd al-Rauf of Singkel. Their attachment to Hindu-Buddhist metaphysical philosophy clothed in anthropomorphic symbolism began to slacken, and they came to participate in the great monotheistic tradition and to lose their faith in the old mythologies. The depth of the change differed from place to place, but by 1800 there had been a decisive shift in the orientation of Indo-Malay civilization.

The most powerful expression of the growing influence of Islam was the spread of the Malay language as a vehicle for literature

▶ *From 1500 Islamic traders continued to foster the expansion of Islam. Throughout the 16th century the* ulama *and* sufis *strove to defend the faith and to promote a purer version of Islam.*

and philosophic discussion, and it did so in the Arabic script. The language was much enriched by Arabic vocabulary and technical terms, becoming widely used along the trade routes of the archipelago and displacing the dominance of Javanese. In other spheres there was much adaptation of old systems to meet new requirements, especially in Java, but the old styles were still discernible. Batik patterns, for instance, became more stylized, mask plays after being banned from the Muslim courts became the property of strolling players, while the magical tradition of women's dance continued but with greater modesty. Pre-Islamic building styles were made to serve the new religious purpose. Thus the 16th-century minaret at Kudus is Hindu-Javanese in style and the roofs of most mosques in Java and Sumatra are layered and pagodalike. But in one sphere there was little adaptation, that of the *wayang* or shadow theater. The traditional cycles of plays, based on the Hindu *Ramayana* or *Mahabharata*, persisted and conceded only the development of a new style, the *wayang golek*, in which the most popular cycle of plays was based on stories about the Prophet's uncle, Amir Hamza.

Africa

Here we are concerned with the areas beyond the effective reach of Ottoman power, from Morocco in the northwest to Africa's Indian Ocean shore. It was free from serious external threat save the occasional Ottoman thrust or the niggling importunity of the European trader. It was not in any way a coherent region; the histories of Morocco, of the western or the Nilotic Sudan, or of the Horn of Africa all followed different patterns. Yet there is a linking theme. All these areas in the early 16th century saw champions of

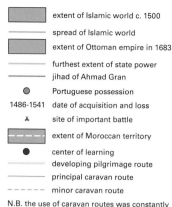

	extent of Islamic world c. 1500
	spread of Islamic world
	extent of Ottoman empire in 1683
	furthest extent of state power
	jihad of Ahmad Gran
●	Portuguese possession
1486-1541	date of acquisition and loss
⚔	site of important battle
	extent of Moroccan territory
●	center of learning
	developing pilgrimage route
	principal caravan route
-----	minor caravan route

N.B. the use of caravan routes was constantly subject to economic and political change

Islam striving to defend the faith or to promote a purer version of Islamic society. Throughout the three centuries from 1500, moreover, where there were states ruled by Muslim princes, *ulama* and sufis were working to consolidate Islam, and not invariably against the royal will, while beyond the boundaries of Muslim power they continued to spread the faith, often hand in hand with trade.

Muslims lived in East Africa from the time of the Prophet. But, except in the Horn where they had spread to the foot of the Ethiopian highlands, they had remained penned in on the coast. There they lived in bustling port cities, for instance, Mombasa, Pate, Kilwa, and Sofala, all of which fell into Portuguese hands soon after 1500. The Horn had its port cities too, notably Mogadishu and Zaila, which escaped Portuguese conquest, but it also had inland Muslim states long tributary to Ethiopia and known collectively as Adal. These rebelled frequently against their overlord, a process which culminated in the early 16th-century jihad of Ahmad Gran (1506–43), the leader of a militant reformist movement which challenged Christian

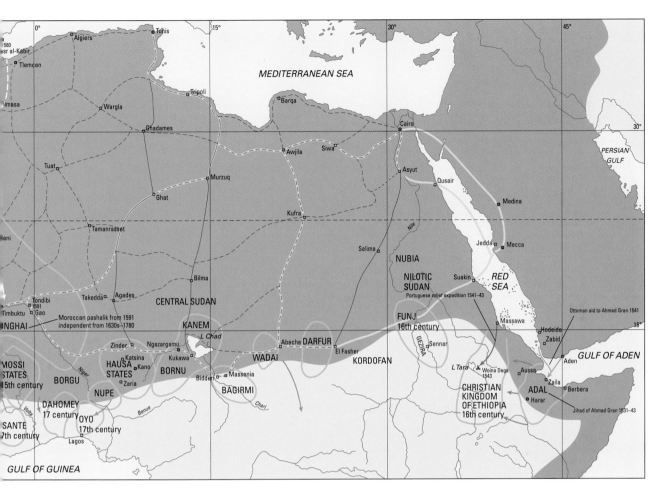

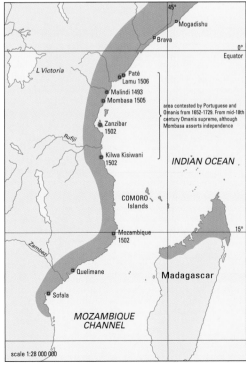

Ethiopia and those who wanted to coexist with it. For 12 years he ravaged the Christian land, strongly supported by the nomadic Somalis, until he was defeated by Portuguese guns and killed. This spelled the end of Adal as an area of inland Muslim states and was followed by a strengthening of the Muslim regimes on the coast. Further south, Muslims continued to strive against the Portuguese until the mid-17th century, when the Omanis became strong enough to drive them out.

The Nilotic Sudan saw a decisive move in favor of Islam as well. Around the beginning of the 16th century the Muslim Arab tribes of Upper Egypt finally conquered the Christian kingdom of Nubia, only to be overwhelmed themselves soon afterward by

◄ Traders had brought Islam to much of Africa's east coast and to the lands south of the Sahara. In the 16th century Europeans began to arrive on the East African shores, yet it would be a long time before they made any great impact.

pagan cattle nomads, the Funj, advancing down the Nile. This defeat, however, was quickly turned into glorious victory when the Funj were converted to Islam and Nubia and the Gezira became Muslim lands. *Ulama* and sufis played a major role in the transformation, and, supported by extensive land grants, were sometimes able to form great dynasties. Thus the land of the pagan Funj became a Muslim sultanate from the mid-16th to the late 18th century when at last it was outshone by a rival sultanate based at Dafur in the far western province of Kordofan.

Even further west there were the little-known kingdoms of Wadai and Bagirmi whose rulers became Muslims in our period. Then around Lake Chad there was the

kingdom of Kanem-Bornu, for long a caravan port on the Sahara's southern fringe and trading much with Egypt and with Tripoli. In the late 15th century the kingdom entered on a new period of strength symbolized by the construction of a permanent walled capital at Ngazargamu on the banks of the Yo. This development reached its height under King Idris Aloma, who reigned between about 1570 and 1619. For a time Kanem-Bornu was a great power in the central Sahara, cultivating the Saadids of Morocco and the Ottomans, and securing military instructions and firearms which gave it the advantage in local wars. At the same time the state was given a sharp push in an Islamic direction, the *Sharia* being widely applied and administered by *ulama*. The state remained powerful to the mid-18th century, by which time its kings were known chiefly for their piety and the *ulama* had come to dominate.

From the time of King Idris Aloma, Hausaland was under the influence of Kanem-Bornu. Here was a clutch of city-states on the savanna lands east of the Niger, some rising, some falling—Katsina, Kano, Gobir, and Zaria being among the more important—and all embroiled in internecine conflict. The long-distance trade was the foundation on which these states were built; east–west along the savanna belt, and from the north down to the Atlantic coast, Islam accompanied this trade and the Hausa peoples came to respect Muslim susceptibilities. Thus King Muhammad Rumfa (reigned 1463–99) of Kano symbolically ceased to follow earlier superstitions by cutting down the city's sacred tree which had grown beside the congregational mosque. Yet in the 300 years which followed, while Islam strengthened its hold, earlier beliefs still flourished.

The greatest state of the west Sudan was the Songhai empire of Gao. At its height in the 16th century it embraced the great bend of the Niger from the Hausa states in the east to Borgu in the south and reached from the Atlantic coastlands in the west across the desert in the north to hold the precious salt deposits of Taghaza and Taodeni almost on the Moroccan frontier. Here too around the beginning of our period there was a shift toward Islam. In 1493 Askia Muhammad, a leading official, challenged the king, who acknowledged the claims of Islam alongside those of many spirit cults, to declare whether he was a Muslim or not. When the king refused, Askia defeated him in battle and seized the throne. He then made much of the *ulama* and set the seal on his revolution by performing the pilgrimage to Mecca between 1495 and 1497. The people of Songhai, however, were loath to accept significant changes in their religious practice, and throughout the 16th century Muhammad's successors were unable, or unwilling, to impose a rigorous Islamic administration. Indeed, the antipathy between the Muslims and those who mixed animism with their Islam formed the basis of debilitating succession struggles. These meant that, when Morocco decided to put an end to the dangerous situation in which a Negro power controlled the two vital Saharan trade commodities of gold and salt, Songhai could not effectively resist. For 40 years from 1591 Morocco controlled the great cities of the Niger bend, and then its interest faded. Nevertheless, Songhai's might was broken, and the trans-Saharan trade which it nourished declined. A mere rump of the old empire, now based on Timbuktu, persisted into the late 18th century. It was famed more for the learning of its *ulama* than the power of its pashas.

Morocco's people had been staunchly Muslim since the early centuries of Islam, and, with its boundaries firmly established on lines which have persisted to the present day, it had long since passed through the processes of state formation which engrossed the regimes of the Sudanic lands. This said, there was at the beginning of the 16th century increasing pressure from the Portuguese along the coast, which stimulated the growth in numbers and in influence of *marabouts*, as Moroccan sufis are called (the term being a French corruption of Arabic and meaning a man "tied" to God), devoted to their expulsion. This movement enabled one holy family, the Banu Saad, to drive the Portuguese out by 1549 and seize power from

the reigning Wattasids by 1553. The Saadids crushed a further Portuguese invasion at al-Qasr al-Kabir in 1578, set about destroying the influence of the very marabouts who had helped them to power, created a centralized administrative system which lasted into the 20th century, and established a brilliant court at Marrakesh. So mighty did the state become that the Ottomans began to scent a rival, and its greatest ruler, Ahmad al-Mansur (1578–1603), felt strong enough just before his death to plan the conquest of Spain with Elizabeth I of England. But there followed succession struggles, weakness, and the resurgence of maraboutic power, until about 1660 another holy family, the Alawites, became predominant. The Saadid machine was revitalized and, as in the central Islamic lands, strengthened with loyal slaves. Henceforth the Alawites grappled with the twin problems of asserting the power of the state over sufi brotherhood and Berber tribe and protecting the integrity of the land from the encroaching European.

In Africa the role of the transmitters of Islam stands forth yet more prominently than in Southeast Asia; this is in part because we know more about them and in part because, leaving Morocco aside, state power was often even weaker than in the sultanates of island Indonesia. These transmitters were sometimes *ulama* and sometimes sufis too, although the great age of the brotherhoods was not to begin till the 18th century. They took their place in verifiable lines of transmission many centuries long, stretching back into the past and forward to the present day. Recent research has revealed how great families often stood at the heart of these lines of transmission, knowledge and blood thus mingling as they flowed down through time. In Timbuktu, for instance, the main lines of

transmission passed through three families, the Aqit, the And-Agh-Muhammad, and the al-Qadi al-Hajj, all of whom emerged in the 15th century and remained prominent in teaching and learning over hundreds of years. Temporal rulers, of course, would move to bring them to heel but over time the contest was rarely equal. Indeed such families could play a leading part in bearing the message of Islam far beyond the reach of Muslim princes.

As one would expect, important centers of Islamic learning flourished. There was Aussa and Harar in east African Adal, Ngazargamu in the center, and Walata further west, but sovereign of them all was Timbuktu, from its early days an Islamic settlement, and one which had literally grown up about its mosques. Here knowledge of the Islamic sciences ran deep and broad. Budding *ulama* studied as rich a course as could be found elsewhere, reading both books and commentaries used widely throughout the Islamic world. At the heart of the educational system lay the study of the law and jurisprudence, an emphasis reflected in the output of the city's most famous scholar, Ahmad Baba (1556-1627), whose works are still preserved in North Africa.

Timbuktu boasted extensive private libraries containing hundreds and even thousands of volumes. Indeed books were the most highly prized items of 16th-century trade. At this time the city had over 150 Quran schools, which suggests that a large proportion of the city's population of 75,000 experienced the first stage of education.

Ulama traveled in the 16th century to Cairo as well as to leading centers of learning in western Asia and the Maghrib to learn from leading teachers of the time. Those who could not travel corresponded. Nor was the

◄ *Timbuktu was the leading center of learning south of the Sahara, and the Sankore mosque was an important focus of advanced teaching.*

▶ *The northern Islamic lands in the 16th century were littered with relatively small states. Elsewhere nomadic peoples roamed freely.*

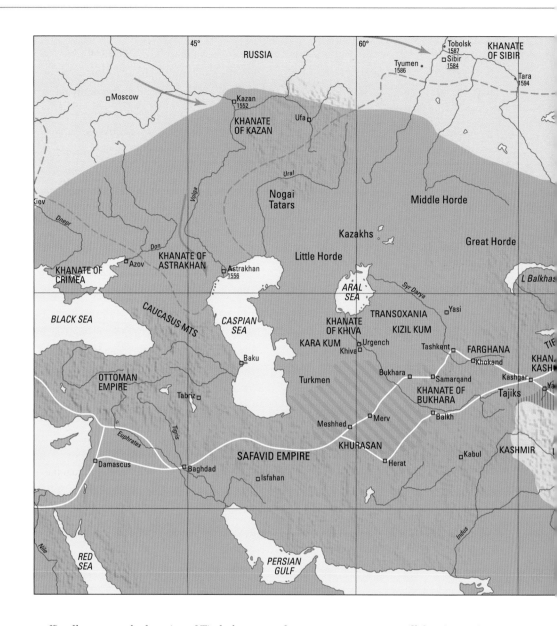

traffic all one way; the learning of Timbuktu was valued highly enough in Morocco for the scholarly Sultan Ahmad al-Mansur to treat Ahmad Baba as a notable prize of his victory over Songhai and to bring him to Marrakesh where Moroccans flocked to sit at his feet.

The vigor and the success of the *ulama* should not lead us to believe that they had everything their own way. Although they stood up for their higher principles, more often than not they also had to stand by while their rulers compromised with pre-Islamic practices. For all the achievements of the *ulama*, many areas were still frontier territory in which the processes of Islamization had but recently begun to operate.

What remains of this distinctive Islamic civilization of the Sudan reflects the role of the *ulama* and of Islam in fashioning it. Arabic was the language of administration, of learning, of correspondence, and of record; it had, moreover, a deep impact on indigenous languages, especially Hausa. More immediately accessible, however, are the clay mosques of the savanna lands, which are striking precisely because indigenous

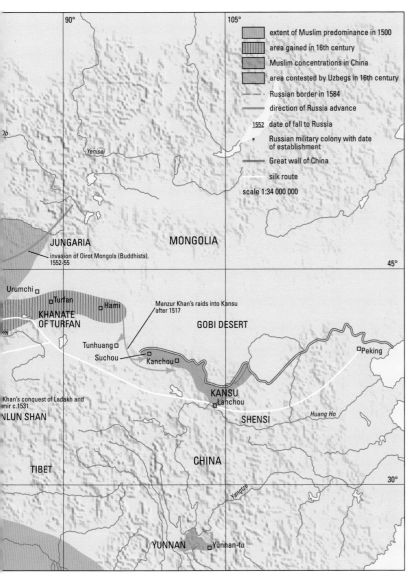

the special maraboutic attribute, *barakat* or divine favor. The countryside became dotted by shrines where the *barakat* of dead marabouts was sought, the people were organized into orders around families whose blood bore *barakat*, and religious practice became dominated by rituals designed to mobilize *barakat*.

Prominent in this movement was a new respect for those who were *sharif*, that is descended from the Prophet. This devotion gained momentum after 1437 when the tomb of Mawlay Idris I (died 791), descendant of the

architectural forms were not completely overwhelmed by those of the central Islamic lands.

If *ulama* figured prominently in the life of sub-Saharan states, it was sufis or marabouts who dominated all aspects of Moroccan life. Until the 15th century they had played a relatively minor part, but then as Moroccans became disenchanted by tribal leadership and alarmed by Christian encroachments, they succeeded in so transforming the consciousness of the people that their religious life became focused on controlling

Prophet and founder of the first Moroccan Islamic state, was rediscovered near Fez. Then it was given specific form by one al-Jazuli whose devotional work, *The Proofs of the Blessings*, was widely used in mystic practice and, more important, focused intense concentration on the Prophet. To be *sharif* became a source of especial spiritual power, for such men most assuredly bore *barakat* in their veins.

It was in this context that the Alawite sharifian family came to establish the dynasty which has persisted to the present day. The sultan was the supreme marabout who demanded complete obedience from his subjects. The educational system no longer emphasized the *Sharia* and the principles of its application but the sufi tradition of imitation and blind obedience to spiritual authority.

Although the Saadians built the largest madrasa in the land at Marrakesh, the great age of madrasa building for which Morocco is famous came to an end. Instead there were vast royal palaces: the el-Badi of the Saadians, the shell of which still stands at Marrakesh, and that of Mawlay Ismail (reigned 1672–1727) at Meknes. Small towns in themselves and separated from their peoples by high walls, they proclaim the power and distant mystery of the sharifian monarchs. But above all there were the royal mausoleums: those of Mawlay Idris I in Fez, of the Saadians in Marrakesh, and of Mawlay Ismail in Meknes. These were the supreme combination of state and maraboutic cult.

Central Asia and China

Here were the northern marches of the Islamic world where by 1500 Muslims were widespread throughout the steppes and

	area of Muslim dominance in 1600
	Russian border in 1584
•	Russian border in 1796
	Russian fortified post
	Russian advance
	Oirot Mongol expansion
	Chinese border c. 1760
	Mughal expedtion
	route of Nadir Shah's raid 1738-39
	boundary of Safavid empire
●	center of learning

▼ *This map shows Central Asia in the 17th and 18th centuries when the area in which Muslims lived freely was steadily reduced.*

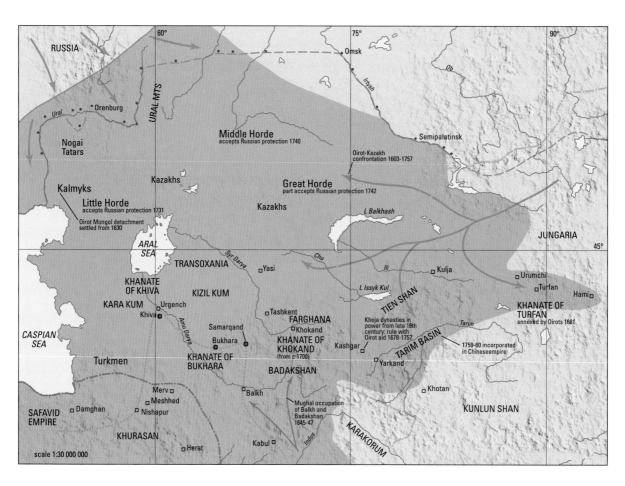

desert oases. In the west there were the khanates of Kazan, Astrakhan, and the Crimea, successor states of the Mongol Golden Horde. In Transoxania, where Tamerlaine and his descendants had presided over glittering courts, the Turkish Uzbeg tribe now ruled and threatened Khurasan. Further east the descendants of Chaghatai, the second son of Gengis Khan, maintained an increasingly precarious hold over Farghana, Jungaria and the oasis cities of the Tarim Basin. In the far east, in Kansu, Shensi, and Yunnan, provinces of China proper, there were notable Muslim communities living under Chinese rule, the descendants of traders and of Muslim officials of the Mongol Yuan dynasty (1280–1368).

Unlike Southeast Asia and sub-Saharan Africa this was not, the lands north and east of the Tien Shan mountains apart, an area in which Islam was still expanding: the features of the three centuries after 1500 were increasing isolation and decline. From the time of the Seljuqs on, steppe peoples had poured through Khurasan into the central Islamic lands. But the Uzbegs, who disdained the use of firearms, found Safavid Iran too firm a barrier. It was, moreover, as much a religious and cultural barrier as a political and military one: while Iran had become Shia, Central Asia had remained Sunni. No longer were the Turkish peoples to be stimulated by the cultural vitality of the cities of the Iranian plateau: indeed, Persian slowly withered and Turkish came to be their favored tongue. Simultaneously, the region was gradually isolated from its major source of wealth, the trade which flowed down the Old Silk route between China and the West. Now this fell into the hands of Europeans, both from western Europe, who developed

ways to China by sea, and from the Russian dominions, who pioneered more northerly routes by land. Furthermore, as these Muslim peoples found their wealth declining, they also found it harder to stand up to Russian and Chinese expansion.

The khanate of Bukhara, the focus of Uzbeg strength, was the most powerful of the Central Asian regimes, capable for much of the 16th century of contesting Khurasan with the Safavids and in the mid-17th century of throwing back a Mughal invasion. Although the great wealth which had been derived from the trans-Asian trade declined, Bukhara remained the most important entrepot for foodstuffs, with merchants working in Siberia and the Tarim Basin. Three dynasties held sway: the Shaibanids until 1599, the Janids, 12 of them, from 1599 to 1785, and then the Mangits. Strong rulers were still able to add to their territories. Thus Abd Allah Khan, who was effective ruler for the second half of the 16th century, could annex Balkh, Tashkent, and Farghana; Shah Murad (1785–1800) could make inroads into the neighboring khanates and Iran. Lands gained, however, were usually lost after a time, the authority of the Bukharan khans being reduced to Transoxania, which in this period became the land of the Uzbegs.

Two weaker Uzbeg khanates survived alongside Bukhara. To the northwest there was that of Khiva, which had been founded after 1512 by a scion of the Shaibanid family. Much less powerful than Bukhara, and protected by the black sand desert of the Kara Kum and the red sands of the Kizil Kum, it remained a bastion of Sunni orthodoxy and of mainly local importance. To the east there was the khanate of Khokand, which was founded around 1700 when another scion of the Shaibanid house, Shah

Rukh (died 1722/3), declared Bukhara's fertile Farghana province independent. Throughout the 18th century this new khanate progressed, especially economically, although after the Manchu conquest of east Turkestan in 1759 it had to acknowledge Chinese suzerainty.

The three Tatar khanates which straddled the Asian border with Europe strove to play an independent role in the politics of the region, but could not long preserve their freedom. That of the Crimea came under Ottoman authority in the late 15th century; Kazan, which controlled the rich corn lands of the middle Volga, and Astrakhan, which controlled the lower Volga, followed suit in the early 16th century. Unable to influence these khanates, which were able to launch devastating expeditions into Russian territory, Tsar Ivan the Terrible annexed Kazan in 1552 and Astrakhan in 1556. The Crimea, which was much more closely attached to the Ottoman empire, suffered the same fate in 1783. The ending of Muslim independence was especially strongly resisted in Kazan. There was good reason: the Russians restructured regional society, redistributing Muslim lands to Russian nobles, reducing Muslims to a minority by importing Russian peasants, destroying mosques and madrasas, and adopting a policy of forced conversion to Christianity. Resistance continued for over 200 years until a *jihad* in 1755 and the Pugachev revolt of 1773–74 made the Russians think again. Catherine the Great ended religious persecution, established an assembly of *ulama*, and rehabilitated the Tatar nobility and merchants. Now the insurgents became partners in empire and wealthy enough to be the enlightened patrons of a Tatar Islamic renaissance in the 19th century.

Turning to east Turkestan, where in the early 16th century Muslim khanates reached out to the borders of China and Tibet, two Chaghatai brothers held sway. One, Manzur Khan, ruled the provinces north of the Tien Shan mountains, the Turfan and Hami oases, and was advancing toward Kansu. The other, Said Khan, ruled the south and west of the Tarim Basin and was invading Ladakh and Kashmir. From the mid-16th century, however, these expanding regimes fell into disarray. Mongol clans occupied the lands north of the Tien Shan mountains, while in the oasis cities to the south Chaghatai dominion faced increasing competition from sufi brotherhoods. The sufi leaders, known as *khojas*, were all descended from a Naqshbandi shaikh and descendant of the Prophet, Makhdum-i Azam, who was greatly venerated in Turkestan and died at the Chaghatai capital of Kashgar in 1540. His descendants split into two factions who struggled for leadership of the brotherhood. In time the oasis cities of the Tarim Basin— Kashgar, Yarkand, Khotan, Aqsu, and so on—became rival city–states in the hands of the various *khoja* clans. In 1678 the last Chaghatai khan, who held Kashgar alone, was toppled by a *khoja* who depended on the aid of the Mongol Oirots (Buddhists) from the north. For the following 80 years the play of Oirot power and the fate of *khoja* factions were intertwined until in 1758/9 the Manchus brought the region within the Chinese empire.

In China, Muslim experiences were different from elsewhere. Scattered in small communities throughout the market centers of the land and most populous in Yunnan and Kansu, where the great trade routes from the south and the west entered China proper, they were always in a minority and without

◀ *Muslims leaving a mosque in Haiyuan, in north-west China. Between the 16th and 18th centuries, Muslims lived in scattered communities throughout China in a state of uneasy coexistence with their Chinese hosts.*

▲ *Tili Kara, built in 1660, is one of three madrasas positioned around Samarqand's central Registan square. Its name means "gold-covered," referring to the lavish decoration of its domed interior.*

power. Nevertheless, they had a strong sense of their own identity. "Arabia, not China, is the center of the world," declared one 17th-century Muslim writer, stressing his allegiance to the community of Islam rather than to the celestial kingdom. They were conscious, moreover, of their superiority: "one Muslim equals five Chinese," the saying went. Of course, this self-awareness was enhanced by their ability to maintain their own religious and educational institutions and their dominance of particular trades such as those in beef or cart transportation. It was further sharpened by the almost universal Chinese contempt for a people they evidently found loud and aggressive. In this light it may seem strange that up to the 19th century Muslims did not

work to create their own religio-political community as they had done from time to time elsewhere. No doubt this is in large part explained by their scattered distribution and the fact that they were left to their own devices. Indeed, some Muslims were prepared to go to considerable lengths to smooth over the differences between Islam and Confucianism. But, after the Manchus came to power in 1644, this uneasy coexistence was harder to maintain. Under the new dynasty government became more effective and more intrusive; by the mid-18th century restrictions had been put on worship, pilgrimage, and other rites. Muslims began to feel that sense of alienation from Confucian society which formed the background to their rebellions in the 19th century.

In these northern Islamic lands from the Caspian Sea to the Tarim Basin the religious spirit was strong, and expressed in a strict Sunni orthodoxy which embraced all, peasants and nomads as much as *ulama* and khans. In the cities the *ulama* were dominant, supported by rich endowments, supplying state administrators from among their number, and teaching in great madrasas whose fame brought students from Russia and from India. In the 1790s, according to tradition, there were as many as 30,000 students in Bukhara alone, which no doubt explains how the city came by the title "pillar of Islam." Rulers found it wiser not to quarrel with their *ulama*; indeed, they tended to reflect in their own actions the orthodox piety of their subjects. Abd Allah Khan II (reigned 1583–98) expelled students of philosophy from Samarqand and Bukhara; some of the Janid khans abdicated so as to be free to pursue a devotional life in the holy cities of Arabia.

Evidently the crucial work of maintaining and transmitting the framework and values of Islamic society was pursued with vigor and without hindrance. Over the three centuries, however, there was a shift in the nature of transmission as sufi orders came increasingly to influence the life of the people, and in places that of the state. The main orders were the Naqshbandiya, the Kubrawiya, and the Qadiriya, which played and continued to play a central role in the conversion of Asia's nomadic peoples. Often shrines would be sited on the edge of the steppe within easy reach of nomadic encampments like that of Shaikh Ahmad Yasavi at Turkestan which was a major place of pilgrimage for Uzbegs and Kazakhs alike. The growing influence of the sufi orders was manifest, as elsewhere in the Islamic world at the time, by increasing emphasis on the life of the Prophet as a model, and so at the beginning of the 18th century we find Liu Chih, most famous of Chinese Muslim writers, composing his *True Annals of the Greatest Saint of Arabia*. It was also manifest in politics. Thus the affairs of the Chaghatai khanate became completely absorbed in the rivalries of two branches of the Naqshbandi order whose *khoja* leaders eventually came to replace the Chaghatai khans. Thus, too, the rulers of Bukhara came to adopt the saintly style; Shah Murad, an unusually successful general, maintained the dress and manners of a sufi, even going so far as to ride into battle on a scraggy pony.

Culturally, the impact of isolation, decline, and the preferences of Sunni orthodoxy were felt more and more strongly. The Central Asian khanates, living with the memories of Tamerlaine's Samarqand and Sultan Husain Baiqara's Herat, had shining examples of artistic and scholarly achievement to follow. Moreover, in Bukhara for much of the 16th century they succeeded in approaching these high standards, largely as a result of the work of the artists and craftsmen who moved there after the destruction of Herat. There was fine painting after the style of Bihzad, which has come to be known as the Bukhara school, there was much poetry and music. Then from the 17th century the isolation from the Iranian springs of inspiration began to tell, and, as in the Ottoman and Mughal lands, there was the steady emergence of local vernaculars to compete with and eventually to overwhelm Persian as the idiom of the courtly arts and polite intercourse. At the same time weakening resources and the narrowing focus of the patronage of intensely religious courts began to leave their mark, and, although some areas are still but lightly studied, the

▶ *Glazed ceramic tiles and blue domes create some of the characteristic features of mosque design throughout central Asia.*

quality of all arts and crafts seems to have declined, except the minting of coins and the weaving of rugs.

Madrasas of Central Asia

The madrasa, where *ulama* learned the Islamic sciences—some to become prayer leaders or teachers themselves, others to become judges or administrators—was the typical building of the age, embodying the profound concern of orthodox society for the maintenance and the transmission of the central traditions of the faith, a concern which was not diverted, as in Morocco, by the rise of sufi influence. Indeed here we can note a marked change, and one which contrasts sharply with contemporary developments in Morocco, from the spirit of the preceding era. Then mausoleums embraced the essence of the age, like those which glorify Tamerlaine and his family at Samarqand, the Ishrat-Khane, the Gur-i Mir, and in the Shah-i Zinde. New mausoleums were still built, but as royal power came to be rivaled by that of the *ulama*, so the tombs of princes came to be overshadowed by the magnificence of the madrasas. Bukhara had three new madrasas in the 16th century and a fourth in the 17th century, which lends weight to the claim that the city entertained tens of thousands of students at a time.

The orthodox ambience apart, however, we should note how the madrasa flourished naturally in Central Asia. The very concept of the madrasa as an institution separate from the mosque had developed here, as had the *pishtaq*, or gateway, glistening with colored tiles which soared up above the roofline of the towns. Furthermore, the typical building plan, with four *iwans*, or halls, open at one end and arranged around a courtyard, belonged to Central Asia too, originating in

the region's grand houses and Buddhist monasteries. The Islamic developments of the period are best expressed by the fate of Samarqand's central Registan square which slowly came to be shut in, although not entirely, by madrasas: the Ulugh Beg (1417–20), the Shir Dar (1619–36), and the Tila Kara (1660).

Rich endowments supported the work of the madrasas, and many were built in the four leading centers of Bukhara, Samarqand, Khiva, and Khokand. Students came from India and Kashmir, from Russia and the cities of eastern Turkestan. Bukhara must have had the atmosphere of a great university city and as such can have had few equals in the contemporary world

Mosques in China

The mosques of China tell a different story, the story of the concessions Muslims had to make to the Confucian world in which they dwelt. Here the mosques were built like pagodas, without domes and without minarets, which were forbidden by the state, the faithful being called to prayer from within the structure. Instead, the roofs were corbeled and gabled, sloping upward at the corners. The interior itself was like those of mosques throughout the Muslim world, neat and serene and with decorative verses in Arabic script and prayers offered in the Arabic tongue. Yet here again the Confucian state imposed its presence on religious practice; on one wall there would be the emperor's tablets which by law had to grace any place of prayer. Before these tablets Muslims were supposed to prostrate themselves in the same way as they did before Allah; but they did not quite, not allowing their foreheads to touch the ground as they did in Islamic prayer.

Decline, Reform, and Revival

From the late 17th century all three great empires which straddled the central Islamic lands declined. In the Safavid dominions the signs were there from the death of Shah Abbas I; indeed, some stemmed from the very solutions which that able ruler had found to the problem of creating strong institutions of central government in a tribal society. The personal army of "slaves of the royal household" which he introduced to check the power of the tribal forces in the state eventually led to a weakening of military competence, while the steady appropriation of state lands by the crown to pay for this new standing army led to overtaxation and the deterioration of provincial administration. The immuring of the royal princes in the female quarters of the palace to stop them plotting against the shah ensured more stable government, but meant that those who did come to the throne had little experience of the world, had been corrupted by harem life, and were in the hands of powerful harem factions. All four of those who ruled from 1629 to 1722 were drunkards; of them two, Shah Safi (reigned 1629–42) and Shah Sulaiman (reigned 1666–94), were notable largely for the slaughter they wreaked among their nobility; a third, Sultan Husain (reigned 1694–1722), was notable for his piety and his buildings; and only Abbas II (reigned 1642–60) displayed the qualities of a ruler.

As royal capacities weakened, the dynasty also began to lose the religious legitimacy which in the 16th century it had so carefully nurtured. *Ulama* began to challenge the partnership of Twelver Shiism and royal ideology which made the shah the "Shadow of God on earth," developing instead the theory that, in the absence of the Twelfth Imam, only a *mujtahid*, who was deeply learned in the *Sharia* and whose life was without blemish, could rule. In the process they were assisted by their growing material independence of the crown, and the failure of the shahs to make effective use of the machinery which existed to control the religious institution. By the reign of Sultan Husain they had gained the upper hand and the leading *mujtahid* of the time, Muhammad Baqir Majlisi, was able greatly to influence government policy, to wipe out the remnants of the Safavid sufi order which had brought the dynasty to power, and to impose his vision of orthodox Shiism on the state to the extent of having the tens of thousands of bottles of wine in the royal cellars publicly smashed.

By the end of the 17th century the empire was rotten to the core. When Sultan Husain went on pilgrimage he did not go on foot and make the journey to Meshhed in 28 days, as Abbas I had done, but took with him his harem and a retinue of 60,000, spent a year in the process, and beggared the provinces through which he passed. When in 1697/8 a band of Baluchis raided to within 200 miles (320 km) of the capital, Sultan Husain had no troops with which to resist them, and, supreme humiliation, was obliged to appeal to a visiting Georgian prince for help. Thus it was a simple matter in 1722 for a young Afghan adventurer, Mahmud of Qandahar, at the head of 20,000 ragged tribesmen, to take Isfahan and effectively destroy the empire.

Iran, however, did not immediately cease to be a focus of Muslim strength. There was, for a brief moment, a brilliant restoration of power. Mahmud and his Afghans failed to establish a dynasty, and instead there arose a former Khurasani bandit, Nadir Khan, who reorganized the Safavid forces and in 1736 felt strong enough to set aside the dynasty and rule as Nadir Shah. Already in 1730 he had defeated the Ottomans and reannexed the Caucasus. In 1739 he invaded India, sacked Delhi, and returned triumphantly with the famed peacock throne. To the north his armies occupied the Uzbeg cities of Transoxania; to the south they occupied Oman, the center of resurgent Arab merchant power. All was quickly lost, however, after his death in 1748, and Iran was delivered over to tribal power. The Luristani chief, Karim Khan Zand, kept the peace in the center and south from Shiraz until he died in 1779. Elsewhere other tribes came to the fore, notably the Qajars, who fought for two decades to succeed the Zand till by 1794 they had established a state based on Teheran in the heart of west Iran. Eventually the Qajars restored effective central government, but the years of anarchy, marked by towers of skulls, mass blindings, and wanton savagery, had greatly impoverished the land. Many villages were deserted, the cities were desolate—only a quarter of late 18th-century Isfahan was occupied—and trade was much reduced.

This same period saw the extinction of Muslim power in India. Initially there was no weakening at the top as there was in Iran. The emperor Awrangzeb was no pampered

▼ *Safavid power in Iran ebbed and advanced during the 18th century, but then quickly declined after the death of Nadir Khan in 1748.*

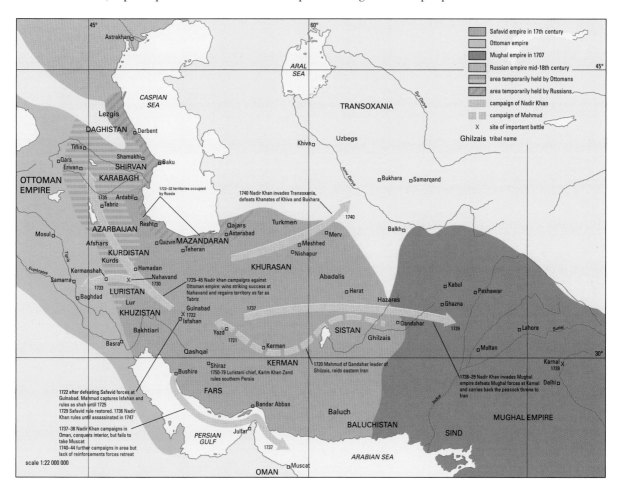

▶ *When the emperor Awrangzeb died in 1707, Mughal power in India had reached its height. Just over half a century later this great empire was lost.*

harem-bred prince but a ruthless man of action who clambered to power over the bodies of his father, whom he jailed, and his brothers, whom he killed. Power waned as *ulama* like Shaikh Ahmad Sirhindi and his Naqshbandi followers came forward to challenge the religious compromises on which the Mughal state was based. Three Mughal emperors chose to ignore them, but Awrangzeb, moved by his own preferences and perhaps supremely confident in the strength of imperial power, did listen to them and abandoned the partnership with the Hindus on which the empire rested. His policies of imposing disabilities on Hindus and of moving the state in an Islamic direction excited opposition. There were revolts of Hindu landlords, of Afghan tribesmen, of Sikhs in the Punjab, of Rajput chiefs resisting Islamization, and of Jat peasants resisting taxation. By far the most serious resistance, however, came from the Marathas, who, under their Hindu chief Shivaji, carved out a state for themselves in the Deccan and refused either to be absorbed in the empire or to coexist with it. To meet this threat, and to appropriate the riches of the sultanates of Bijapur and Golkonda, Awrangzeb campaigned in the Deccan from 1680, thus shifting the focus of government from Delhi to central India. By the time he died in 1707, Bijapur and Golkonda were conquered but the Marathas still raided from Gujarat to the far south.

Weaknesses in the military patronage system aggravated the effects of the ideological shift that Awrangzeb brought to the empire: the empire had established itself in India largely by incorporating provincial warrior elites into its political system, and it could only continue to win the loyalty of its *mansabdars* (that is, the imperial service elite

composed of holders of commands in the military household) as long as it could reward them. These two factors were inexorable. When the Maratha warrior elite refused to come to terms with the empire, Awrangzeb had no choice but to move south to subdue them. When he failed to do so, in part it seems because the Marathas had technological advantages in musketry, he resorted to bribery, bestowing high *mansabs* on more and more of them. The result was that the empire was handing out *mansabs* without having won the fresh lands to pay for them. There was a growing number of *mansabdars* supported by a static pool of resources, which meant that the peasantry was impoverished by the growing exactions of government, the army was weakened because the *mansabdars* were unable to meet their military commitments, the *mansabdars* themselves were demoralized by their unaccustomed failure to win victories, and the emperor was increasingly less able either to impose his authority at home or to meet threats on the frontier.

After Awrangzeb's death the ruling class fell apart. The *mansabdars* divided into factions supporting rival claimants to the throne. Emperors squandered their lands in rewarding clients and favorites rather than in sustaining a body of loyal troops able to enforce their will. The countryside became increasingly disorderly as neither the *mansabdars* nor the emperor could raise sufficient force to hold it in awe. By the 1740s there had been the humiliation of Nadir Shah's invasion, the Marathas had helped themselves to Gujarat and Malwa, the governors of the Punjab, Awadh, Bengal, and Hyderabad had converted these imperial provinces into their own domains, and the Mughal writ hardly ran beyond Delhi. Three

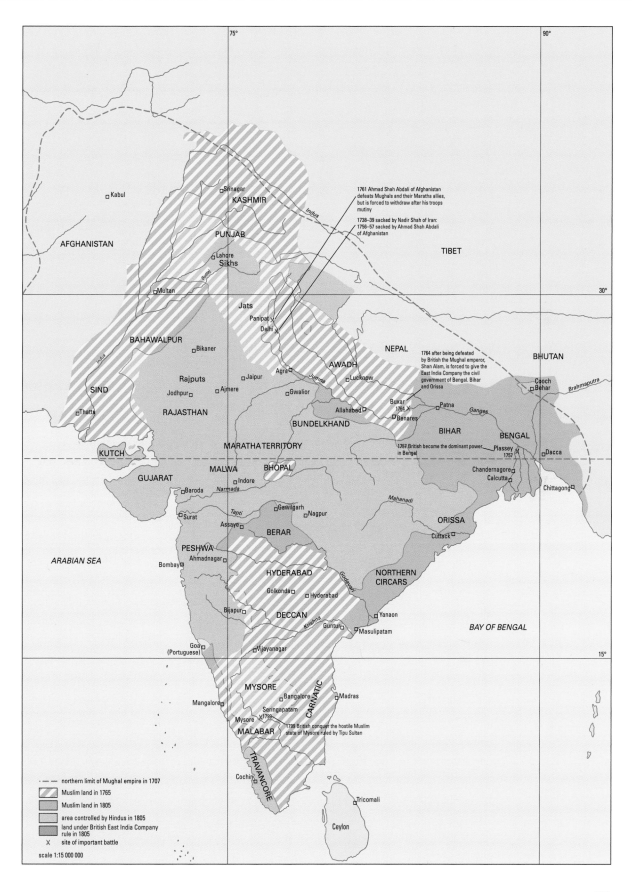

75°

90°

□ Kabul

Srinagar □

KASHMIR

Indus

PUNJAB

AFGHANISTAN

Lahore □

Sikhs

TIBET

1761 Ahmad Shah Abdali of Afghanistan
defeats Mughals and their Maratha allies,
but is forced to withdraw after his troops
mutiny

1738–39 sacked by Nadir Shah of Iran;
1756–57 sacked by Ahmad Shah Abdali
of Afghanistan

□ Multan

Sutlej

30°

Jats

BAHAWALPUR

□ Bikaner

Panipat ✗

Delhi ✗

NEPAL

BHUTAN

Agra □

AWADH

Jumna

Lucknow □

1764 after being defeated
by British the Mughal emperor,
Shan Alam, is forced to give the
East India Company the civil
government of Bengal, Bihar
and Orissa

Cooch
Behar

Brahmaputra

SIND

Rajputs

Jaipur □

Indus

Jodhpur □

□ Ajmere

□ Gwalior

Allahabad □

Buxar
1764 ✗

Patna □

Benares □

Ganges

□ Thatta

RAJASTHAN

BUNDELKHAND

BIHAR

BENGAL

□ Dacca

KUTCH

MARATHA TERRITORY

1757 British become the dominant power
in Bengal

Plassey
1757

MALWA

BHOPAL

Chandernagore □

Calcutta □

GUJARAT

□ Indore

□ Chittagong

□ Baroda

Narmada

Surat □

Tapti

Gawilgarh □

□ Nagpur

Mahanadi

Assaye □

BERAR

ORISSA

PESHWA

Ahmadnagar □

Cuttack □

Bombay □

HYDERABAD

NORTHERN
CIRCARS

ARABIAN SEA

Golkonda □

□ Hyderabad

Godavari

Bijapur □

DECCAN

BAY OF BENGAL

Krishna

Guntur □

Yanaon □

Goa
(Portuguese)

□ Vijayanagar

Masulipatam □

15°

MYSORE

Mangalore □

Bangalore □

□ Madras

CARNATIC

Seringapatam
✗1799

Mysore □

1799 British conquer the hostile Muslim
state of Mysore ruled by Tipu Sultan

MALABAR

TRAVANCORE

Cochin □

Tricomali □

northern limit of Mughal empire in 1707

Muslim land in 1765

Muslim land in 1805

area controlled by Hindus in 1805

land under British East India Company
rule in 1805

✗ site of important battle

scale 1:15 000 000

Ceylon

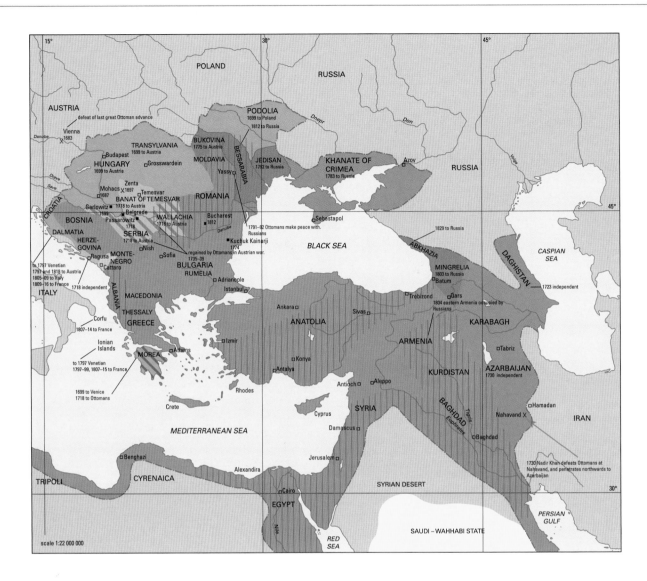

▲ This map shows the decline of Ottoman power during the 18th century.

— ·— boundary of Ottoman empire in 1683

losses to 1699, treaty of Carlowitz

losses to 1718, treaty of Passarowitz

losses to 1774, treaty of Kuchuk Kainarji

losses to 1812, treaty of Bucharest

Ottoman empire in 1813

area under autonomous or tribal rulers c. 1800

■ 1699   site and date of treaty

✕   site of important battle

▶ Fath Ali Shah (reigned 1797– 1834), second king of the Qajar dynasty, playing polo. He encouraged the arts, particularly painting.

more decades saw the murder of two emperors, Ahmad Shah (1748–54) and Alamgir II (1754–59), the flight of a third, Shah Alam (1759–1806), and the sacking of Delhi in 1761 by the invading forces of Ahmad Abdali, king of Afghanistan (1747–73). All the while, non-Muslims took increasing control of India. By 1800 the Marathas ruled the subcontinent from Rajasthan in the north to the Deccan in the south, and from the Arabian Sea in the west to the Bay of Bengal in the east as they had done for 60 years. In the Punjab the gifted Sikh leader, Ranjit Singh, had just secured Lahore. Throughout most of the Gangetic plain the British ruled. Only two significant Muslim states remained, Awadh and Hyderabad, and they both acknowledged British paramountcy. Never before in Islamic history had Muslims surrendered so much power to their former subjects and other infidels. Shah Abd al-Aziz, the leading

scholar of Delhi, symbolically acknowledged the disaster when in 1803, the year General Lake defeated the Mughal emperor's Maratha allies under the city walls, he announced India to be no longer *dar al-Islam*, the land of Islam, but *dar al-harb*, the land of war.

The decline of the Ottoman empire took much longer than that of its Safavid and Mughal contemporaries. If the Safavid empire fell as the result of one battle, and the Mughal crumbled away over a century, the Ottoman took 300 years to die. It was, of course, much stronger, with a more deeply rooted and more highly developed version of the military patronage state; it also had quite remarkable recuperative powers. Thus in 1683, after nearly a century of administrative decline, we find the empire at its point of furthest expansion, revitalized by the Koprulu viziers and threatening central Europe even more seriously than in the days of Sulaiman the Magnificent. Yet soon afterward, though interrupted by brief moments of recovery and extensive periods of stability, the long retreat began once more. In the treaty of Carlowitz of 1699 the Ottomans surrendered Hungary, Transylvania, and Podolia; this was the first time that they had

signed a peace as the defeated power in a clearly decided war. In the treaty of Passarowitz of 1718 they surrendered the Banat of Temesvar, Serbia, and Wallachia. In the 1720s they tried to regain former territories in northwest Iran but were humiliatingly rebuffed in 1730 by Nadir Khan. There was some respite when they managed to regain Serbia and Wallachia in the Austrian war of 1735–39; moreover the Habsburgs were able to make only one more significant gain in the 18th century, that of Bukovina in 1775.

By now a much more dangerous enemy had come forward, Russia, who after 1768 subjected Ottoman forces to massive defeats on land and sea. In the subsequent treaty of Kuchuk Kainarji in 1774 the Ottomans lost control of a large chunk of the Black Sea shore, conceded to Russia the right to intervene on behalf of the sultan's Greek Orthodox Christian subjects, but most shamefully surrendered political control for the first time over a wholly Muslim people, the Tatars of the Crimea. Then Russian control of the Black Sea's northern shore was completed by the annexation of Jedisan in 1792 and Bessarabia in 1812. By this time a

▼ *From the mid-17th century the great sultanates of Aceh and Mataram declined, and the Dutch began to assert their power.*

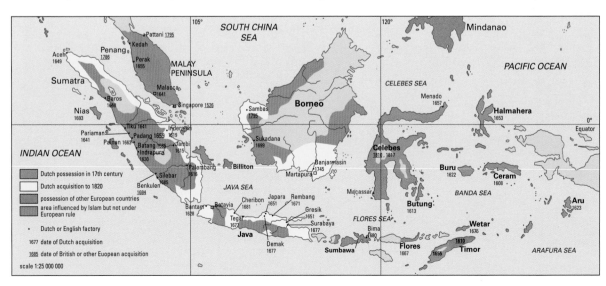

curious paradox had emerged. The Ottoman empire was the only remaining Muslim great power and the sultan was coming to be seen as the *khalifa*, or successor of the Prophet, as the leader of the Muslim community. Yet the empire was no longer strong enough even to defend itself single-handed against a major power. Indeed, in the 18th century and throughout the 19th century, its capacity to survive as the standard-bearer of Islam depended on its ability to ally itself with infidel states and to play a part in the European balance of power.

Within the empire the weakening of central authority, which had been the hallmark of decline from the late 16th century, continued in the 18th century and defied all attempts to reverse the process.

One manifestation was the bestowal on Christian powers of privileges within the empire, beginning in 1740 with the French, who were being repaid for diplomatic services against the Habsburgs. The most important of these was the extension of certificates of protection to non-Muslim Ottoman subjects which enabled them to gain the privileges of foreign nationals. Christians and Jews, placing themselves in droves under the protection of one or the other European power, came to control the growing trade with Europe, and to edge out their Muslim rivals. As most traders moved from Ottoman to privileged foreign jurisdiction, government lost the capacity to tax or to control much of the commerce of its territory. A second manifestation lies in the

▼ *Ottoman and Habsburg cavalry clash outside Vienna during the siege of 1683 in this painting by Franz Geffels. The siege represented the high point of Ottoman expansion: from now on the empire entered a long period of decline.*

▲ *Selim III (1789–1807) holds a reception at his court. Influenced by the French Revolution, he embarked on large-scale military and administrative reform of the Ottoman empire along European lines.*

growing subordination of the ideal of service to the state to self-interest. "No business can be accomplished in this country without a bribe," declared an Indian visitor in 1802, "even the Government departments are ruined by this nefarious system. The army is without discipline, the ordnance unfit for use, the regulation of the post office totally neglected.... The persons at the head of all these departments are only anxious to procure money and deceive the

Government." Indeed the interests of almost all seemed to be served by the maintenance of weak central authority: the leading *ulama*, who had formed themselves into a hereditary and closed corps, the Janissaries, who had also become hereditary and whose special privileges were enjoyed by many throughout the land; the valley lords of Anatolia and the new notables of Rumelia, who had turned government posts into semi-autonomous principalities; and the governors of distant

Arab provinces, who were virtually independent. When men strove to strengthen central authority, as did the vizier Ibrahim Pasha (vizier 1718–30) and the sultan Selim III (reigned 1789–1807), they were given short shrift. Both sought to create new power bases beyond the reach of sectional interests by opening windows on Europe and by training new army units along European lines. Both were stopped by an alliance of Janissaries and of *ulama* who were quick to see the threat to their independence and no less quick to raise the cry of Islam in danger. Nevertheless, some Ottomans were clearly coming to feel that infidel knowledge was needed to bolster the standardbearer of Islam from within, just as infidel allies were needed in the world at large. The Turks had begun their long flirtation with the West.

In the further Islamic lands there was a similar story of waning power, of threats from infidel culture, of Muslims actually falling under infidel rule. In Central Asia holy men ruled where once there had been mighty Mongol khans, and the former center of world empire slid into a lethargic provincialism, while all the while the Russian line crept forward and the nomad peoples of the steppe slipped into vassalage. In China Muslims suffered an energetic attempt to assimilate them to the dominant Confucian culture, while between 1758 and 1760 those of the Tarim Basin came to feel the weight of Chinese rule for the first time. In Java by 1800 the sultanate of Mataram had been all but gobbled up by the Dutch; the fragment which survived had been cut off from the Islamized north coast and formed a central state in which Hindu–Javanese culture was definitely preeminent and the progress of Islam was checked. In Sumatra the once great power of Aceh was restricted to the

northern coastal strip and scattered ports in the southwest, while a weakening of royal authority in Minangkabau was breeding social and political discontent. In West Africa Islam was still expanding, it is true, borne forward by the spears of the Fulani holy warriors of Senegal and the acumen of the Dyula who traded through much of the region. But there were startling reverses too: the cities of the Niger bend, Jenne, Timbuktu, Gao, the heart of Muslim empire for 500 years or more, had fallen beneath the sway of the heathen Bambara. Moreover, where Muslims ruled, as they did in most places where they had in the past, they no longer challenged pagan beliefs so strongly.

Reform and revival

The unprecedented political decline in the Muslim world of the 18th century provided the context for the most important development in Islam since sufism first took widespread hold 600 years before. This was a movement of inner renewal, of reform of religious practice, of revival of religious élan, which sprang up in and spread to almost every part of the Islamic world from the mid-18th century to the beginning of the 20th century. As Muslim power waned and Muslim princes no longer seemed to command the fate of humankind, *ulama* and sufis, guardians of the central traditions of the faith, seized the initiative and strove as they had never done before to promote a purer vision of the Islamic life and society. This led on occasion to declarations of *jihad*, and these holy wars were waged with that especial ferocity which seems reserved for the times when coreligionists fall out. Sometimes these movements collided with expanding European empires and turned to give the intruder the full force of their

▼ *During the 18th and 19th centuries as Muslim power waned, ulama and sufis strove to promote a purer vision of Islam.*

religious fury, adding yet more lurid colors to the Western understanding of the faith.

The *ulama* and sufis responded to the decline of Muslim power by returning to first principles for guidance, to the word of God in the Quran and to the actions of the Prophet in the *Hadiths*, and by rejecting much of the scholastic and mystical superstructure built up as Islam had encountered other civilizations down the centuries. Closely involved with this process was an Islamic "right wing" which had habitually opposed

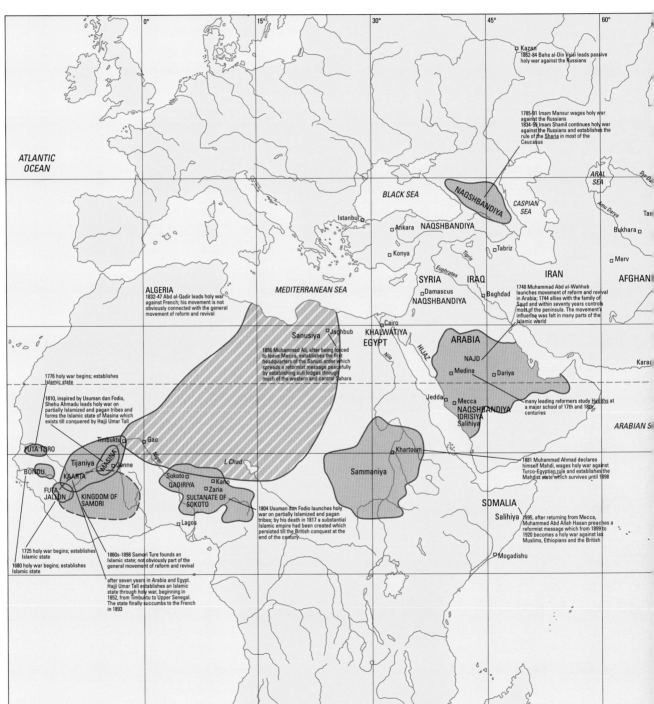

ATLANTIC OCEAN

BLACK SEA

CASPIAN SEA

ARAL SEA

□ Kazan
1862-84 Baha al-Din Vaisi leads passive holy war against the Russians

1785-91 Imam Mansur wages holy war against the Russians
1834-59 Imam Shamil continues holy war against the Russians and establishes the rule of the Sharia in most of the Caucasus

NAQSHBANDIYA

□ Istanbul

□ Ankara   NAQSHBANDIYA

□ Konya

□ Tabriz

□ Merv

□ Bukhara

Tas

SYRIA   IRAQ   IRAN   AFGHAN

ALGERIA
1832-47 Abd al-Qadir leads holy war against French; his movement is not obviously connected with the general movement of reform and revival

MEDITERRANEAN SEA

□ Damascus
NAQSHBANDIYA

□ Baghdad

1740 Muhammad Abd al-Wahhab launches movement of reform and revival in Arabia; 1744 allies with the family of Saud and within seventy years controls most of the peninsula. The movement's influence was felt in many parts of the Islamic world

Sanusiya □ Jaghbub

□ Cairo
KHALWATIYA
EGYPT

ARABIA
NAJD
□ Medina   □ Dariya

many leading reformers study Hadiths at a major school of 17th and 18th centuries

1856 Muhammad Ali, after being forced to leave Mecca, establishes the first headquarters of the Sanusi order which spreads a reformist message peacefully by establishing sufi lodges through much of the western and central Sahara

HIJAZ

Jedda □
□ Mecca   NAQSHBANDIYA
IDRISIYA
Salihiya

ARABIAN S

1776 holy war begins; establishes Islamic state

1810, inspired by Usuman dan Fodio, Shehu Ahmadu leads holy war on partially Islamized and pagan tribes and forms the Islamic state of Masina which exists till conquered by Hajji Umar Tall

FUTA TORO

Timbuktu □ Gao

Tijaniya

BONDU

KAARTA

FUTA JALLON

KINGDOM OF SAMORI

Jenne

MASINA

Niger

Sokoto □
QADIRIYA   □ Kano
□ Zaria
SULTANATE OF SOKOTO

□ Lagos

L Chad

Sammaniya

□ Khartoum

1881 Muhammad Ahmad declares himself Mahdi, wages holy war against Turco-Egyptian rule and establishes the Mahdist state which survives until 1898

SOMALIA

Salihiya   1895, after returning from Mecca, Muhammed Abd Allah Hasan preaches a reformist message which from 1899 to 1920 becomes a holy war against lax Muslims, Ethiopians and the British

□ Mogadishu

1804 Usuman dan Fodio launches holy war on partially Islamized and pagan tribes; by his death in 1817 a substantial Islamic empire had been created which persisted till the British conquest at the end of the century

1725 holy war begins; establishes Islamic state

1680 holy war begins; establishes Islamic state

1860s-1898 Samori Ture founds an Islamic state; not obviously part of the general movement of reform and revival

after seven years in Arabia and Egypt, Hajji Umar Tall establishes an Islamic state through holy war, beginning in 1852, from Timbuktu to Upper Senegal. The state finally succumbs to the French in 1893

the extravagances of sufism; it was represented by those who had always limited their sources of authority to the Quran and the *Hadiths* and by the followers of the Hanbali school of law who from the beginning had rejected the speculative innovations of the other schools. These, and those who thought like them, now attacked the widely held beliefs in the powers of saints and holy men and the practices connected with them: the worship of and at saints' tombs, prayers for the intercession of the Prophet and the saints, all aspects in fact of popular religion which challenged the unity of God. They also attacked, though not with such unanimity, Ibn al-Arabi's philosophy of the unity of being which had so long made it possible for half-Islamized peoples to be made comfortable in the faith.

Ironically, although directed against dubious sufi practices and fed by an ancient suspicion of sufism, this movement was spread throughout much of the Islamic world by sufi orders. Sufis responded to the reformist challenge by absorbing within the sufi framework the orthodox emphasis on the Quran and the *Hadiths*, and by stripping their rites of ecstatic practices and their beliefs of

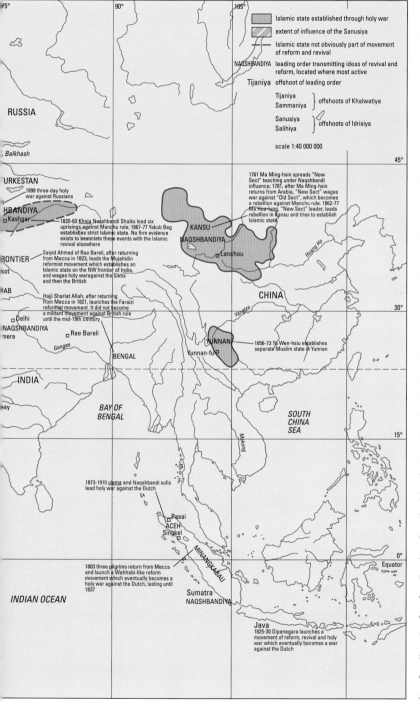

Islamic state established through holy war

extent of influence of the Sanusiya

Islamic state not obviously part of movement of reform and revival

NAQSHBANDIYA leading order transmitting ideas of revival and reform, located where most active

Tijaniya offshoot of leading order

Tijaniya
Sammaniya } offshoots of Khalwatiya

Sanusiya
Salihiya } offshoots of Idrisiya

scale 1:40 000 000

RUSSIA

Balkhash

TURKESTAN
1898 three-day holy war against Russians

NAQSHBANDIYA
Kashgar
1820-63 Khoja Naqshbandi Shaiks lead six uprisings against Manchu rule; 1867-77 Yakub Beg establishes strict Islamic state. No firm evidence exists to associate these events with the Islamic revival elsewhere

FRONTIER
Saiyid Ahmad of Rae Bareli, after returning from Mecca in 1823, leads the Mujahidin reformist movement which establishes an Islamic state on the NW frontier of India, and wages holy war against the Sikhs and then the British

PUNJAB
Hajji Shariat Allah, after returning from Mecca in 1821, launches the Faraizi reformist movement. It did not become a militant movement against British rule until the mid-19th century

Delhi
NAQSHBANDIYA
Rae Bareli
Ganges
BENGAL

INDIA

BAY OF BENGAL

1761 Ma Ming-hsin spreads "New Sect" teaching under Naqshbandi influence; 1781, after Ma Ming-hsin returns from Arabia, "New Sect" wages war against "Old Sect", which becomes a rebellion against Manchu rule. 1862-77 Ma Hua-lung, "New Sect" leader, leads rebellion in Kansu and tries to establish Islamic state

KANSU
NAQSHBANDIYA
Lanchou
Huang Ho

CHINA

Yangtze

YUNNAN
Yunnan-fu
1856-73 Tu Wen-hsiu establishes separate Muslim state in Yunnan

Mekong

SOUTH CHINA SEA

1873-1910 ulama and Naqshbandi sufis lead holy war against the Dutch

Pasai
ACEH
Singkel

MINANGKABAU

1803 three pilgrims return from Mecca and launch a Wahhabi-like reform movement which eventually becomes a holy war against the Dutch, lasting until 1837

Sumatra
NAQSHBANDIYA

INDIAN OCEAN

Equator

Java
1825-30 Dipanegara launches a movement of reform, revival and holy war which eventually becomes a war against the Dutch

metaphysical tendencies. The concern of the *ulama* with Quran and the *Hadiths*, moreover, was matched by the sufis in a new emphasis on the person of the Prophet. It became a notable feature of the reformed sufism, the spread of which can be traced in the steady increase of the literary genre devoted to the life of the Prophet and in the institution of *mawlid* ceremonies to celebrate his birthday. Some orders actually gave themselves the title *Tariqa Muham-madiya* (the order of Muhammad), thus symbolizing their intention of following the path laid down by the Prophet and of forsaking the degraded practices of the past. All of this amounted to a sufi revival, as old orders were revitalized and new orders were founded. This purified sufism subsisted side by side with with the old form. It tended, however, to be less attractive to the masses.

From the movement's attention to the *Hadiths* and the example of the Prophet came a new emphasis on action. Just as the Prophet had himself gone to cast out the idols from the Kaaba, so they would act to stop men worshiping false gods. Action could lead to violence—holy war in the way of the Lord—because at times only through force might the object be achieved.

This movement did not spring into existence all of a sudden in the mid-18th century. There had been a slow spiritual and scholarly preparation over many years. There was the reaction led by Mawlana Abd al-Haqq and Shaikh Ahmad Sirhindi in the early 17th century to the compromises Mughal rulers made with Hindus and Indian Muslims with Hinduism. There was the great debate at the court of Aceh in the mid-17th century over the interpretation of Ibn al-Arabi's thought which attracted the attention of leading scholars in Medina. There was the

steady assertion of the power of the *ulama* against the shah in Safavid Iran which led by the end of the century to the almost dictatorial position of Muhammad Baqir Majlisi. In Syria Abd al-Ghani of Nablus (1641–1731), a prolific scholar and a Naqshbandi shaikh, strove to create a revitalized theology and a reformed sufism. In India Shah Wali Allah (1702–60), a Naqshbandi too and a considerable scholar of *Hadiths*, strove not only to achieve the same ends as Abd al-Ghani but also to persuade Shah Ahmad Abdali of Afghanistan to wage holy war against the Hindus in order to bring about a restoration of Muslim power. The Naqshbandi sufi order deriving from Shaikh Ahmad Sirhindi and bearing his purified sufi message, if somewhat diluted, spread from India to Mecca, Damascus, Istanbul, and the Balkans. The Damascene scholar Mustafa al-Bakri (died 1749), the chief pupil of Abd al-Ghani of Nablus, revived the Khalwati sufi order, making it a vehicle for his reformist ideas. Based in Cairo, it gained great influence at the university of al-Azhar, where al-Bakri's leading pupil, Muhammad al-Hifnawi, was rector from 1758 to 1767, and was the framework within which reformist ideas developed in Egypt. But above all stands a leading group of teachers of *Hadiths* in 17th-and 18th-century Medina, strategically placed to influence those on pilgrimage, as many reformers did. Major figures in this group, and also Naqshbandis, were Ibrahim al-Kurani, who settled the great debate at Aceh, and the Indian Muhammad Hayya al-Sindi. Pupils of the group included many leading reformers: Abd al-Rauf of Singkel, Shah Wali Allah of Delhi, Mustafa al-Bakri, Muhammad Abd al-Wahhab (1703–92), and Shaikh Muhammad Samman (1717–75).

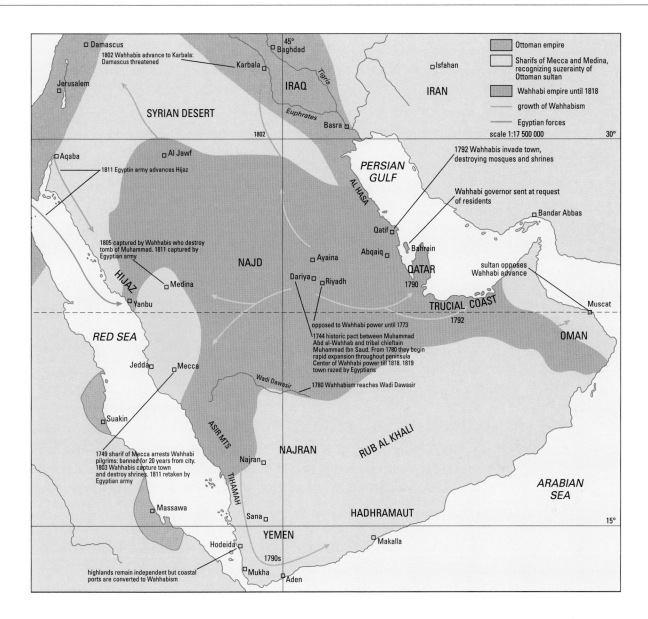

Map labels:

Damascus
1802 Wahhabi advance to Karbala: Damascus threatened
Karbala
45°
Baghdad
Isfahan
IRAN
Jerusalem
SYRIAN DESERT
IRAQ
Tigris
Euphrates
Basra
1802
Aqaba
Al Jawf
1811 Egyptin army advances Hijaz
PERSIAN GULF
1792 Wahhabis invade town, destroying mosques and shrines
Wahhabi governor sent at request of residents
Bandar Abbas
AL HASA
1805 captured by Wahhabis who destroy tomb of Muhammad. 1811 captured by Egyptian army
NAJD
Qatif
Abqaiq
Bahrain
QATAR
1790
sultan opposes Wahhabi advance
HIJAZ
Medina
Ayaina
Dariya
Riyadh
Yanbu
TRUCIAL COAST
1792
Muscat
RED SEA
opposed to Wahhabi power until 1773
1744 historic pact between Muhammad Abd al-Wahhab and tribal chieftain Muhammad Ibn Saud. From 1780 they begin rapid expansion throughout peninsula Center of Wahhabi power till 1818. 1819 town razed by Egyptians
OMAN
Jedda
Mecca
Wadi Dawasir
1780 Wahhabism reaches Wadi Dawasir
Suakin
ASIR MTS
NAJRAN
RUB AL KHALI
ARABIAN SEA
1749 sharif of Mecca arrests Wahhabi pilgrims: banned for 20 years from city. 1803 Wahhabis capture town and destroy shrines. 1811 retaken by Egyptian army
Najran
THIMAH
Massawa
Sana
HADHRAMAUT
15°
YEMEN
Makalla
Hodeida
1790s
highlands remain independent but coastal ports are converted to Wahhabism
Mukha
Aden

Legend:
Ottoman empire
Sharifs of Mecca and Medina, recognizing suzerainty of Ottoman sultan
Wahhabi empire until 1818
growth of Wahhabism
Egyptian forces
scale 1:17 500 000
30°

Muhammad Abd al-Wahhab was the first to steer the movement on to the field of action when in the middle of the 18th century he led a campaign for purification and renewal in Arabia. In his youth, as a sufi, he had traveled widely in Iran, Iraq, and the Hijaz in search of knowledge. As a result he came to be strongly influenced by the orthodox scholarship of his time, adopting the Hanbali legal position and the anti-sufi polemic of the 14th-century Hanbali scholar, Ibn Taimiya. Around 1740 he returned to the Najd and began to preach against the corruption of religion among the Bedouin, saint worship and all other sufi innovations. He was determined to put an end to practices which threatened the oneness of God. This meant that he even opposed reverence for Muhammad's tomb at Medina which was a favorite object of devotion for many pilgrims to Mecca.

In 1744 his campaign acquired explosive energy when he allied himself with Muhammad Ibn Saud, a petty chieftain of Dariya in the Najd, who accepted the reformer's religious views and significantly

▲ *This map shows the rise and spread of Saudi-Wahhabi power in Arabia between 1744 and 1818.*

121

sealed the compact with the same oath that the Prophet and the men of Medina had sworn in making their alliance in 622 CE. The Wahhabis steadily expanded through central and western Arabia. In 1802 they advanced into Iraq and Syria, occupying Karbala, the burial place of Husain, and destroying much that was holy to the Shias. In 1803 they occupied Mecca and in 1805 Medina where they tried to destroy all sacred tombs, including that of the Prophet, massacred the inhabitants, and imposed their unbending standards on those performing pilgrimage. A mighty challenge was delivered both to Islam, as Muslims generally had come to understand it, and to the Ottoman empire. By 1818 the European-style army and modern artillery of Muhammad Ali, the viceroy of Egypt, had managed to break Wahhabi power, raze their capital at Dariya, and restore the sultan's authority.

However, the Wahhabis succeeded in sustaining a nucleus of power in the Najd from which in the 20th century they were able to launch a second great expansion which culminated in the foundation of the Saudi Arabian state. In addition, many were influenced by the Wahhabis' puritanism and inspired by their religious zeal, although not all sympathized with their extremism and intolerance. Many too were attracted by the Wahhabi theological position, which dismissed the medieval superstructure of Islam and sought authority in the Quran and *Hadiths* alone.

Ripples from these developments in Arabia mingled with the endemic conflict between the supporters of the Islamic ideal and the supporters of accommodation to the local milieu in southeast Asia. In the Minangkabau region of Sumatra, for instance, as royal power declined in the late 18th century, *ulama* were beginning to assert their independence. Then in 1803 three pilgrims returned from Mecca and launched a Wahhabi-like reform movement, known to the Dutch as the Padri movement ("padre" being Portuguese for "clergyman"). They attacked moral looseness, insisted that Muslims should observe the duties of the faith, and required women to go veiled and men to wear white clothing after the Arab fashion. For 15 years the Padris steadily imposed their will, until they became became entangled with the expansion of Dutch power and their campaign of purification became a war against the interloper, which only ended in 1837.

A second notable reformist movement broke out in Java between 1825 and 1830. This conflict was due to the way in which the long-standing antipathy between the Islamic orthodox and the syncretic Hindu–Javanese elite was being exacerbated by the economic and cultural impact of the Dutch, who allied with the latter. One Dipanegara, of royal blood and religious temper, was moved to attack the European ways of the aristocracy and the growing misery that European rule brought the peasantry. He took to wandering through the countryside in Arab dress and meditating in holy places. Voices told him of his mission to purify Islam and save the people; the people hailed him as the long-awaited *ratu adil* or just ruler. Holy war was declared with support from the *ulama*. At first the struggle was mainly against the Hindu–Javanese elite, but it came to be a war of all against the foreigner, and although the Dutch gained the upper hand, the outcome, as in Minangkabau, gave a powerful thrust to the process of Islamization.

There was a third great holy war in the area in the 19th century, the Aceh war of

1873–1910, which would seem to have been primarily a war of resistance to Dutch expansion into northern Sumatra, but it was stiffened by the active involvement of the Naqshbandi sufi order as well as by pan-Islamic ideas broadcast from Istanbul. It was led by *ulama*, the most important being of Arab descent, who greatly strengthened their hold on Acehnese society, at least for the duration of the war.

Turning to India, we find two notable reformist movements in the 19th century. The first was the Mujahidin movement of Saiyid Ahmad of Rae Bareli (1786–1831). After returning from pilgrimage to Mecca in 1823, he raised support throughout India and in 1826/7, following the example of the Prophet's flight to Medina, fled pagan-dominated India to establish his ideal Islamic state on the Northwest Frontier. Although he waged holy war first against the

Sikh kingdom in the Punjab, it was clear that his campaign was no less directed against British expansion. Saiyid Ahmad died in 1831 at the battle of Balakot. His followers continued to spread his message, fighting in the great uprising of 1857 and remaining active on the frontier down to World War I.

The Faraizi movement of the eastern Bengal province was more profoundly influenced by reformist ideas in the wider Islamic world, probably Wahhabi ones. After returning from his second pilgrimage to Mecca, the founder, Hajji Shariat Allah (1781–1840), urged Bengalis to observe their duties (*faraiz*) according to the Quran and the example of the Prophet, and attacked Hindu influence on Islamic practice. He also attacked the British presence, but did not declare holy war against the foreigner. After his death, however, the movement transferred its attentions to the foreign ruler, became

▲ *A Dutch judge and local dignitaries witness the execution of criminals in Java. In the 19th century Wahhabi reformers clashed with the Dutch, who were expanding their power base.*

organized as a military brotherhood, and maintained an underground organization which worked quite independently of British law for most of the 19th century.

The Naqshbandiya in Asia

Many of those involved in reformist thought or action were members of the Naqshbandi sufi order, and indeed they were at the heart of Muslim activism throughout Asia. Some of the drive came from India as a result of the expansion of the order under Sirhindi's influence in the 17th and 18th centuries. In the 19th century the westward transmission of the Naqshbandi way received a second fillip from Mawlana Khalid Baghdadi (1776–1827), who, after studying in Delhi at the feet of the spiritual successors of Sirhindi, returned to western Asia where within a few years large numbers came to follow his guidance in Syria, Iraq, the Hijaz, Kurdistan, Anatolia, and the Balkans. Later

his influence spread to East Africa, Ceylon (Sri Lanka), and Southeast Asia.

Two striking movements of reform which merged into resistance to alien rule took place in the Caucasus. The first was led by Imam Mansur (died 1794) who, though it cannot be proved he was a Naqshbandi, is regarded as one by popular tradition and in fact preached a pure Naqshbandi message. From 1785 to 1791, supported in particular by the people of Daghistan, he waged holy war against the Russians until defeated and captured. The second movement emerged 50 years later and was led by Imam Shamil (c. 1796–1871), who was third in a line of Naqshbandi shaikhs which derived from northeastern Turkey. In 1834 he came to lead the order of Daghistan and, continuing the work begun by Imam Mansur, spread his rule over most of the Caucasus, imposed the *Sharia* so effectively that his reign came later to be known as "the period of the *Sharia*,"

and for nearly 30 years resisted mighty Russian invasions. But eventually, after cutting down the forests on which Shamil's forces depended for cover, the Russians gained the upper hand, and the imam surrendered. Still the Naqshbandis continued sporadically to resist.

In Central Asia, activity was by comparison feeble in the extreme. Quite exceptional was the three-day holy war against Russian rule, led, organized, and financed by the Naqshbandis,

▼ This map shows the distribution of Muslims in China, excluding the Tarim Basin, in about 1900.

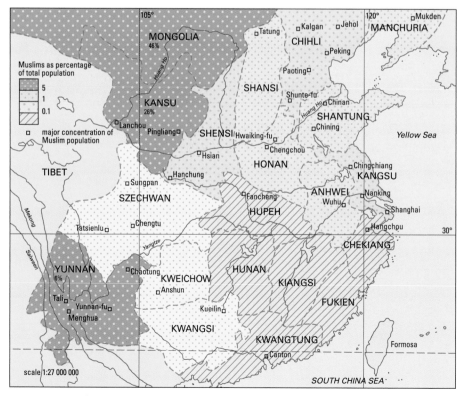

which broke out in Andijan in 1898. In the Volga Basin, a passive holy war was launched in 1862 in Kazan by Baha al-Din Vaisi (1804–93), who had just returned from Turkestan where he had entered the Naqshbandi order. Shocked by the way in which the local Islamic leadership was being absorbed into the Russian state, he conducted his fight with the infidel power by refusing to pay taxes or to perform military service. His message was so well received among the Tatars that by 1884 the government had to move; it broke up his organization, transported its leaders to Siberia, and committed Baha al-Din to a mental hospital. His movement, however, did not die, reemerging 20 years later and being marked by increasing puritanism as well as by involvement with Tatar nationalism.

China, by contrast, saw extraordinary Muslim activity in the 19th century. In east Turkestan holy wars against Manchu rule were led by the *khoja* Naqshbandi shaikhs living in exile in Khokand. Their record is impressive—five uprisings in 1820–28, 1830, 1847, 1857, and 1861. Then, after the Muslim rebellions in Kansu isolated the region from the rest of China in 1862, the *khojas* were able to reoccupy the whole of east Turkestan in 1863, only to be thrust aside by their brilliant subordinate, Yakub Beg (1820–77), who imposed a strict Islamic regime on the area which he ruled from 1867 to 1877.

Among the remaining Muslims scattered throughout China there was striking evidence of Naqshbandi influence, reform, and revival: Chinese Muslims adopted the Prophet's color of green, emphasized his example as the model for the rightly conducted life, and for the first time wrote on religious matters in Chinese, so important had it become to make every Muslim aware of his religious duty. Then around 1761 Ma Ming-hsin (died 1781) returned from study in Kashgar and began to spread the teaching of what came to be called the "New Sect" (as opposed to the "Old Sect" which embraced long-accepted Chinese Muslim doctrines of accommodation to Confucian society), which aimed to root out vestiges of acculturation to the Chinese environment in religious practice, and was behind every major Muslim rebellion down to the 20th century.

Muslims of the "New Sect" showed their first signs of real militancy after Ma Ming-hsin returned from a visit to Arabia, and in 1781 armed conflict with the "Old Sect" around Lanchou, known as the "Mecca of Chinese Islam," merged into rebellion against Chinese rule. This militancy grew in the 19th century as the "New Sect" spread throughout China and its message was probably reinforced by returning pilgrims from Arabia and reformist influences from India. Its vitality was revealed in two great rebellions. The first raged across Kansu and Shensi from 1862 to 1877, during which time its leader, Ma Hua-lung, tried to establish a Muslim state, and according to one estimate over 90 percent of the population were killed. In the second, which racked Yunnan from 1856 to 1873, the rebel leader, Tu Wen-hsiu, actually succeeded in establishing a separate Muslim state for 16 years in which he ruled over half the province as Sultan Sulaiman. So powerfully did this revivalist current run that for a time it even swept along with it members of the "Old Sect." The first leader of the Yunnan rebellion was Ma Te-hsin, member of the "Old Sect" and major scholar of the day: he was the first to translate the Quran into his native tongue.

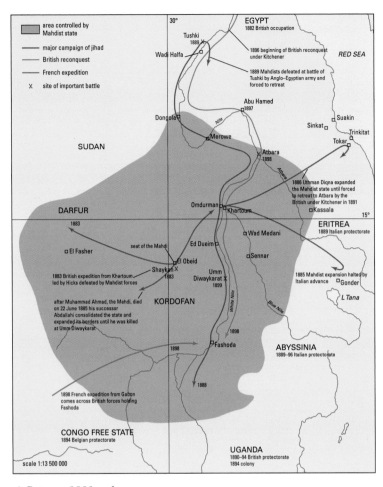

The map legend reads:

- area controlled by Mahdist state
- major campaign of jihad
- British reconquest
- French expedition
- X site of important battle

EGYPT
1882 British occupation

Tushki 1889

Wadi Halfa

1896 beginning of British reconquest under Kitchener

RED SEA

1889 Mahdists defeated at battle of Tushki by Anglo-Egyptian army and forced to retreat

Abu Hamed 1897

Dongola

Nile

Merowe

Sinkat

Suakin

Trinkitat

Tokar

SUDAN

Atbara 1898

Atbara

1886 Uthman Diqna expanded the Mahdist state until forced to retreat to Atbara by the British under Kitchener in 1891

DARFUR

Omdurman

Khartoum

Kassala

15°

ERITREA 1889 Italian protectorate

1883

seat of the Mahdi

Wad Medani

El Fasher

Ed Dueim

El Obeid

Sennar

Shaykan X 1883

1883 British expedition from Khartoum led by Hicks defeated by Mahdist forces

Umm Diwaykarat 1899

White Nile

1885 Mahdist expansion halted by Italian advance

Gonder

L Tana

after Muhammad Ahmad, the Mahdi, died on 22 June 1885 his successor Abdallahi consolidated the state and expanded its borders until he was killed at Umm Diwaykarat

KORDOFAN

Blue Nile

1898

1898

Fashoda

ABYSSINIA 1889–96 Italian protectorate

1888

1898 French expedition from Gabon comes across British forces holding Fashoda

CONGO FREE STATE 1894 Belgian protectorate

UGANDA 1890–94 British protectorate 1894 colony

scale 1:13 500 000

▲ Between 1881 and 1898 the Mahdist movement created a theocratic state in Sudan that was eventually overcome by British forces.

The Khalwatiya and Idrisiya

In the western Islamic world the Khalwatiya and the Idrisiya took up reformist ideas. The former was an ancient order given new life by Mustafa al-Bakri. The latter was a new order founded by the Moroccan Ahmad Ibn Idris (1760–1837) who settled as a sufi shaikh in Mecca, where he taught a sufi way which embraced an almost Wahhabi program and emphasized the importance of following the path beaten by the Prophet. Hence it was called, like that of Saiyid Ahmad of Rae Bareli, Tariqa Muhammadiya. These two streams of reformist vigor spread throughout Islamic Africa in the 19th century, having a dynamic impact on the relations between those who strove to realize the Islamic ideal and those who did not. They also helped to sustain and on occasion to satisfy the expectation that at the end of each Muslim century (in this case 1199 AH /1784–85 CE and

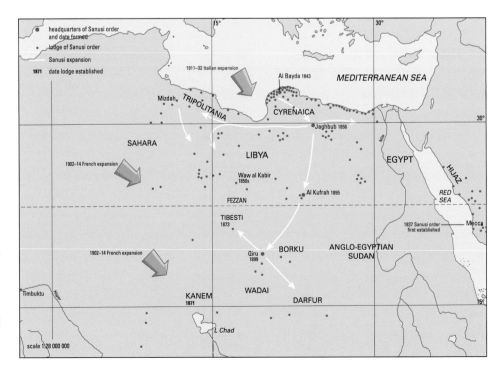

The map legend reads:

- headquarters of Sanusi order and date formed
- lodge of Sanusi order
- Sanusi expansion
- 1871 date lodge established

1911–32 Italian expansion

Al Bayda 1843

MEDITERRANEAN SEA

Mizdah

TRIPOLITANIA

CYRENAICA

Jaghbub 1856

30°

SAHARA

LIBYA

EGYPT

Nile

HIJAZ

1902–14 French expansion

Waw al Kabir 1850s

Al Kufrah 1895

RED SEA

FEZZAN

TIBESTI 1873

1837 Sanusi order first established

Mecca

Qiru 1899

BORKU

ANGLO-EGYPTIAN SUDAN

1902–14 French expansion

Timbuktu

Niger

KANEM 1871

WADAI

DARFUR

15°

L Chad

scale 1:28 000 000

▶ This map shows the expansion of the Sanusi sufis' system of lodges in the later 19th century as they sought to convert and coordinate the many Saharan tribes.

1299 AH/l881–82 CE) a Mahdi would appear who would "fill the world with justice, as it was previously filled with injustice and oppression."

One important offshoot of the Khalwatiya was the Tijaniya, founded by the Algerian Ahmad al-Tijani (1737–1815), who had been taught by Mahmud al-Kurdi (1715–80), a leading pupil of both al-Bakri and al-Hifnawi. His order spread to Algeria and Morocco and to the Nilotic and central Sudan, but it spread most widely in West Africa. At the heart of its success in this region was Hajji Umar Tall (1794–1864), a Fulani from Futa Toro in Senegal, a state long established by holy war. On pilgrimage in the 1820s he became caught up in the reformist movement after spending three years in Medina as a pupil of the Tijani shaikh, Muhammad al-Ghali, who made him his successor in the Sudan, and four years among the Khalwatis in Egypt from whom he learned his practice of retreat into prayer [*khalwat*], which he often practiced before battle. He returned to the western Sudan and founded a theocratic state just outside Futa Jallon. In 1852 he began his holy war, fighting the pagan Bambara of Karta, and by 1863, after he had captured Timbuktu, he commanded an empire which stretched from the bend in the Niger to Upper Senegal. Indeed only the French on the coast had prevented him from "dipping the Quran in the Atlantic." The state survived to 1893, when it was absorbed by the French, but the Tijaniya continued to flourish, becoming the most popular order in West Africa.

The second important offshoot of the Khalwatiya was the Sammaniya, which was founded by Shaikh Muhammad Samman and spread in the Nilotic Sudan, Eritrea, and southwest Ethiopia. Out of the spiritual tradition of this order there flowed the Sudanese Mahdiya. Muhammad Ahmad (1840–85), who declared himself to be the expected Mahdi on June 29, 1881, spent his life from 1861 under the instruction of two leading Sammaniya shaikhs of the Sudan and became renowned for his asceticism and his rigor in observing the *Sharia*. His movement was nourished by local resentments against the Turko-Egyptian regime which had ruled since 1821; the Sudanese resented the *ulama* imported from Lower Egypt, the "Western" innovations of the administration, and the abolition of the slave trade. So he waged a holy war against the regime which led to the capture of Khartoum in 1885 and the establishment of a separate Mahdist state in the Sudan. The ideas he promulgated and the institutions he founded were full of the reformist spirit. Muhammad Ahmad was the successor of the Prophet, the divinely elected Mahdi, and his followers were the successors of the companions of the Prophet, the *Ansar*—hence the name of the sufi way flowing from the Mahdi, the Ansariya. All formed the basis of an effective theocratic state, which only fell in 1898 because its simple armaments were exposed to the overwhelming power of a modern army.

The Tdrisiya also produced two offshoots with notable records. Strangely enough they both stemmed from those who lost a dispute for the succession in Mecca after the death of Ahmad Ibn Idris. One was Muhammad Ali al-Sanusi (1787–1859), who was forced to leave Mecca and eventually in 1856 came to establish his headquarters at Jaghbub deep in the Libyan desert. From here he spread a reformist message, which emphasized reliance on the Quran and the *Hadiths* and the need to purify sufism. In marked contrast to many reformists, he strove to create a

▶ *This map shows the campaigns of Usuman dan Fodio in his holy war to establish and expand the caliphate of Sokoto.*

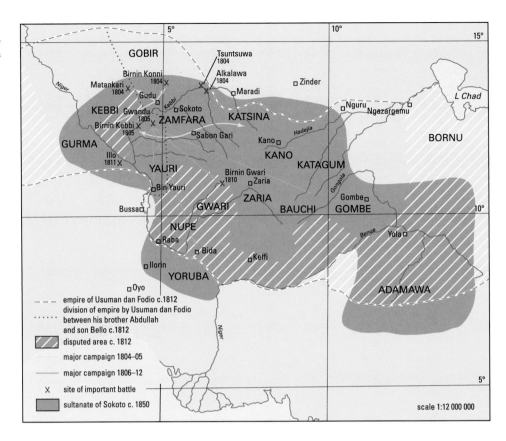

theocratically organized society by peaceful means. His method was to establish sufi lodges (*zawiya*). Each lodge was regarded as belonging to the tribe in whose region it was placed and from whom increasing numbers of adherents were won. Steadily in the 19th century a vast network of lodges, coordinating in one organization the once contentious tribes, spread down the Saharan trade routes till they stretched from Cyrenaica to Timbuktu and the kingdom of Wadai. They came, of course, to collide with the French as they expanded across the Sahara, and with the Italians as they invaded Libya. Nevertheless, they survived to become the basis of Libyan resistance to foreign domination, while their hereditary leaders became the first rulers of an independent Libyan state.

The second of those who failed to succeed Ahmad Ibn Idris was Ibrahim al-Rashid

(died 1874). His pupil and nephew, Muhammad Ibn Salih, founded the Salihiya, based in Mecca, whose most notable product was the Somali leader Muhammad Abd Allah Hasan (1864–1920), described most inaccurately by his British opponents as the "mad mullah." A gifted scholar, he traveled widely in search of knowledge. He studied in Mecca for five years, where he joined the Salihiya. On returning to Somalia in 1895 he began to preach a particularly puritan message: justice could only flow from the Quran and the *Hadiths*; holy war was a perpetual obligation; intercession at saints' tombs must end; those who missed their prayers risked mutilation or even death. By 1899 Abd Allah Hasan was waging holy war on all sides: against the laxer Qadiri order, against the Ethiopians, and against the British. He died unbeaten after 20 years.

Local movements in West Africa

In West Africa, the work of Hajji Umar Tall apart, the prime reformist drive was locally generated. The main leaders came from the Fulani, who had been converted to Islam before the 14th century. From the 15th century groups of Fulani began a long migration east to Hausaland. Like the *ulama* of Timbuktu or the Hausa city–states, they coexisted uneasily with those who mixed pagan rites with their Islamic practice.

The first Fulani holy war broke out in Bondu around 1680 and ended in the creation of an Islamic state; the second, which began in 1725, led to the founding of a Muslim dynasty in Futa Jallon; while the third, which began in 1776, brought an Islamic theocracy to Futa Toro. Then the focus switched 1,000 miles (1,600 km) east to Hausaland, where the preaching of Usuman dan Fodio (1754–1817) excited increasing tension with local rulers. In 1804 dan Fodio launched a holy war, in which Hausa as well as Fulani supported him, and which led to the formation of the sultanate of Sokoto out of the Hausa city–states. Nor did the holy war end here. After driving unsuccessfully into Bornu, Sokoto with local Fulani help was able by 1850 to draw Adamawa to the southeast, Nupe to the south, and Ilorin to the southwest into its Islamic empire. Usuman's achievement was noted by Fulani elsewhere. Between 1810 and 1815 Shehu Ahmadu (1775/6–1844) led a holy war on the Upper Niger against partially Muslim chiefs and pagan Bambara which led to the creation of the Islamic state of Masina reaching down river to Timbuktu.

These developments were felt beyond reforming circles. It helped sufi orders expand in East Africa; stiffened resistance against French expansion in Algeria; and encouraged Samori Ture (1830–1900) to transform the kingdom he built in the Guinea highlands from the 1860s into an Islamic state. Moreover, it stimulated a revival of activity among those whose Islam was in no way touched by ideas of reform. In the Maghrib, for instance, the most popular sufi ways from the 19th century onward were those which stemmed from the ecstatic master, Ahmad al-Darqawi (1760–1823).

This great movement of reform and the revival it stimulated were inspired in part by crises in the enduring tensions between the Islamic ideal and local conditions, and in part by the impact of ideas of reform as they spread throughout the Islamic world. No development in Muslim affairs since 1500 demonstrates more clearly the central role of *ulama* and of sufis as the principal sustainers of the Islamic community.

▶ *(overleaf) The tomb in Khartoum, Sudan, of Muhammad Ahmad, who in 1881 declared himself the divinely elected Mahdi, or successor of the Prophet.*

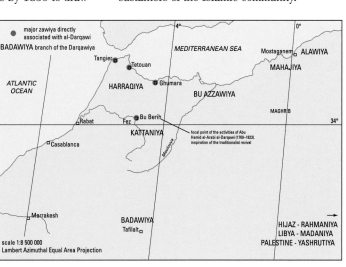

◀ *Not all revived religious feeling in the 18th and 19th centuries was reformist. This map shows the centers of activity of the major sufi ways flowing from Ahmad al-Darqawi which were the most popular in the Maghrib from the 19th century.*

Europe's Rise and Islam's Response

In the 19th and 20th centuries the Muslims experienced disaster. The slow erosion of power on the margins of their world during the 18th century became a rampant decay as European empire came to envelop the community. This brought a series of threats to the very heart of Islamic civilization: Christian missionaries, secular philosophies, rational learning, purely earthly visions of progress, and all supported by unprecedented material prosperity and power. Muslims were ill equipped to respond. Even the revivalist movements, products of the new vitality which surged through the Muslim world from the mid-18th century, could offer only temporary resistance. Nevertheless, their new spirit and ideas did provide some lasting basis for Muslim responses, which was important because the processes unleashed by Europe were powerful enough to make Muslims march to their tempo. Muslims now faced a civilization strong enough to transform them in its own image.

The symbolic beginning of the new era came when the French invaded Egypt in 1798. The revolutionary army represented the new forces of reason, nationalism, and state power; their action epitomized the new confidence of the Europeans, who had not dared to violate the eastern Mediterranean shore since the crusades. Within three years the British and the Ottomans had chased the intruders away, but the great forward thrust of Europe had now begun. In island Southeast Asia the Dutch government took over from its East India Company in 1800 and spread Dutch authority throughout the archipelago until the process was completed by the end of the Aceh war in 1908. In India the British were recognized as paramount by 1818 and 40 years later ruled all Indians either

Russian territory 1801
Islamic lands lost by 1825
Islamic lands lost by 1855
Islamic lands lost by 1881
Islamic lands lost by 1914
Russian protectorate prior to annexation in 1920
—·—· boundary of Russia 1920
1873 date of loss
Russian line of fortification (19th century)

▼ *During the 19th and 20th centuries Russia gradually conquered the northern Islamic lands as this map shows.*

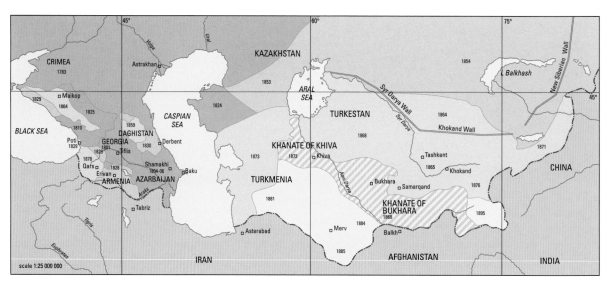

directly or though Indian princes. The strategic demands of this vast possession inexorably drew them into other Muslim lands. The Afghans, fortunate in their terrain, their warlike habits, and their position as a buffer between the ambitions of British India and tsarist Russia, were able to maintain their independence. In the Gulf, on the other hand, British power steadily grew, as it did in southern Iran and along Arabia's Indian Ocean shore. Further west the construction of the Suez Canal in 1869 and European competition for power resulted in the government of huge Muslim territories. In 1882 the British occupied Egypt; this in turn led to the establishment in 1898 of an Anglo-Egyptian "condominion" over the Nilotic Sudan, where they held effective power. On the East African coast they shared out the considerable possessions of the sultans of Zanzibar with Germany and Italy, while far away on the other side of the Indian Ocean they had from the 1870s begun to assert their hegemony over the sultans of the various Malay states.

Tsarist Russia was one of four European powers—together with Holland, Britain, and France—to come to rule large numbers of Muslims. In the Caucasus Russia made large steps forward at the beginning of the 19th century when it conquered the Iranian territories of northern Azarbaijan and by 1864 the whole region was effectively occupied. In Central Asia the lands of the

Eduard Riou painted the inauguration of the Suez Canal, opened by Empress Eugenie of France in 1869. The canal heralded new competition among European powers for influence in the Muslim world.

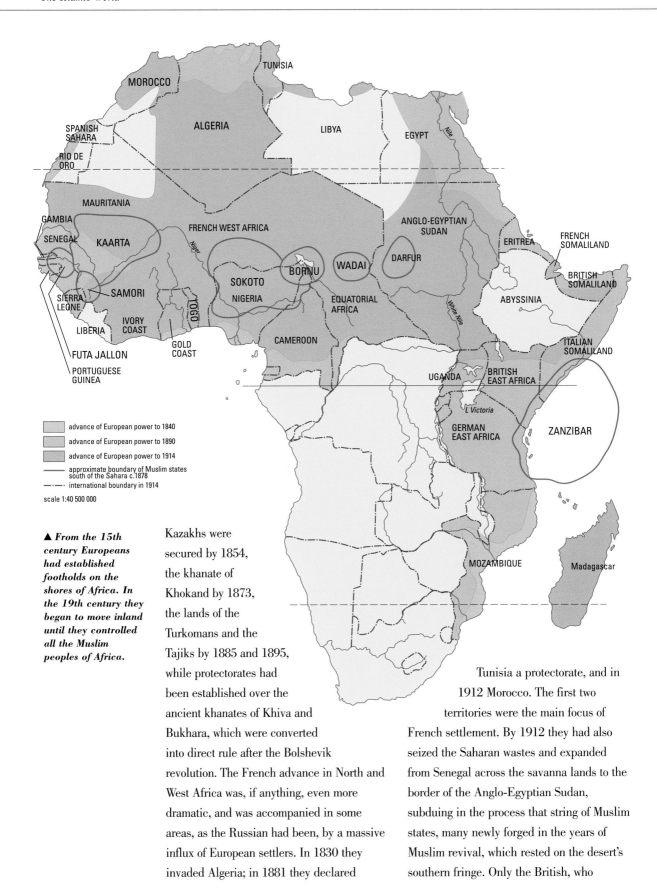

advance of European power to 1840
advance of European power to 1890
advance of European power to 1914
approximate boundary of Muslim states
south of the Sahara c.1878
international boundary in 1914

scale 1:40 500 000

▲ *From the 15th century Europeans had established footholds on the shores of Africa. In the 19th century they began to move inland until they controlled all the Muslim peoples of Africa.*

Kazakhs were secured by 1854, the khanate of Khokand by 1873, the lands of the Turkomans and the Tajiks by 1885 and 1895, while protectorates had been established over the ancient khanates of Khiva and Bukhara, which were converted into direct rule after the Bolshevik revolution. The French advance in North and West Africa was, if anything, even more dramatic, and was accompanied in some areas, as the Russian had been, by a massive influx of European settlers. In 1830 they invaded Algeria; in 1881 they declared

Tunisia a protectorate, and in 1912 Morocco. The first two territories were the main focus of French settlement. By 1912 they had also seized the Saharan wastes and expanded from Senegal across the savanna lands to the border of the Anglo-Egyptian Sudan, subduing in the process that string of Muslim states, many newly forged in the years of Muslim revival, which rested on the desert's southern fringe. Only the British, who absorbed the sultanate of Sokoto in their main West African colony of Nigeria, also ruled large numbers of Muslims in the region. Other European powers picked up what crumbs they could; in 1912, for instance, Spain asserted a protectorate over the northern tip of Morocco, and Italy conquered Libya. By the outbreak of World War I all the Muslims of Africa were under infidel rule.

Throughout the 19th century the Ottoman empire remained the only significant focus of Muslim power. But even here Muslims were falling steadily into the hands of unbelievers. The European powers, all equally intent on expanding their influence but all also determined that not one of their number should gain an advantage over the rest, used every financial, political, and military device to build up influence in the empire. The direct results were that Christian peoples of the Balkans—Greeks, Serbians, Romanians, Bulgarians—supported by one European power or the other, threw off Ottoman rule, and that the sizeable and long-established Muslim populations of the region lost their lands and sometimes their lives. By the outbreak of World War I only Rumelia remained of the once-vast empire in Europe. The war itself saw Arab peoples of the empire also fall under the European rule as the British, with Arab help, rolled the Ottoman forces back into Anatolia and divided the spoils with their French allies. By 1920 the Ottomans, whose subjects were now mainly Turks, were fighting to hold on to their Anatolian heartland, which the Europeans according to the treaty of Sèvres proposed to dismember by seizing chunks for themselves and by creating a Greek Christian province in the west and an Armenian Christian state in the east. This

was the lowest point of Muslim fortunes. No great Muslim power existed any longer to protect the community. Only Afghanistan, the Yemen, and the Muslims of central Arabia could pretend to any kind of independence. The great Muslim cities so redolent of past glories—cultural and political centers such as Damascus, Baghdad, Cairo, and Samarqand—had all been conquered by infidel powers. Only Istanbul remained free, but was no longer willing or able to take a lead in Muslim affairs. The future, moreover, looked bleak; although the Europeans trumpeted words of freedom to the people of Europe, they seemed to consider only further bondage for the peoples of Islam.

The European challenge

In the beginning the rise of Europe did not seem to demand a fundamental transformation of the way in which Muslims thought and lived. All that seemed necessary for independent Muslim states, such as Selim III's Ottoman empire or Muhammad Ali's Egypt, was that they should take from the Europeans what had made them strong and install it in their societies. All they had to do was to buy European weapons or Europeans machines, and their armies would automatically be stronger and their industries more productive. No concomitant changes in the organization of society or in the nature of its aspirations were seen to be necessary. For those Muslims who were conquered there was the considerable trauma of defeat and of rule by infidel powers; there might also be worrying attentions of Christian missionaries. It should be realized, however, that conquest rarely meant, in the 18th and the first half of the 19th centuries, any radical transformations of Muslim society. The old ruling class might have been swept away, in

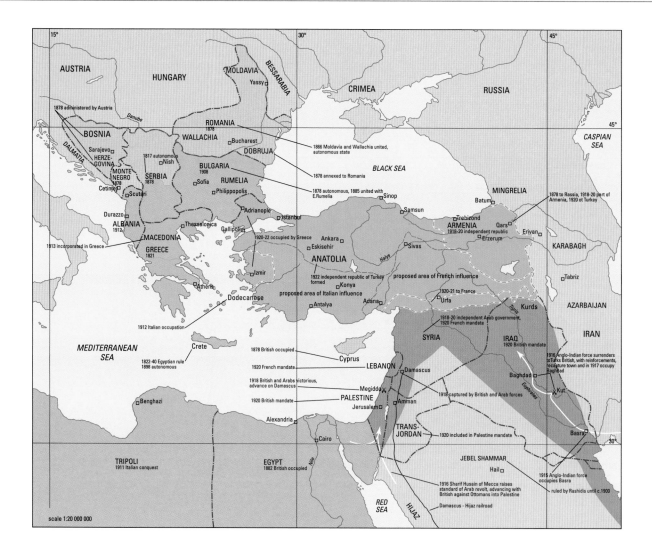

remainder of Ottoman empire in 1923
—— boundary of Turkey after treaty of Sèvres 1920
—— boundary of Turkey after treaty of Lausanne 1923

land lost from the Ottoman empire

to 1830
to 1878
to 1915
to 1923

—— proposed boundary for division of Anatolia between French, Italian and Turks

1878 date of independence

▲ *Between 1812 and 1923 almost all the Ottoman lands fell beneath European rule. Only the Anatolian heartland remained, becoming the focus of the modern Turkish state.*

part at least, but underneath Muslim life continued very much as before: the schools still taught the traditional Islamic sciences, government was still served in large part by Muslims, and the law was still the *Sharia*. Indeed, in the early stages of colonial rule, Europeans often adapted themselves considerably to the societies to which they had come, learning their language, using their systems of law, and even marrying their women.

As European power grew, however, the fundamental nature of the challenges offered to Islam was revealed. There were the challenges posed by Western philosophical and scientific theories to God, to his

relationship with nature and man, and to the life hereafter. There was the more general challenge as to whether faith could ever be reconciled with reason. Beyond this, moreover, there was the implicit challenge for men, who for 13 centuries had known history to be on their side, of the material and political success of societies in which Allah and his revelation played no part.

There were challenges which questioned the organization of Muslim society and Muslim values. These, furthermore, were severe because Islam, unlike other major religions, established rules of social conduct in minute detail; God had ruled very precisely on the behavior of the first Muslim community at Medina. But some of Europe's most cherished beliefs and practices seemed to clash violently with his commands. European capitalism challenged the Quranic prohibition on the taking of interest; the new European commitment to the rights of man challenged the Quranic acceptance of slavery; most importantly of all, the new European belief in the equality of all human souls challenged the inferior position which the Quran seemed to have designated for women: a man's right to four wives, his right to easy divorce, and the injunction to keep women in seclusion.

The most obvious set of challenges, however, came at the level of the state. From 1800 the pressing problem for Muslims was one of power—power to command their own destinies. The prime instrument of the new European strength was the modern state. It was aspects of this state which Muslims introduced to make their regimes strong enough to keep the Europeans out and which Europeans introduced to exploit the resources of their colonies. The key feature of the modern state was its capacity to control available physical and human resources. There followed the increasing involvement of the people in the activities of the state and the spread of the idea of the people as the legitimizer of those activities, of popular sovereignty. The meaning of these developments should be clear. The growth of state power meant the development of machinery to direct the minds and energies of the people in the service of the state. It meant the creation of an educational system to transmit the modern knowledge the state needed, a code of law which would make it strong, and a political structure which would express in some form or other the popular will. It meant, in fact, the creation of a

framework for Muslim lives and minds which need owe nothing to Quranic revelation. The spread of the idea of popular sovereignty, on the other hand, challenged the sovereignty of God. In Islam only God was sovereign, only God could make law, and the legitimacy of the state was measured according to the extent that it administered his law. The duty of humans was to come up to God's standards, not to establish their own. But the struggle for power seemed to demand that the strongest aspirations of the people be expressed in terms of the state, in terms of some national state within the community, and not in terms of their relationship to God. "The country is the darling of their hearts," wrote the Indian philosopher-poet Muhammad Iqbal, "vanished is humankind; there but abide the disunited nations. Politics dethroned religion...."

Muslims had a choice. They could ignore the European challenge, in which case they risked conquest and, if conquered, continuing servitude. On the other hand, they could strive to seize hold of the new sources of power Europe had revealed; they could learn the new knowledge, train the new armies, build the new factories, construct the machinery of the modern state, and fashion a "modern" outlook on the world. They could, moreover, work to reconcile all these things with the patterns for a Muslim life revealed in the Quran. But in doing so they ran the risk that the central institutions of Islamic society would wither away. The *Sharia* would seem redundant, *ulama* and sufis would seem irrelevant, and Muslims would no longer know how to submit. They ran the risk, in trying to absorb the new forces within the Islamic frame, of being transformed themselves by what they hoped would make them strong, of being just a Muslim husk of language, memory, and culture which enclosed a spirit secular, materialistic, and quasi-European.

Europe and the Ottoman lands

One theme emerges from the various strategies adopted by Muslims to answer the European challenge. Presented first and most strikingly in terms of power, it was taken up by those primarily concerned with power. *Ulama* and sufis, if they played a role at all,

played a minor one. The result was that in the continuing tension between the powerful and the transmitters in Muslim society there was a marked shift in favor of the former.

Ottoman leaders tried to build a system strong enough to prevent the steady encroachment of the Europeans on the empire. Work began in earnest under Sultan Mahmud II (reigned 1808–39) who set about destroying the semiautonomous groups which had so long defied and limited the central

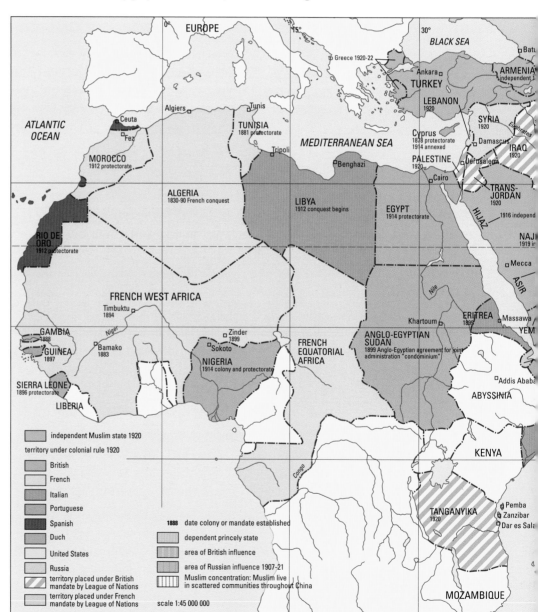

▶ *This map shows the territory controlled by European powers c. 1920. Very few Muslim areas were truly free.*

power. He first used the Janissaries to help him bring to heel local notables, valley lords, and provincial pashas, except for Muhammad Ali of Egypt, and then on June 15, 1826, used a new European-trained force to wipe out this historic elite corps of the Ottoman army turned hereditary corporation. There followed a slow, halting, but in the long run successful construction of a new state system of Western character, quite distinct from those remnants of the old order which managed to survive. There was a modern army, trained by Prussian officers, who began the close association between Germany and the Turkish people which has existed to the present day. Schools teaching European learning, often in European languages, were established to provide capable officers for this army as well as competent civil servants. By the end of the century these schools formed an empire-wide system, headed by the university of Istanbul, the

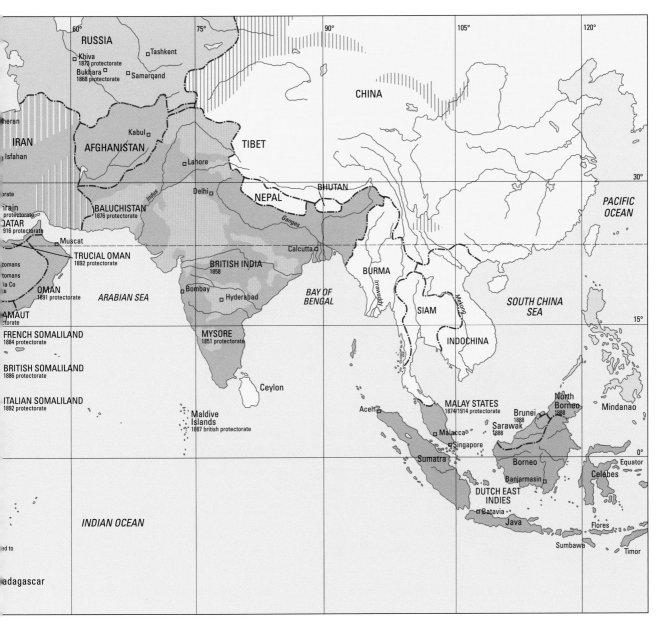

▶ *When Mahmud II became sultan in 1808 he set about destroying the Janissaries, the elite corps of the Ottoman army, and replacing them with a new European-trained force. Uniforms too became European in style.*

first truly indigenous modern university in the Muslim world, and controlled by a ministry of education. Rather earlier, indeed by 1863, all criminal, commercial, maritime, and land law was based on codes of French origin. The meaning of these changes for the *ulama* and for the transmission of the molding forces of an Islamic society should be evident. The Ottoman state which had once existed to spread Islam now treated Islamic knowledge as irrelevant to its purposes; the Turkish state, which had gone further than any other toward putting the *Sharia* into effect, was now thrusting it to one side. The *ulama* themselves, moreover, found their endowments expropriated, and their standing, now that they were just state pensioners, much lowered in the eyes of ordinary Muslims.

The growth of this heavily centralized secular government continued throughout the century and was much helped by improved communications, by railroads, and by the telegraph. It was not diluted by the espousal by Sultan Abd al-Hamid II (reigned 1876-1909) of a pan-Islamic ideology, which was as much for external as internal consumption. It was not deflected by moves to involve the people in government which led to the abortive Ottoman constitution of 1876 and the attempt of the Young Turks to restore it in 1908. By World War I the latter, who formed the Committee of Union and Progress, had shown themselves as despotic as any of their predecessors in commanding the new state machine, which was alien in spirit and out of sympathy with the mass of the people.

As we might expect, the development of the new secular Ottoman state created problems of identity. Would it be able to

reconcile and to represent the aspirations of the various peoples and religions which made up the empire? The 19th century reformers backed the idea of an Ottoman nationality. The great edicts of the time, the Noble Rescript of the Rose Chamber of 1839 and the Imperial Rescript of 1856, both declared that all the sultan's subjects, whether Muslim or not, were equal before the law. The state offered itself as the object of the affections of all, rejecting its old Islamic basis and bidding to overcome the religious divisions which had weakened it from the 17th century. Such a policy, combined as it was with the dismantling of the old Islamic fabric, was bound to antagonize Muslims. Thus Abdul Hamid II felt able to experiment with an Islamic identity, to distinguish again between Muslim and non-Muslim, to restore esteem to the *ulama*, though not their power, and to promulgate the idea that he was the caliph with spiritual authority over the whole Muslim community. The attempt was wrecked by its internal contradictions: Islam was a dangerous identity for an absolutism which fostered Western education and Western law; it was a liability for a ruler striving to cope with rebellious Christian subjects within and meddlesome Christian powers without. When the Young Turks came to power in 1908 the Islamic option was finished. There were two further possibilities: they could return to the supra-communal Ottoman identity, or they could turn to a completely new option, a Turkish identity. The theorist of Turkism was Ziya Gokalp (1876–1924) who, influenced by French sociologists, saw language as the only effective basis of nationality and argued that the genius of the Turkish speakers would be most fully expressed through the medium of Western civilization. At first the Young Turks

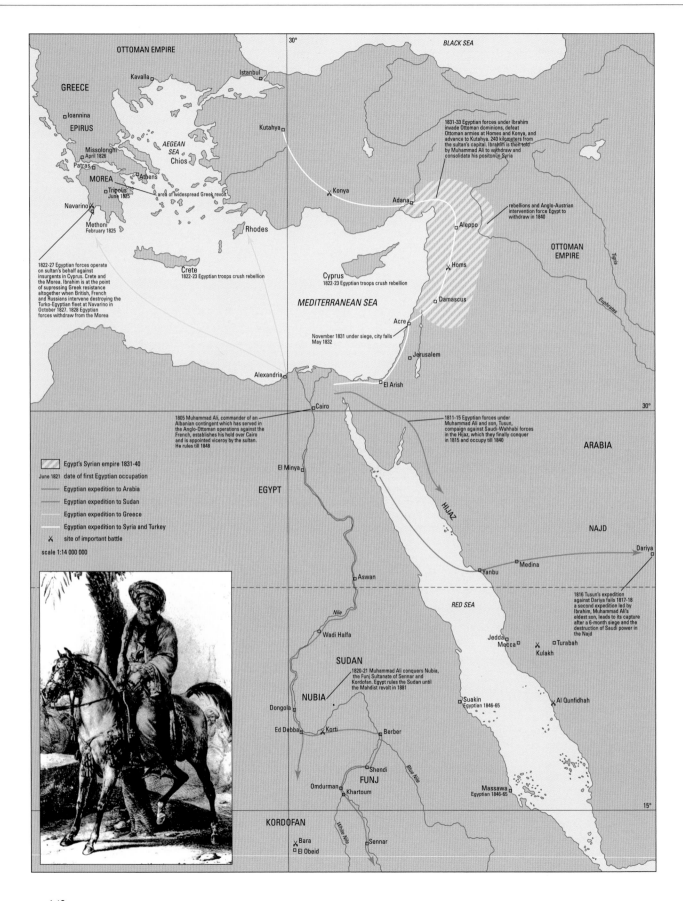

OTTOMAN EMPIRE

BLACK SEA

GREECE

□Kavalla

□Istanbul

□Ioannina

EPIRUS

Missolonghi
April 1826
□Patras

□Kutahya

AEGEAN
SEA

Chios

MOREA

□Athens

Tripolis
June 1825

☓Konya

1831-33 Egyptian forces under Ibrahim
invade Ottoman dominions, defeat
Ottoman armies at Homes and Konya, and
advance to Kutahya. 240 kilometers from
the sultan's capital. Ibrahim is then told
by Muhammad Ali to withdraw and
consolidate his position in Syria

Navarino☓

area of widespread Greek revolt

Adana□

Aleppo□

rebellions and Anglo-Austrian
intervention force Egypt to
withdraw in 1840

OTTOMAN
EMPIRE

Methoni
February 1825

☓Homs

1822-27 Egyptian forces operate
on sultan's behalf against
insurgents in Cyprus. Crete and
the Morea. Ibrahim is at the point
of supressing Greek resistance
altogether when British, French
and Russians intervene, destroying the
Turko-Egyptian fleet at Navarino in
October 1827. 1828 Egyptian
forces withdraw from the Morea

Crete
1822-23 Egyptian troops crush rebellion

Rhodes

Cyprus
1822-23 Egyptian troops crush rebellion

□Damascus

MEDITERRANEAN SEA

Acre□

November 1831 under siege, city falls
May 1832

□Jerusalem

Alexandria□

□El Arish

30°

30°

□Cairo

1805 Muhammad Ali, commander of an
Albanian contingent which has served in
the Anglo-Ottoman operations against the
French, establishes his hold over Cairo
and is appointed viceroy by the sultan.
He rules till 1848

1811-15 Egyptian forces under
Muhammad Ali and son, Tusun,
compaign against Saudi-Wahhabi forces
in the Hijaz, which they finally conquer
in 1815 and occupy till 1840

ARABIA

Egypt's Syrian empire 1831-40

June 1821 date of first Egyptian occupation

Egyptian expedition to Arabia

Egyptian expedition to Sudan

Egyptian expedition to Greece

Egyptian expedition to Syria and Turkey

☓ site of important battle

scale 1:14 000 000

El Minya□

EGYPT

HIJAZ

NAJD

□Dariya

□Aswan

□Yanbu

□Medina

RED SEA

1816 Tusun's expedition
against Dariya fails 1817-18
a second expedition led by
Ibrahim, Muhammad Ali's
eldest son, leads to its capture
after a 6-month siege and the
destruction of Saudi power in
the Najd

Nile

□Wadi Halfa

□Jedda
□Mecca

□Turabah
☓
Kulakh

SUDAN

1820-21 Muhammad Ali conquers Nubia,
the Funj Sultanate of Sennar and
Kordofan. Egypt rules the Sudan until
the Mahdist revolt in 1881

NUBIA

□Dongola

□Suakin
Egyptian 1846-65

□Al Qunfidhah

Ed Debba□

☓Korti

□Berber

Blue Nile

□Shendi

FUNJ

□Massawa
Egyptian 1846-65

15°

Omdurman□
□Khartoum

White Nile

KORDOFAN

☓Bara
□El Obeid

□Sennar

backed the Ottoman identity; they could not find much in common with the Turkish peasants and they still ruled an empire which also consisted of Greeks, Armenians, and Arabs. The nature of the problem, however, was changed dramatically by the final European assault which reduced the empire to its Anatolian heartland. Now only the Turkish option was left.

The man who gave his life to this option was Mustafa Kemal (1881–1938), who later came to be called Atatürk, meaning "Father Turk." The most successful Turkish general of World War I, he led his people to victory in 1922 against the Greeks who occupied Rumelia and western Anatolia. After making peace with the Allies in 1923, when they recognized the existence of a Turkish national state, he then set about bringing to fruition within this purely Turkish frame the modern secular system which the Ottomans had been building from the early 19th century and also pointing it firmly toward Western civilization. The sultanate was abolished in 1923, the caliphate in 1924, the last ruler of the august house of Osman being packed unceremoniously into the Orient Express for Paris. Religious schools and religious courts were swept away; the last vestiges of the *Sharia* were replaced by the Swiss legal code; state training of *ulama* ceased; sufi orders were abolished; their mosques and convents became museums; the Perso-Arabic script was replaced by the Roman; and the Turks were compelled to abandon their multifarious headgear in favor of the hat, which had long been a symbol of Europeanization and in which it was impossible to perform the Muslim prayer. Henceforth Islam was to be a purely private affair, a matter of individual conscience. The whole process, moreover, was imposed by a

Westernized elite. They succeeded in removing the last traces of the old high religious culture of Islam based on the *Sharia*, but among the people at large both sufi orders and a vigorous piety survived.

Egypt's response

Egypt also answered the European challenge by striving to modernize the army and to strengthen the state. In the beginning, moreover, the Egyptians were more vigorous than the Ottomans, which was to be expected as they had felt European military power more sharply. Their leader was Muhammad Ali, who ruled from 1805 to 1848; he was the commander of an Albanian contingent serving in the Anglo-Ottoman operations against the French invasion, who after becoming master of Cairo was appointed viceroy by the sultan. He created strong central government. By 1809 the *ulama* had submitted, and by 1811 the Mamluks, the old slave soldiery, had been massacred in a fashion which presaged the fate of the Janissaries. The endowments and tax farms of both groups were resumed, a huge system of monopolies was introduced to exploit trade and attempts were made to generate an industrial revolution. In command of new resources and new power, Muhammad Ali directed Egypt along a European road. A new conscript army was trained by foreign instructors. Egyptians were sent to study technical subjects in Europe, the rudiments of a state educational system imparting European knowledge were established, and participation in it was made the key to posts in the army and the bureaucracy.

Egypt gained in strength and wealth, but her growth was stunted by Europe. Muhammad Ali's armies spread his power to Arabia, the Sudan, Palestine, Syria, and

◀ *This map shows the growth and extent of Egyptian power under Muhammad Ali 1805–48. However, even before the death of this remarkable ruler (inset), European powers were beginning to acquire massive influence over the Egyptian economy.*

▶ *The courtyard of Cairo's al-Azhar, which maintained a network of traditional Islamic schools but which was challenged by government attempts to bring it under control after 1925.*

Greece, but when he threatened to advance into the Ottoman heartland, the European powers intervened. The new enterprises of Muhammad Ali and his successors encouraged European intervention in the economy, which withered its expansion at the roots and shackled it to European finance and industry. By 1882 European involvement had led to British military occupation. They found a situation in Egypt in which there was a "modern" layer of society which had Western education, served the state, and administered the law which was entirely based on French codes except in personal matters where the *Sharia* still held; there was also a "traditional" Islamic layer trained at al-Azhar and the great network of schools attached to it, which survived Muhammad Ali's assault on the income of the *ulama* and which still taught 95 percent of those Egyptians attending school.

The existence of these two distinct social and cultural layers was reflected in the 70 years of Egyptian history that followed. The campaign to free Egypt from British control was led by the heirs, in spirit at least, of Muhammad Ali; there was, for instance, Saad Zaghlul (1860–1927) who in 1919 founded the Wafd, the first mass nationalist party. This forced Britain to grant a limited degree of independence in 1922. In the following decades it was Wafdists and other secular nationalists who led the fight to remove the last vestiges of British influence from Egypt. At the same time they strove to extend the frontiers of the secular state into Egypt's still essentially Islamic society. The new constitution, promulgated in 1923, and based on Belgian and Ottoman models, asserted the sovereignty of the people as opposed to that of God. Vigorous measures were taken, after years of British neglect, to expand the state educational system which offered compulsory free elementary education from 1925. Active steps were also taken to bring al-Azhar, its curriculum, its *ulama*, and its subject schools under government control. The *ulama*, on the other hand, played only a small role in the nationalist struggle. After participating in the mass agitations of 1919,

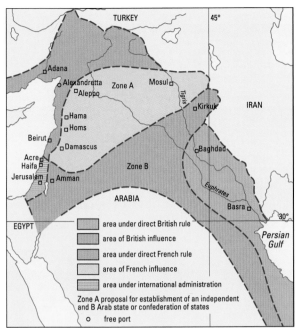
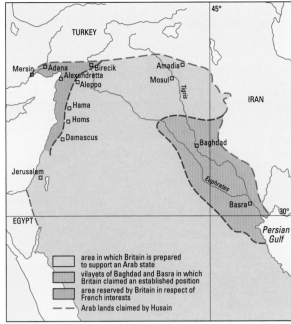

Arab aspirations

We now turn to the eastern Arab provinces of the Ottoman empire. Their first attempt to throw off foreign rule failed, blocked by the ambitions of Britain and France. The opportunity came in 1914 after the Ottomans declared war on the Allies. Sharif Husain (died 1931), the hereditary ruler of Mecca and descendant of the Prophet, asked the British to support independence for Arab lands from the Taurus mountains to the Indian Ocean and from the Mediterranean Sea to the Iranian Frontier. The British pledged support with the main exceptions of the *vilayats* of Baghdad and Basra, and of areas on the Mediterranean coasts north of Palestine. The sharif compromised, which meant shelving some key issues, and raised the standard of Arab revolt on June 10, 1915. His forces advanced into Palestine with the British. They took Damascus on October 1, 1918, where, amid wild rejoicing, one of his sons, Prince Faisal, established an independent Arab government. Arabs thought their dreams had come true. But the

which their countrywide network of pupils made possible, they withdrew from the struggle against their governors.

Identifying the secular nationalists as their chief enemy, the *ulama* went so far in their efforts to preserve their independence as to support the crown, even though that meant implicitly accepting the continued British presence. Religious-minded Egyptians did come forward, however, who were not content with the limp attitude of the *ulama* and the compromises with imperialism they seemed prepared to make. In the 1930s and 1940s a militant political organization grew up, the Muslim Brethren founded by Hassan al-Banna (1906-49), which aimed to impose on Muslims in Egypt and elsewhere, including by violence if necessary, a theocratic Islamic government. On the eve of the Free Officers' revolution in 1952 Egyptian society was still deeply divided. If the balance of power had come to lie with those who looked to a secular future, there was still powerful support in organization and in spirit for an Islamic vision.

▲ *Two maps reflecting the changing shape of postwar Arabia: (left) the Sykes-Picot agreement of 1916 and the Balfour Declaration of 1917; (right) areas in which Sharif Husain of Mecca wanted to establish Arab independence in 1915, and the more limited area in which the British pledged support for such an ambition.*

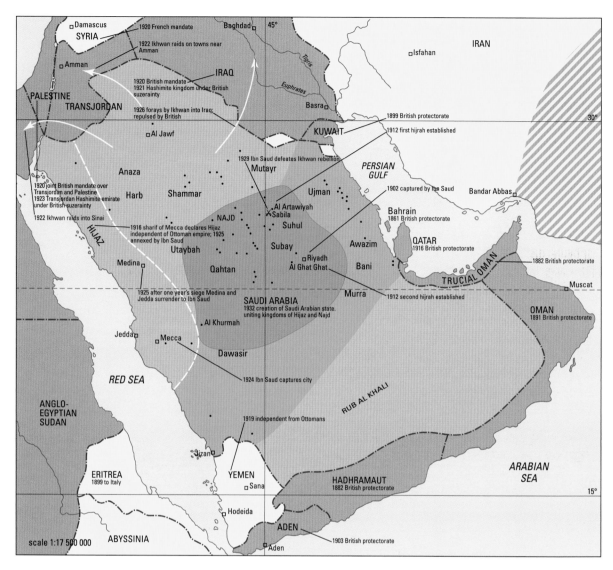

extent of Ibn Saud's territory

- in 1912
- in 1920
- in 1925

sharif of Mecca and Medina

· hijrah (a representative distribution, after Habib)

Harb tribal name

area under British mandate or protection

area of British influence

▲ *This map shows the growth of the Saudi Arabian state under Abd al-Aziz Ibn Saud between 1902 and 1925. In 1932 the land he had conquered was called the Kingdom of Saudi Arabia.*

British had made other promises which conflicted with their pledges to Sharif Husain—in May 1916 the Sykes-Picot agreement with the French, and in November 1917 the Balfour Declaration, which supported the establishment of a Jewish national home in Palestine. The Arabs had barely tasted the sweets of freedom before the Allies locked them away again. In 1920 the League of Nations gave the French mandates to rule Lebanon and Syria, and after 21 months of independent government Faisal was chased out of Damascus by the French army.

Churchill and other leading British statesmen had the grace to be embarrassed. In the same year the British received mandates for Iraq, for Transjordan, and for Palestine, with the obligation to create in the last a Jewish national home.

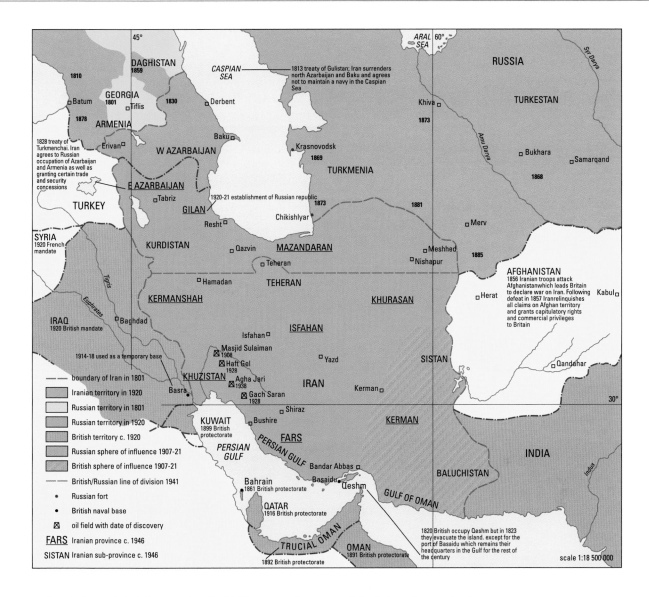

The map labels and annotations:

DAGHISTAN 1859 · 1810 · CASPIAN SEA · 1813 treaty of Gulistan; Iran surrenders north Azarbaijan and Baku and agrees not to maintain a navy in the Caspian Sea · ARAL SEA 60° · RUSSIA · Syr Darya · GEORGIA 1801 · Batum · Tiflis · 1830 · Derbent · Khiva · TURKESTAN · 1873 · 1878 · ARMENIA · Baku · Krasnovodsk · Amu Darya · Bukhara · Samarqand · 1828 treaty of Turkmenchai. Iran agrees to Russian occupation of Azarbaijan and Armenia as well as granting certain trade and security concessions · Erivan · W AZARBAIJAN · 1869 · 1868 · TURKMENIA · E AZARBAIJAN · 1920-21 establishment of Russian republic · 1873 · 1881 · Merv · TURKEY · Tabriz · GILAN · Chikishlyar · Meshhed · 1885 · SYRIA 1920 French mandate · Resht · KURDISTAN · Qazvin · MAZANDARAN · Nishapur · AFGHANISTAN 1856 Iranian troops attack Afghanistan which leads Britain to declare war on Iran. Following defeat in 1857 Iran relinquishes all claims on Afghan territory and grants capitulatory rights and commercial privileges to Britain · Teheran · Tigris · Hamadan · TEHERAN · Herat · Kabul · KERMANSHAH · Euphrates · Baghdad · KHURASAN · IRAQ 1920 British mandate · ISFAHAN · Isfahan · Masjid Sulaiman 1908 · Haft Gel 1928 · Yazd · SISTAN · Qandahar · 1914-18 used as a temporary base · KHUZISTAN · Agha Jari 1938 · IRAN · boundary of Iran in 1801 · Basra · Gach Saran 1928 · Kerman · Iranian territory in 1920 · Shiraz · Russian territory in 1801 · Bushire · KERMAN · Russian territory in 1920 · KUWAIT 1899 British protectorate · FARS · PERSIAN GULF · INDIA · British territory c. 1920 · PERSIAN GULF · Russian sphere of influence 1907-21 · Bandar Abbas · BALUCHISTAN · Indus · British sphere of influence 1907-21 · Bahrain 1861 British protectorate · Basaidu · Qeshm · British/Russian line of division 1941 · GULF OF OMAN · Russian fort · QATAR 1916 British protectorate · 1820 British occupy Qeshm but in 1823 they evacuate the island. except for the port of Basaidu which remains their headquarters in the Gulf for the rest of the century · British naval base · oil field with date of discovery · TRUCIAL OMAN · OMAN 1891 British protectorate · FARS Iranian province c. 1946 · 1892 British protectorate · scale 1:18 500 000 · SISTAN Iranian sub-province c. 1946

The dashing of Arab hopes after World War I brought a new militancy to Arab nationalism which was now nourished by a lively resentment both of Anglo-French domination and of Jewish settlement. There was also a growing secularism of thought as those who had had the education of the last Ottoman years and of the mandatory regimes began to make their mark in public life. We can see their impact in the changing relationship between Arab nationalism and Islam. Arabs could not circumvent the problem of Islam in the same way as the Turks. Islam was the great Arab contribution

to history, and it had given them unity, law, and culture. It was even possible to regard Muhammad as the first Arab nationalist: his message was not easily ignored. There were potential advantages here in that *ulama* could try to reconcile Islam to an Arab national state. Muhammad Abduh (1849–1905), a brilliant rector of al-Azhar, laid the foundation by demonstrating that Islam and modern European thought were reconcilable. His pupil, the Syrian Rashid Rida (1865–1935), went further and asserted at the time of the Arab rising in World War I that the political interests of the Arabs were

▲ *From 1800 to 1946 the development of Iran was subject to the commercial ambitions and strategic rivalries of Britain and Russia.*

the same as those of the community as a whole, and that an independent Arab state would put new life into the language and into the *Sharia* which would form its law. But by the 1930s very different views were coming to dominate. Islam was no longer seen as the binding agent of an Arab national state, but just as a strand in a broader Arab culture. Arabic, men argued, was the foundation of national solidarity. This transformation was of major significance. It enabled Christians, who after all had been the earliest promoters of secular nationalism, to appropriate the Arab Muslim heritage. Egyptians and other North Africans could be included in the Arab nation as well and whatever non-Islamic ideas were useful could be exploited. One outcome was the foundation of the socialist Baath, or resurgence party, which came to power in Syria and Iraq in 1963. Arabs could now build a modern state or states, and treat Islam purely as culture.

Developments in the Arabian peninsula offer a totally different picture. It is indeed, one unique in the 20th century history of Islam, the major processes deriving not from the interactions between Islam and the European world but entirely from a rekindling of the spirit of revival which had awoken there in the 18th century. The actors were the same as before, the Saudi family allied to Wahhabi *ulama*. For much of the 19th century their fortunes had fluctuated and the end of the century found the Saudi house in exile in Kuwait. Then the family produced one of the greatest Muslim leaders of the 20th century, Abd al-Aziz Ibn Saud (1880–1953), who from 1902 began to rebuild Saudi-Wahhabi power in the Najd. From 1912 his strength was greatly enhanced as he began to wield a weapon of his own devising, the *Ikhwan* or Brothers. For some

time he had been sending Wahhabi *ulama* among the Bedouin to persuade them to forego their un-Islamic practices and shiftless nomadic habits and settle in self-sufficient missionary and military agricultural communities. Here they lived lives of extreme asceticism and literal adherence to the *Sharia*, beating, for instance, women who wore silks or men who were late for prayers. Over 200 such communities were founded whose members' highest ambition was to die fighting to raise men to their own puritan Islamic standard. With the aid of this remarkable force and unimpeded by the desire of any great power to intervene, Abd al-Aziz gradually spread his rule over Arabia until by 1925 he had emulated the achievement of his ancestors over a century before by conquering the Hijaz and by imposing their fundamentalist views on religious practice in the holy cities of Mecca and Medina.

Once Abd al-Aziz had achieved power and declared himself king, the *Ikhwan* became an embarrassment. They objected to his introduction of motor cars and telephones and they knew no international frontiers in their campaigns against unbelievers, coming to blows with the British in Iraq and Transjordan. He was forced to destroy the demon he had created and most of the *Ikhwan* died at the battle of Sabila in 1929. Nevertheless the basis of his state, known as Saudi Arabia from 1932, was the *Sharia* which was administered in full through the courts. Modernization took place within the framework of divine law, royal decrees regulating areas where the *Sharia* did not run. In this respect the development of modern Saudi Arabia was quite different from that of any other Muslim state. After oil was discovered in 1938 and power returned to the birthplace of Islam, it was to be a difference of the first significance for Muslims throughout the world.

Iran's struggle for independence

The responses of Iran to Europe make interesting comparison with the Ottoman empire and with Egypt. There were similarities, but there were also important differences, notably the later drive for modernization, the weaker power of the state, and the greater power of the *ulama*.

Pressure from Britain and Russia was continuous throughout the 19th century. The

◄ *Fath Ali Shah Qajar (r. 1797– 1834) was the last Iranian monarch truly confident in his world beyond the reach of Europe.*

149

Russians aimed to extend their possessions in Iran as far as was feasible and to lay the foundations for the remainder of the country. By 1828 they lived in Iran under their own law, not the *Sharia*. By the 1870s they had made considerable territorial gains on both sides of the Caspian Sea. Between 1907 and 1921 they asserted a sphere of influence in northern Iran and again during World War II. The British were concerned with the defense of India and the development of commerce. They wanted a strong independent Iran able to keep the Russians away from the Persian Gulf and the borders of India. Between 1907 and 1921 they asserted a sphere of influence in southeastern Iran which was extended to the whole of southern Iran in World War II. From the 1870s Anglo-Russian commercial rivalry was also intense. In 1872 Baron de Reuter, a British subject, was granted a countrywide monopoly including railroad construction, mining and banking. Russian counter-demands quickly followed and in 1878 they were granted permission to raise, equip and train an Iranian Cossack regiment. By far the most pervasive and disliked foreign commercial presence was the Anglo-Iranian Oil company, later British Petroleum, which first struck oil in 1908 and quickly grew to be the country's dominant economic enterprise.

The main reason why Britain and Russia were able to penetrate Iran with such ease was that central government was weak. Iranian society at this time is best seen as a collection of semiautonomous estates: religious and ethnic minorities (Armenians, Assyrians, Jews, Zoroastrians, amounting to about 10 per cent of the population), tribes (Kurds, Lurs, Bakhtiars etc., amounting to between 25 and 50 per cent of the population), merchants who formed close

networks across the land and were the major source of loans to government, and *ulama* whose power, in stark contrast to that of their contemporaries in the Ottoman empire and Egypt, was increasing. We have already seen how under the later Safavids the *ulama* had begun to promote the theory that in the absence of the Twelfth Imam only a *mujtahid*, a scholar deeply learned in the *Sharia* and whose life was without blemish, could rule. The theory was further elaborated in the 18th century so that most *ulama* and most Iranians came to believe that they must seek guidance from a living *mujtahid*. *Ulama* who achieved this status had extraordinary power. It was bolstered, moreover, by the social functions and economic strength of the group as a whole. They had total control over education, the law and the administration of charitable works. They had huge endowments large landholdings and received annually one fifth of the disposable income of each devout Shia, half to support the poor and half to support their work. Religious specialists with such powers might well have found popular support hard to win. These *ulama*, however, had a symbolic relationship with the people; they progressed towards the rank of the *mujtahid* not by government appointment, nor by the election of their peers but through a combination of scholarship and popular standing. They formed a great independent corporation firmly rooted in the people. No ruler could afford to ignore them.

Like the Ottoman sultans and the Egyptian khedives the Qajar shahs strove to build up the power of central government. The work really began in the reign of Nasir al-Din (1848–96) and as elsewhere attention was paid first to the army. The equivalent of the massacres of the Janissaries and the

◄ *Kurdish horsemen salute on their way to the coronation of Riza Khan as shah of Persia in 1926. Riza Khan seized the throne from a weak king and crowned himself shah in a ceremony of remarkable opulence.*

Mamluks was Nasir al-Din's abolition of the old feudal army and his raising of battalions whose first loyalty was to the state and not to landowners or tribal leaders. A college was established in 1851 to give army officers and bureaucrats Western learning. In the 1860s central government was further strengthened by bureaucratic reforms and the introduction of the telegraph, and in 1873 Nasir al-Din felt secure enough to make the first of his three visits to Europe. Then he tried to hasten the pace of modernization by granting concessions to Europeans: the Reuter concession and the Cossack brigade, as well as rights granted to Christian missionaries to establish schools and hospitals, were part of the process. *Ulama* were bound to oppose such developments. The growth of Western education, the presence of missionaries, increasing European influence and the extension of royal power threatened their position. They led a successful protest against the Reuter concession in 1873. They led another successful protest against a British tobacco

monopoly in 1891/2, persuading Iranians to forego smoking for several months, and they led the early stages of the constitutional revolution of 1905–11, in which, allied with the merchants of Teheran and a small group of Western educated radicals, they succeeded in imposing a democratic constitution on the royal regime. At first sight their leadership of the revolution seems paradoxical. It was not. They were concerned to defend the *Sharia* and the Islamic quality of Iranian life against royal government and Western-educated radical alike. They inserted provisions to meet these ends in the constitution which was promulgated in 1906, and when it became clear that their Western-educated allies did not intend to uphold them, they went into opposition.

A dramatic increase in the authority of central government took place after Colonel Riza Khan (1878–1942) of the Cossack brigade seized power in 1921 and used it to make himself shah in 1926. At the heart of this greater government power was a new unified standing army which was both to curb the forces of decentralization and to help modernize society. A secular pattern of development was now imposed. In 1921 a comprehensive and compulsory system of state education with a Westernized curriculum was introduced; in 1935 the university of Teheran was founded; Iranians were sent abroad for further studies. Secular codes of law replaced the *Sharia*, religious courts were stripped of their functions, and only Western-educated men could sit as judges. Like Atatürk, whom he admired, Riza Shah wanted Iranians to adopt the outward symbols of secular society. From 1928 men who were not *ulama* had to wear Western dress. From 1935 they had to wear hats with brims. From 1936 women had to go unveiled, and police were employed to rip the veils from those who ignored the shah's command. Overall, his achievements were considerable. Iran was freed from much foreign political and economic domination, a modern state of secular style was firmly established in Iranian life and the power of the *ulama* was greatly curtailed. That the *ulama* did not come to suffer the same fate as their Turkish contemporaries was in large part due to World War II, which brought about the shah's abdication and ushered in two decades of relatively weak government. The *ulama* were able to regain some of their losses and to preserve the fabric of an Islamic society within the modernizing Iranian state.

Other parts of the world

For the most part so far we have been studying the responses of Muslims concerned to keep the foreigner out of their lands. Now we turn to the responses of Muslims in a different situation, those already under alien rule in Central, southern, and Southeast

Asia, and in Africa. Here responses depended in part on the impact of the colonial power and in part on the position of Islam in society. Two points are clear: because Muslims were being ruled by non-Muslims, whether Christians or atheists, Islam, or at least Islamic culture usually moved closer to the center of their identity than in Turkey or even Iran; and because colonial regimes often felt weak and developed a healthy respect for their subjects' religious susceptibilities, they were often cautious in attacking Islamic institutions. Russian policy in the northern Islamic lands stimulated a revival of Islam in the 19th century, led by the Tatars; however, that revival came to an end with the Revolution of 1917; mosques were closed and schools closed down. In India, Muslims saw their position challenged by Christian missionaries and secular educational institutions; the leadership of India's 20 percent Muslim population passed to the United Provinces in the north, paving the way for the eventual creation of the Muslim state of Pakistan there in 1947. In Southeast Asia, Islam would emerge from Dutch rule having carved out a place at the center of modern Indonesian life by becoming a focus of protest against the colonial government. Meanwhile, in sub-Saharan Africa Islam expanded more under colonial rule than anywhere else in recent times, particularly in West African nations such as Senegal and Nigeria. The most important aids to the spread of Islam in Africa cam from the indirect influence of colonial rule: the extension of peace and stable government over large areas enabled people to mix as never before and Islam to gain new importance as a set of beliefs and values which might be widely shared.

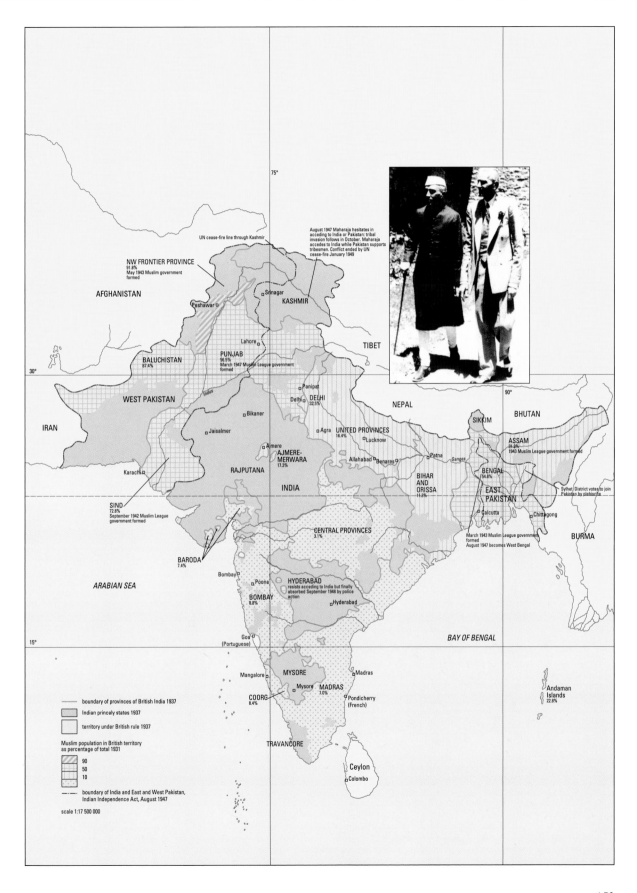

August 1947 Maharaja hesitates in
acceding to India or Pakistan: tribal
invasion follows in October. Maharaja
accedes to India while Pakistan supports
tribesmen. Conflict ended by UN
cease-fire January 1949

UN cease-fire line through Kashmir

NW FRONTIER PROVINCE
91.8%
May 1943 Muslim government
formed

AFGHANISTAN

Peshawar □

□ Srinagar

KASHMIR

TIBET

Lahore □

PUNJAB
56.5%
March 1947 Muslim League government
formed

BALUCHISTAN
87.4%

WEST PAKISTAN

□ Panipat

Delhi □ DELHI
32.5%

NEPAL

SIKKIM

BHUTAN

IRAN

□ Bikaner

□ Jaisalmer

□ Agra   UNITED PROVINCES
16.4%
□ Lucknow

ASSAM
-31.8%
1943 Muslim League government formed

Karachi □

Ajmere □ AJMERE-
MERWARA
17.3%

RAJPUTANA

Allahabad □ □ Benares

Patna □   *Ganges*

BENGAL
54.8%

EAST
PAKISTAN

BURMA

INDIA

BIHAR
AND
ORISSA
11.3%

Sylhet District votes to join
Pakistan by plebiscite

SIND
72.8%
September 1942 Muslim League
government formed

CENTRAL PROVINCES
3.1%

□ Calcutta

□ Chittagong

March 1943 Muslim League government
formed
August 1947 becomes West Bengal

BARODA
7.4%

ARABIAN SEA

□ Bombay

□ Poona

HYDERABAD
resists acceding to India but finally
absorbed September 1948 by police
action

BOMBAY
8.8%

□ Hyderabad

Goa □
(Portuguese)

BAY OF BENGAL

Mangalore □

MYSORE

□ Madras

□ Mysore   MADRAS
7.0%

Andaman
Islands
22.8%

COORG
8.4%   □ Pondicherry
(French)

boundary of provinces of British India 1937

Indian princely states 1937

territory under British rule 1937

Muslim population in British territory
as percentage of total 1931

TRAVANCORE

90
50
10

Ceylon

□ Colombo

boundary of India and East and West Pakistan,
Indian Independence Act, August 1947

scale 1:17 500 000

Belief and Practice

There is no systematic exposition in the Quran of what Muslims should believe and do, yet, taken as a whole, it expresses a consistent body of doctrine and duties. These are contained in the "five pillars," or basic observances, of Islam: (1) the observance of the creed, which demands belief in God, his angels, his books, his prophets, and the last day on which men will be judged; (2) the performance of prayer; (3) the giving of alms; (4) the observance of fasting; (5) the performance of pilgrimage, There was nearly a sixth pillar, *jihad* or "striving in the way of God." The Quran often urges Muslims to "fight in the way of God against those who fight you but be not aggressive… and fight them until there is no persecution, and religion is only for God" (Quran 2: 190 and 193). Muslims are aware of the exhortation to "strive in the way of God," although they have come to see it not just as holy war against the unbeliever but also against the enemy within, humans' baser instincts.

The Creed

It is widely agreed that anyone who utters the *shahada*, or testimony, "There is no God but God and Muhammad is the Prophet of God," may be regarded as Muslim. This formula comprises the irreducible minimum of Muslim belief. Many Muslims, however, might point to the Quran chapter 4 verse 136 as providing the basic outline of what they should believe: "Oh you who believe, believe in God and his messenger and the book which he revealed before. And whoever disbelieves in God and his angels and his books and his messengers and the last day, he indeed strays far away."

◀ *(previous pages) Muslims pray during Friday prayers at a mosque in Malaysia.*

God

The one God, the Arabic Allah, is but a shortened version of al-ilan, "the God," who has no partners, is utterly transcendent, creator of all things, judge of all men, all-knowing, all-powerful. He exists from eternity to eternity, beyond the reach of men's minds. He is the ultimate reality to whom Muslims give total allegiance.

Angels

As God was beyond all physical perception, angels were needed to bring his messages to man. It was Gabriel who communicated the Quran to Muhammad, and it was Gabriel who announced the birth Jesus to the Virgin Mary. Along with the angels there were also devils, evil spirits, or jinns, the chief among whom is known as Iblis.

Prophets

The men who received God's messages from the angels were the prophets, men of piety and models of good behavior. The Quran mentions 28, of whom 21 also appear in the Bible, and of these Adam, Noah, Abraham, David, Jacob, Joseph, Job, Moses, and Jesus are given especial honor. Particular stress is laid upon Jesus's immaculate conception and his miracles, although his claim to divinity is denied. Muhammad is, of course, the seal of the prophets; his message is for all men.

Books

The messages transmitted by the prophets are harmonious in fundamentals and represent a steady progress toward the perfect revelation of Muhammad. The Quran names and recognizes the scriptures of

Abraham, the Torah of Moses, the Psalms of David, and the Gospel of Jesus as books revealed by God.

The last day

The trumpet will sound the last judgment when men will be raised from the dead and called to account. Those who have believed the messages of the prophets and have struggled to follow God's path will be summoned to enter paradise where they will live for ever in a garden with cool streams, beautiful women, couches adorned with silk, flowing cups, and luscious fruit, although all these will be as nothing compared with the ultimate reward, the sight of God. Those who have ignored the messages and followed other gods will be cast into hell where they will be burned by fire, drink boiling water, eat of the vile zaqqum tree and endure other torments without hope of release through

death. Only God can save men, believers or not, from further torment and in the Quran he often reassures men of his merciful intent.

Prayer

Prayer, the remembrance of the sovereignty of God on earth, is to be performed five times a day: on rising, and the Muslim should rise early, early in the afternoon, late in the afternoon, at sunset, and at night before going to bed. Spontaneous extra prayers are encouraged; so too is ritual prayer in the company of other Muslims; indeed, it is prescribed that the early afternoon prayer each Friday should be in congregation and should be led by the chief Muslim of the locality who also delivers a sermon.

The ritual of prayer symbolizes the humility of men in the presence of God. First the Muslim ritually purifies himself by washing, and then orientates himself toward

▲ *Muslims pray at the Damascus Gate in the Old City of Jerusalem. Some Muslims develop a distinctive callus or mark of prayer on their foreheads from repeated contact with the ground over many years.*

Mecca, the direction of which is indicated in a mosque by the mihrab, or niche in the wall facing Mecca. Then he performs the number of *rakats* or "bowings" prescribed for the prayer time, each "bowing" consisting of a sequence of seven movements accompanied by recitations. He begins by placing his hands on each side of his face and reciting "God is most great"; continuing to stand upright he recitates the opening chapter of the Quran, which may be followed by other passages; he bows from the hips; he straightens up; he moves to his knees and prostrates himself face to the ground; he sits back on his haunches; and finally he makes a second prostration. Thus the Muslim, the submitter, by word of mouth and graphic gesture demonstrates the meaning of the word Islam: "submitting."

Alms

"Keep up prayer and pay the poor rate" (58:13) is one of many reminders in the Quran that benevolence is one of the chief virtues of the true believer; indeed prayer and the giving of alms (*zakat*) are often linked. The amount which the Muslim should pay was fixed at one-fortieth of his revenue for the year in cash or kind. The object of giving alms was twofold: on the one hand to purify or legitimize the gaining of private property by devoting a proportion of what was gained to the common need, the word *zakat* being derived from the root *zaka*, to be pure; and on the other hand as a manifestation of the believer's sense of social responsibility, of his will to help cement the community. The revenue from alms is to be spent on the poor, the needy, the collectors of alms, those who might become Muslims, the freeing of prisoners of war, debtors, travelers, and those who strive in the "way of God."

Fasting

The Muslim is required to observe the ninth month of the lunar year, Ramadan, as a period of fasting in which he abstains from eating, drinking, smoking, and sexual relations during daylight hours. The purpose is to subjugate the body to the spirit and to fortify the will to enable the believer to come closer to God, and in harmony with this purpose the devout will offer extra prayers during the month and make recitations of the Quran. This shared physical privation and spiritual discipline foster each year a renewed sense of community.

Pilgrimage

The final pillar is the pilgrimage to Mecca, where Muslims believe Abraham rebuilt the house of Adam, which all Muslims must perform at least once in a lifetime providing they have the means. The pilgrimage takes place each year. Before entering Mecca, the pilgrim puts off his ordinary clothes and dons two plain white sheets, symbolizing his abandonment of ordinary life and his will to annihilate self as he presents himself to God. Then, with thousands of fellow pilgrims, he walks seven times around the central sanctuary in the great mosque of Mecca; runs seven times from Mecca toward Marwa and back, recalling the desperate search for water for her son Ishmael by Hagar, Abraham's wife; stands on the plain of Arafat outside Mecca in remembrance of the standing of Abraham against idolatry; stones the pillars at Mina in remembrance of Abraham, Hagar, and Ishmael's rejection of the temptation of Satan; and finally sacrifices an animal and shaves his head. No rite has done more to foster the solidarity of the Muslim community. It is described in greater detail on pages 169–171.

◄ A pilgrim prays before the Kabaa, the sanctuary in the great mosque at Mecca which Muslims believe was first built by Abraham.

The Stages of Life

Birth

No sooner is a baby born than the call to prayer is whispered into his or her right ear and the commencement of prayer into the left. Thus the very first word the child hears is God, and he begins his Muslim life with a double exhortation to worship him.

Seven days later the child is named in a ceremony called *aqiqah*. Friends and relatives are invited, the object being to introduce the new Muslim into the immediate world in which he will grow up as well as to give him a name. The head of the baby is shaved completely; a weight in gold, silver or money, equivalent to the weight of the hair, is given to the poor; an animal is sacrificed. The name will generally be chosen from those of the Prophet's family, other prophets mentioned in the Quran, or great Muslims of the past. If the family is especially devoted to a particular saint, the choice of name may be left to a representative of the saint's family.

Growing up

Two ceremonies mark childhood, although neither is mentioned in the Quran. The first is the *basmala*. When a child is ready to begin learning, soon after he is four, a family feast is held at which he receives his first lesson. The basmala and the first words revealed to the Prophet are recited. The child is then made to recite them, and his education has begun.

The second ceremony is circumcision, generally performed on boys between 7 and 12, although it is permitted to circumcise a child seven days after birth. In parts of the Islamic world girls also are circumcised, a controversial practice for which religious authority is weak. It is not done much in India, Russia, China, Iran, Afghanistan, Turkey, or Arabia. It may be the persistence of a pre-Islamic custom.

Marriage

"When the servant of God marries," said the Prophet, "he perfects half of his religion." Muhammad laid such emphasis on marriage and so strongly condemned celibacy that even members of ascetic sufi orders tend to be married rather than single.

Marriage is a contract, not a sacrament. Nevertheless, non-Muslims should not think that it is undertaken lightly. Great emphasis is placed on the importance of mutual love and respect and the care of children; it is preferred that a man remain with one wife throughout his life. The barriers to divorce are also high.

Death

When a man is near to death, he is encouraged to say the confession of faith; just as God was the first word he heard, so it should be the last he utters. After death the body is washed, shrouded, and carried to a mosque where the burial service is said. Then the bier is taken quickly to the grave; the Prophet said that the righteous should arrive soon at happiness. The body is then buried with the face turned toward Mecca.

Muslims are encouraged not to grieve too much, and among Sunni Muslims mourning continues for no more than seven days. Death is not the end of life; Muslims are only briefly separated from those who die. Through God's grace all who truly submit will enjoy life after death.

▶ *Veiled brides wait for the start of a mass wedding in Amman, Jordan. Such ceremonies are arranged by charities to help poorer couples by allowing them to share the cost of the wedding.*

The Quran

▶ *A young girl studies Koranic verses at a madrasa in Libya. Traditionally men have been the interpreters of Islam, but the spread of literacy has enabled women to play a greater role in Quranic studies.*

▼ *The art of calligraphy is highly valued in Muslim society, especially for copying the Quran. This page is from a 9th century Quran.*

Muslims believe that the Quran is the word of God, the direct expression of divine will. Its revelation was a miracle, attested by Muhammad's illiteracy and his ignorance of many of the matters with which it deals, no less than by its literary form. God's revelation through Muhammad is his last word before the day of judgment. The Quran is thus the supreme authority for all mankind, the only road to salvation. It is the measure of truth and the best model for conduct. It is always right and is the purest and most beautiful form of speech.

The Quran accompanies the believer through his life. As a child he will begin to learn it as he begins to talk. He will hear it recited during daily prayers, at his marriage, and at the death of loved ones. He will turn to it for consolation. He will perhaps know the whole text by heart and recite it from day to day. One of his greatest pleasures will be to hear a well-voiced *Qari* chanting the holy word in slow melodic phrases, revealing new beauty and uncovering layers of meaning.

The Quran is witness of God's care for humankind. The words are to be remembered with precision; they are to be copied in the fairest of hands. The book is to be made beautiful. It is cherished, wrapped in a fine cloth, and always given a place of honor.

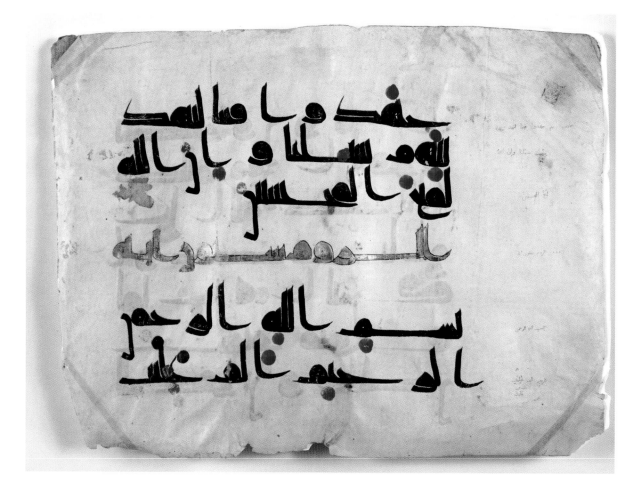

The Mosque

▶ *The mihrab, the niche which indicates the direction of Mecca, is usually the most decorated part of a mosque. Unlike an altar, it is not sacred itself: it is the direction it indicates that is sacred.*

At dawn, at midday, in the afternoon, just after sunset and in the evening the muezzin calls Muslims to prayer: On hearing the call Muslims should prepare for prayer, either in their homes, where women generally pray, or in the mosque, a term derived from the Arabic *masjid* meaning place of prostration, where it is preferred that men should pray if they possibly can; they are obliged to attend for midday prayer on Friday when they will also listen to a sermon.

The design of the mosque and its features directly reflect their functions in public worship. Essentially the mosque is a wall so orientated that a line drawn directly from Mecca would strike it at right angles. This ensures that the Muslim knows which way he should face to pray; the niche made in the wall by the *mihrab* emphasizes that direction.

The tendency of the building to be square rather than long stems from the desire of all of the worshipers to pray as close to the mihrab wall, and therefore to Mecca, as possible: there is no need, as in a Christian church, to accommodate processional worship. The minaret developed to call the people to prayer, and the higher it is, the further the muezzin's voice will carry across the surrounding area. Some kind of tank or fountain is essential so that worshipers can perform their ablutions; so also is the *minbar*, or pulpit, from which the imam delivers his Friday sermon. The *dikka*, or platform, is needed so that respondents can transmit the posture of the imam and the appropriate response to a large congregation, although the introduction of the loudspeaker has tended to make it redundant. The *kursi*, or lectern, holds the Quran.

▶ *Shoe racks stand at the entrance to the mosque to avoid worshipers defiling the building with ritually impure substances; some worshipers carry their shoes with them.*

▶ *A tank or fountain is necessary for ritual cleaning. Should a Muslim fail to wash correctly, his or her subsequent prayer has no value.*

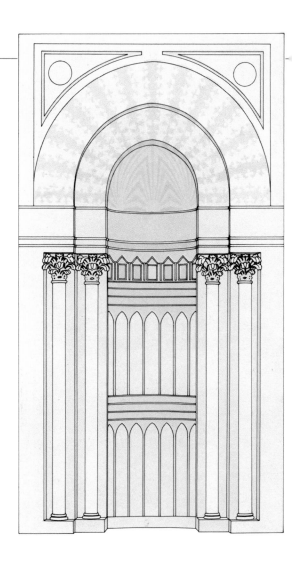

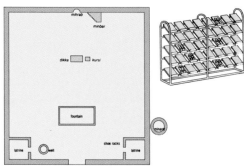

◄ *The dikka, or platform, is usually placed in line with the mihrab. Here muezzins from the mosque speak the responses to transmit the stages of prayer to a large audience.*

▲ *The kursi, or lectern, holds the Quran, which in a mosque may be very large. The kursi is usually placed next to the dikka.*

▲ *The imam gives his sermon from one of the lower steps of the minbar, or pulpit: only the Prophet preached from the topmost step.*

► *A mosque does not have to have a minaret—the call to prayer can be made from a courtyard— but in central Islamic lands most do.*

The Believer's Year

The Muslim year is based on a lunar cycle, containing 354 days, and so changes annually by 10 or 11 days in relation to the Christian solar calendar. It is divided into 12 lunar months of 29 or 30 days. Each day begins immediately after sunset.

The two festivals that Muslims must keep, because the Prophet instructed them to do so, are the Id al-Fitr and the Id al-Adha. Fasting in Ramadan is also obligatory.

HIJRA, migration, 1 Muharram, the first day of the Muslim year, celebrates the very first day of the Muslim era when in 622 CE Muhammad left Mecca to start a new community in Medina. Hence AH denotes the years of the Muslim era, meaning "After the Hijra," after the migration.

RAMADAN, the month when all Muslims who have reached puberty observe their religious obligation to abstain from eating, drinking, smoking and sexual relations during daylight hours.

LAILAT AL-QADR, the "Night of Majesty," 27 Ramadan. Ramadan is the month in which the first revelation of the Quran was made to Muhammad.

ID AL-FITR, the "festival of breaking the fast," I Shawwal, used to be the less important of the two Ids; but so great is the joy at the end of Ramadan that Muslims have come to celebrate it with more festivity than the major festival. Id means " "time of happiness" in Arabic. Muslims begin the day by bathing and changing into new clothes before going to the mosque for prayers. After prayers they exchange presents, visit friends and relations, and try to bury any differences so they can make a new start in peace. They are also obliged to give to the poor.

MAWLID AL-NABI, the birthday of the Prophet, 12 Rabi al-Awwal. For sufis, with their especial regard for Muhammad as the "perfect man," the day is particularly important and its observance may be the culmination of celebrations which begin on 1 Rabi al-Awwal.

LAILAT AL-MIRAJ, the "Night of the Ascent," 27 Rajab, commemorates the night in the tenth year of Muhammad's prophethood when the Archangel Gabriel conducted him through the Seven Heavens, where he spoke with God, and from which he returned the same night with instructions that included the five daily prayers.

ID AL-ADHA, the "festival of sacrifice," 10 Zul-Hijja. Its origins go back to the Prophet Abraham who demonstrated his willingness to sacrifice all that he loved most dearly for God's sake, which act is commemorated in the last rite of the pilgrimage to Mecca. Muslims begin the festival by attending communal prayer, and then sacrifice a sheep, a cow, or a camel, usually keeping one-third of the meat and giving the rest to the poor. Celebrations may last three or more days.

Three further festivals should be noted: the last Friday in Ramadan, when Muslims make a point of attending the mosque to bid farewell to the month of fasting; Shab i-Barat, 15 Shaaban, when God is said to register each year all the actions of humankind, which is celebrated particularly by Indian Muslims; and Ashura, 10 Muharram, when Muslims remember that Noah left the Ark, Moses saved the Israelites from Pharaoh, and Husain was martyred at Karbala. It is the most important festival of the Shia year.

▶ *The year begins with the month of Muharram. Reading from left to right, the believer moves through the months until he reaches the last month of Zul-Hijja.*

166

MUHARRAM

Monday		7	14	21	28
Tuesday	1	8	15	22	29
Wednesday	2	9	16	23	30
Thursday	3	10	17	24	
Friday	4	11	18	25	
Saturday	5	12	19	26	
Sunday	6	13	20	27	

SAFAR

Monday		5	12	19	26
Tuesday		6	13	20	27
Wednesday		7	14	21	28
Thursday	1	8	15	22	29
Friday	2	9	16	23	30
Saturday	3	10	17	24	
Sunday	4	11	18	25	

RABI AL-AWWAL

Monday		3	10	17	24
Tuesday		4	11	18	25
Wednesday		5	12	19	26
Thursday		6	13	20	27
Friday		7	14	21	28
Saturday	1	8	15	22	29
Sunday	2	9	16	23	30

RABI AL-AKHIR

Monday	1	8	15	22	29
Tuesday	2	9	16	23	30
Wednesday	3	10	17	24	
Thursday	4	11	18	25	
Friday	5	12	19	26	
Saturday	6	13	20	27	
Sunday	7	14	21	28	

JUMADA AL-AWWAL

Monday		6	13	20	27
Tuesday		7	14	21	28
Wednesday	1	8	15	22	29
Thursday	2	9	16	23	
Friday	3	10	17	24	
Saturday	4	11	18	25	
Sunday	5	12	19	26	

JUMADA AL-AKHIR

Monday		5	12	19	26
Tuesday		6	13	20	27
Wednesday		7	14	21	28
Thursday	1	8	15	22	29
Friday	2	9	16	23	30
Saturday	3	10	17	24	
Sunday	4	11	18	25	

RAJAB

Monday		3	10	17	24
Tuesday		4	11	18	25
Wednesday		5	12	19	26
Thursday		6	13	20	27
Friday		7	14	21	28
Saturday	1	8	15	22	29
Sunday	2	9	16	23	

SHAABAN

Monday		2	9	16	23
Tuesday		3	10	17	24
Wednesday		4	11	18	25
Thursday		5	12	19	26
Friday		6	13	20	27
Saturday		7	14	21	28
Sunday	1	8	15	22	29

RAMADAN

Monday	1	8	15	22	29
Tuesday	2	9	16	23	30
Wednesday	3	10	17	24	
Thursday	4	11	18	25	
Friday	5	12	19	26	
Saturday	6	13	20	27	
Sunday	7	14	21	28	

SHAWWAL

Monday		6	13	20	27
Tuesday		7	14	21	28
Wednesday	1	8	15	22	29
Thursday	2	9	16	23	
Friday	3	10	17	24	
Saturday	4	11	18	25	
Sunday	5	12	19	26	

ZUL-QAADA

Monday		5	12	19	26
Tuesday		6	13	20	27
Wednesday		7	14	21	28
Thursday	1	8	15	22	29
Friday	2	9	16	23	30
Saturday	3	10	17	24	
Sunday	4	11	18	25	

ZUL-HIJJA

Monday		3	10	17	24
Tuesday		4	11	18	25
Wednesday		5	12	19	26
Thursday		6	13	20	27
Friday		7	14	21	28
Saturday	1	8	15	22	29
Sunday	2	9	16	23	

Pilgrimage to Mecca

As pilgrims get their first glimpse of the Kaaba, the central sanctuary in the great mosque at Mecca, they cry "Labbaika! Labbaika!"—"Here I am (God), here I am (God), present before you, before you." This is the zenith of a Muslim life, the culmination of years spent striving in the way of the Lord, the moment when yearning can end. "I long for Mecca and its bright heavens," declares the pious Rizwan in Najib Mahfuz's Egyptian novel, *Midaq Alley*. "I long for the whisper of time at every corner and to walk down its streets and lose myself in the holy places ... I can see myself now, my brothers, walking through the lanes of Mecca, reciting verses from the Quran just as they were first revealed, as if I was listening to a lesson given by the Almighty Being. What joy!"

Every Muslim, who is sane, healthy, free from debt, and able to pay both his expenses and those of his dependents while he is away, must perform the pilgrimage at least once in his lifetime. The observances are based on the Quran (2: 196–200; 5: 95-97; 22: 26–33) and the practice of the Prophet Muhammad. They commemorate events in the lives of Abraham, Hagar his wife, and Ishmael his

son. The spirit of the rite is one of total self-abnegation. The pilgrim, as he presents himself to God, sacrifices all those things which mark him in the world of men: wealth, family, friends, distinctions of dress, birth, and race. He also celebrates the brotherhood of all Muslims. All are equal in dress and in what they must perform, just as they will all stand equal before God on the day of judgment. Nothing has done more to foster Muslim solidarity than the coming together of this vast gathering each year through which fresh spiritual energy is transmitted to the Muslims of the world.

The pilgrimage takes place in Zul-Hijja, the last month of the Muslim year. Before entering the sacred territory around Mecca, the pilgrim puts on the *ihram*, two plain white sheets which symbolize his abandonment of worldly life. He walks seven times around the Kaaba. He runs seven times from Mecca to Marwa and back, recalling Hagar's desperate search for water for Ishmael, and drinks from the Zamzam well where Hagar eventually found water gushing at Ishmael's feet. Soon after sunrise on 9 Zul-Hijja he sets out for the plain of Arafat,

◀ *These Persian tiles illustrate a schematic view of Mecca, showing the Kaaba standing in the great mosque.*

▼ *This sketch map shows the route taken by pilgrims, on 9 and 10 Zul-Hija, from Mecca to the plain of Arafat, and then back via Muzdalifa and Mina.*

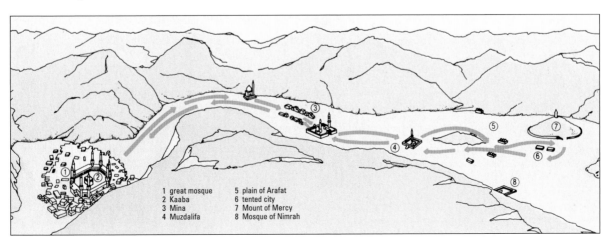

1 great mosque	5 plain of Arafat
2 Kaaba	6 tented city
3 Mina	7 Mount of Mercy
4 Muzdalifa	8 Mosque of Nimrah

where from noon until dusk he stands before God and worships him. After sunset he goes to Muzdalifa for the night. Then on 10 Zul-Hijja he moves on to Mina, where he stones three pillars in memory of the way Abraham, Hagar and Ishmael rejected Satan's temptings to disobey God. He sacrifices an animal in memory of Abraham's willingness to submit to God's will, and then shaves and takes off the *ihram*. He makes seven more circuits of the Kaaba and returns to ordinary life. The prayer he offers on his sixth circuit conveys the submission which marks the performance of the whole rite:

O God, thou hast much against me in respect of my relations with thee and with thy creation. O God, forgive me what is due unto thee and unto thy creation and take it off from me. By thy gracious glory make me well-satisfied without what thou hast disallowed. By obedience unto thee keep me from rebelliousness against thee and by thy goodness keep me from any save thee, O thou who art of wide forgiveness. O God, verily thy house is great and thy countenance is gracious. Thou, O God, art forbearing, gracious, and great. Thou lovest to pardon: therefore, pardon me.

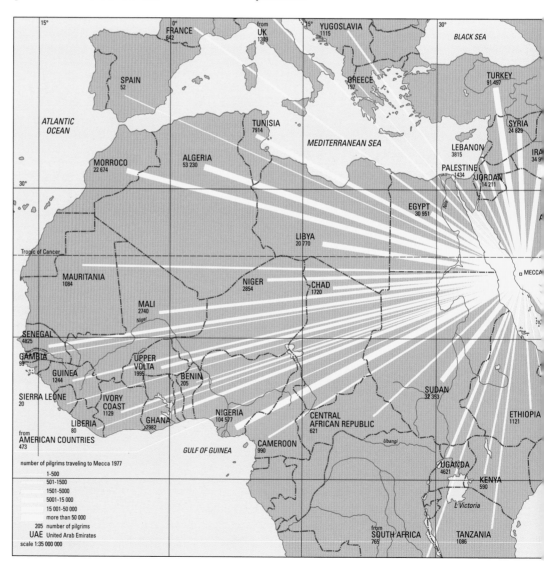

▶ **This map shows the origins and numbers of pilgrims to Mecca in 1997. The vast majority were not Saudi Arabian nationals.**

Pilgrims wearing the ihram arrive in Mecca on an overcrowded bus.

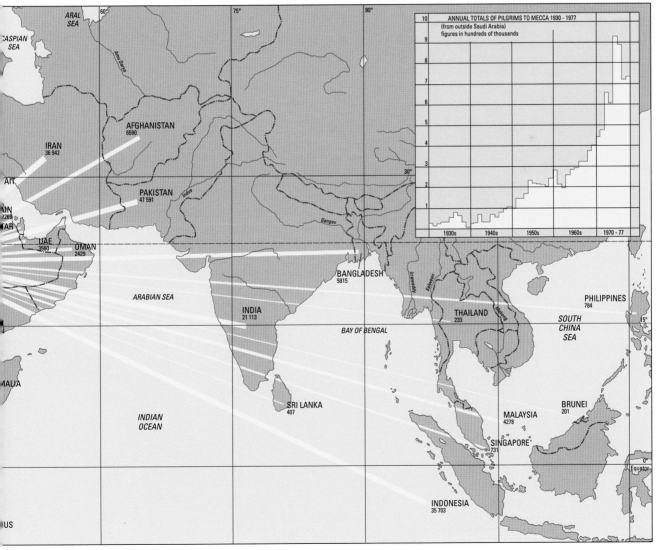

Arts and Society

Calligraphy

◄ (previous pages)
(previous pages) Detail of a rug woven in Persia, one of the five main centers of carpet-making in the Islamic world.

Calligraphy is the highest of the Islamic arts, the most typical expression of the Islamic spirit. "Thy Lord," declares the very first revelation, "… taught by the pen—taught man that which he knew not." Moreover, as God spoke in Arabic and his words were first written in the Arabic script, the Arabic language and script were treasured by all Muslims. Only by understanding them could men hope to understand God's meaning. There was no more important task than preserving and transmitting this precious gift; Muslims showed their gratitude by doing so with all the art at their command. "Good writing," declares a tradition of the Prophet, "makes the truth stand out."

The Arabic script, it is widely agreed, relates directly to the Nabataean script which was itself derived from the Aramaic script. The Arabic alphabet has 29 letters; they are written from right to left, and most letters change shape, depending on whether their position in the word is at the beginning, in the middle, or at the end.

In the 650s the first full versions of the Quran were written down in a form called Jazm which reveals Nabataean influence. This in turn influenced the development of Kufic, a powerful, angular script, which became for centuries the most popular medium for recording the Quran. At the same time cursive scripts developed for bureaucratic and private purposes, and by the mid-10th century the six classical scripts of Islamic calligraphy had been established: Thuluth, Naskhi, Muhaqqaq, Raihani, Tawqi, and Riqa. Soon these too were used for Quranic writing, bringing many new

► Because the Quran is considered to record the words of God, copying it is a sacred act. This richly decorated page is from a 14th-century Mamluk version of the book.

possibilities for decorative effect. There were four other important scripts: Tumar, Ghubar, which was often used for miniature Qurans; Taliq, which was greatly encouraged by the Safavids; and Nastaliq, which, although it has not been popular among Arabs, has for nearly four centuries been the favorite script of Iranian, Turkish and Indian Muslims.

Examples of calligraphy have been, and are, highly prized. Tamerlaine and his descendants were notable patrons of the art; so too were the Safavids, Mughals, and Ottomans. As decoration it is found on tombstones and textiles, on pots, weapons, and tiles, fashioned into strange shapes and adorning buildings. The words of the Quran are as important a means of beautifying mosques as the figure of Christ in churches: both are gifts of God to humans.

Calligraphers were highly esteemed by the most powerful of Muslim rulers. The Ottoman sultan Bayazid II valued the work of Hamd Allah al-Amasi so highly that he would hold the inkpot as Hamd Allah wrote. Calligraphers often sat on the ground to work, with one knee drawn up on which to rest the paper. Tools included scissors or a knife for cutting pens, brush and reed pens, and an inkpot. The ink was usually made from lamp black mixed with vinegar.

Calligraphers have used their imaginations to create all kinds of shapes from combining Arabic characters, particularly in writing the articles of faith. In one representation, for example, the seven articles of faith become the hull of a boat and its rowers, while the sail represents the declaration of faith, "There is no god but God and Muhammad is his messenger."

وَأَمَّا مَنْ خَافَ مَقَامَ رَبِّهِ وَنَهَى النَّفْسَ عَنِ الْهَوَى فَإِنَّ الْجَنَّةَ هِيَ الْمَأْوَى

يَسْأَلُونَكَ عَنِ السَّاعَةِ أَيَّانَ مُرْسَاهَا فِيمَ أَنتَ مِن ذِكْرَاهَا إِلَى رَبِّكَ مُنتَهَاهَا إِنَّمَا

أَنتَ مُنذِرُ مَن يَخْشَاهَا كَأَنَّهُمْ يَوْمَ يَرَوْنَهَا لَمْ يَلْبَثُوا إِلَّا عَشِيَّةً أَوْ ضُحَاهَا

سُورَةُ عَبَسَ اثنان وأربعون آية مكية

بِسْمِ اللَّهِ الرَّحْمَنِ الرَّحِيمِ

عَبَسَ وَتَوَلَّى أَن جَاءَهُ الْأَعْمَى وَمَا يُدْرِيكَ لَعَلَّهُ يَزَّكَّى أَوْ يَذَّكَّرُ فَتَنفَعَهُ

الذِّكْرَى أَمَّا مَنِ اسْتَغْنَى فَأَنتَ لَهُ تَصَدَّى وَمَا عَلَيْكَ أَلَّا يَزَّكَّى وَأَمَّا مَن

جَاءَكَ يَسْعَى وَهُوَ يَخْشَى فَأَنتَ عَنْهُ تَلَهَّى كَلَّا إِنَّهَا تَذْكِرَةٌ فَمَن شَاءَ ذَكَرَهُ

فِي صُحُفٍ مُّكَرَّمَةٍ مَّرْفُوعَةٍ مُّطَهَّرَةٍ بِأَيْدِي سَفَرَةٍ كِرَامٍ بَرَرَةٍ قُتِلَ

Ceramics

Muslims have used color in architecture as no other people, clothing buildings both inside and out with brilliant hues and rich patterns. Glazed tiles are the common medium. The art reached its height under Tamerlaine and his descendants in the cities of Central Asia and Afghanistan. Then there was a late but very fine flowering in the Safavid and Ottoman empires. In North Africa another tradition, no less fine, was maintained. There are four main styles of tile decoration: calligraphic, geometric, floral, and arabesque. Arabesques are twining patterns that resemble stylized plant stems. Floral tiles were a specialty of Iznik, from where they were exported throughout the Ottoman empire, including to the Topkapi palace in Istanbul. Geometric patterns were characteristic of the Maghrib. There are two main ways of using tiles: in mosaics, where

pieces of different tiles are cut to fit a pattern, and as whole tiles, colored and patterned to form part of a larger design.

Carpets

The knotting and weaving of carpets and rugs is the classic art of nomads, whose possessions need to be easy to pack and transport, who typically have access to fibers or wool from their animal herds, and who need floor coverings for their tents and other accommodations. From earliest times, carpet weaving found favor among Muslims at large as well as in the non-Muslim world beyond. No product stems more directly from the possibilities and the needs of nomadic life. Women spin into yarn and weave into carpets the wool and hair from the herds managed by their menfolk; they find natural dyes in the plants and insects around them. The products of their looms are the superbly

▲ *Arabesque patterns are characterized by a long stem that splits regularly into leafy stems that may, in turn, split into more leafy stems. The curving lines give this tiled background from Uzbekistan a sense of movement, rhythm and balance.*

◀ *This image of people and animals sharing an earthly paradise was created in Persia in 1567 to illustrate the Shahnameh ("Book of Kings") written five centuries earlier by the poet Ferdowsi, a favorite subject for Persian calligraphers and artists.*

functional furnishings of those who live their lives in tents and on the ground.

Among settled Islamic communities carpets were adopted to serve new purposes, covering the sacred areas of shrines and mosques, demonstrating the wealth and connoisseurship of merchants and princes, and producing the stuff of lucrative exports to Europe. Patterns created in both tent and town remained extraordinarily rich and varied, from stylized shapes and geometrical designs to prayer rugs reproducing the mihrab niche and realistic compositions of men, animals, and flowers.

There are five major carpet-producing areas in the Islamic, world: Iran, south Asia, Turkey, the Caucasus, and Central Asia. Iran has both sustained a rich tradition in the work of its nomadic tribes, for instance the Qashqai, the Lur, and the Bakhtiari, and revealed the highest achievement in the hunting, vase, and garden carpets of the early Safavid period, when leading painters from the royal studios played a key role in designing the carpets. The climate of south Asia is much less hospitable to carpet manufacture than the dry highlands of Iran and Central Asia, and the Mughals found no strong manufacturing tradition there after they invaded. However the emperor Akbar,

determined that Mughal glory should not suffer by comparison with the Safavids, introduced 200 Iranian artisans and started a carpet-making industry in Lahore. Like the painters who came from Iran to work in the studios at Akbar's spiritual city of Fatehpur Sikri, the Iranian weavers quickly absorbed indigenous artistic preferences and began to produce identifiably south Asian work. Turkish carpets reflected the austere religious ideals of the crusading Ottoman state. The typical form of Turkish carpet was the prayer rug depicting the mihrab niche, although in the 18th century patterns of stylized flowers, particularly tulips, began to proliferate, in part as a result of European influence. Most notable are the carpets of Ushak and those of Ghiordes, supreme examples of the prayer rug whose sevenfold borders represent the seven gardens of paradise. Caucasian carpets are almost entirely geometric in design. They are the especial product of this land of high mountains and deep valleys which harbor many different peoples, languages, and traditions. Central Asia from the Caspian's eastern shore to Kashgar in the Tarim Basin is the final area. Its designs were often influenced by China; Bukhara and Samarqand are the best-known types.

◀ *Washed carpets dry on a cliff in Iran. It is thought that Cyrus the Great introduced carpet weaving to Iran in c. 500 BC. Carpet weaving is still the most widespread handicraft in the country.*

▼ *This map shows the five main areas and the major centers of carpet production in the Islamic world.*

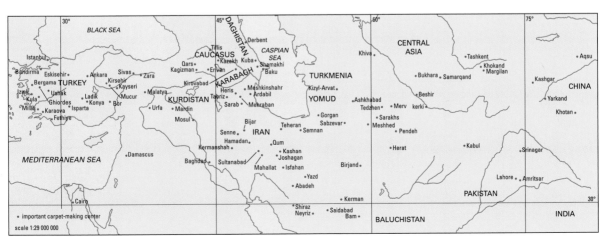

Glossary

alim (plural *ulama*) A learned man, in particular one learned in Islamic legal and religious studies.

amir Military commander, provincial governor.

ayatullah Literally "sign of God." A title conferred by his followers upon a distinguished **mujtahid** among the Shias.

barakat Holiness, divine favor, often attributed to sufi saints.

basmala Formula with which Muslims begin all important acts: "In the name of God, the merciful, the compassionate."

bida Innovation on a point of law; as close as Islam goes to the Christian concept of heresy.

caliph (Arabic *khalifa*, "vicar," "successor") Successor of Muhammad as head of the Muslim community. The title implies continuous religious and political suzerainty over all Muslim peoples but not direct divine revelation.

chador "Tent," the veil worn by women in Iran.

dar el-harb "The land of war," i.e. all territory outside **dar al-Islam** ("the land of Islam"). All territories which did not recognize Islam were under threat of **jihad**.

dar al-Islam "The land of Islam," i.e. all territory which recognizes the law of Islam.

devshirme System of recruitment and training of slaves (especially Christians) for government service in the Ottoman empire. About 10 percent were sent to the palace school to train for the highest positions in the sultan's service. The rest were set to work on the land and hardened for military service.

dhikr "Recollection" of God, a spiritual exercise to render God's presence throughout one's being.

dhimmi A protected religious minority under the Ottomans until the 17th century. Comprising the Jews and Coptic, Greek, Armenian, and Syrian Christians, they were allowed to organize themselves as separate communities, or **millets**.

dikka Platform from which men, usually the **muezzins** of the mosque, repeat and amplify the words and actions of the **imam** for the benefit of the congregation.

Fatiha Opening **sura** of the Quran, which Muslims use as Christians would the Lord's Prayer.

fatwa Decision or opinion on a point of Islamic law issued by a **mufti**.

Fulani The largest nomadic society in the world and generators of religious reform in West Africa. In 1680 they began a series of holy wars that led to the establishment of the Islamic states of Futa Jallon, Futa Toro, Khasso, Kaarta, Masina, and Sokoto.

ghazi Holy warrior; later a title of honor.

Ghulam Member of an exclusive force of military or palace slaves in the Safavid empire.

Hadith Report of a saying or action of the Prophet, or such reports collectively. The body of *Hadiths* is one of the principal sources of the **Sharia**.

Hajj Pilgrimage to Mecca which every adult Muslim of sound mind and body must perform once in his or her lifetime.

Hanafi One of the four **Sunni** schools of law, founded by Abu Hanifa (died 767). It was the dominant legal system in the Ottoman empire, Central Asia, and India.

Hanbali One of the four **Sunni** schools of law, founded by Ahmad Ibn Hanbal (died 855) and known for its opposition to the speculative and rationalist approaches of the other three schools.

Hijaz Northwest part of the Arabian peninsula, bordering on the Red Sea, which includes the holy cities of Mecca and Medina.

Hijra Flight of the Prophet and his followers from Mecca to Medina in 622 CE from which point the Muslim calendar begins.

Idrisiya Sufi order founded by the Moroccan, Ahmad Ibn Idris, whose influence spread through Africa in the 19th century.

ijaza License or diploma, granting a pupil permission to teach a skill, knowledge of a book perhaps, or a particular sufi way. The certificate records how knowledge has been transmitted from the original fount to the present.

ijma Consensus of the scholarly community on a point of law.

ijtihad Exercise of human reason to ascertain a rule of **Sharia** law. In the l0th century Sunnis considered *ijtihad* permissible only on points not already decided by recognized authorities. The Shias, on the other hand, usually permit full *ijtihad* to their leading scholars.

ikhwan Shock force of "brothers," created by Abd al-Aziz Ibn Saud and committed to die fighting for Islam. Established in over 200 missionary and military communities, or *hijrab*, they enabled him to spread his rule over Saudi Arabia from 1912 to 1929.

imam Leader of mosque prayers, or the leader of the Muslim community. Among Sunnis any great *alim* might be called imam. Among Shias one of the 12 successors of the Prophet, descended from Ali, the legitimate leaders of the Muslim community.

iwan Vaulted hall, an important element of pre-Islamic Central Asian architecture which was adopted for use in mosques and madrasas of the region.

Iznik pottery The chief glory of Ottoman ceramics. It developed in three phases: 1490–1525 blue and white only; 1525–50 Damascus and Golden Horn ware introduced more blues and a sage green; 1550–1700 Rhodian ware employed a full range of design and seven colors.

Janissary Ottoman infantryman, a member of an elite corps of highly trained men, raised initially through the **devshirma** but later hereditary.

jihad "Striving in the way of God," hence holy or "just" war. This may be waged against unbelievers; it may also be waged by an individual against his baser instincts. War on Muslims, or on protected minorities (**dhimmis**), is forbidden.

jizya Tax levied by holy law on unbelievers in Muslim territory, abolished by Akbar.

Kaaba Cube-shaped building in the center of the sanctuary of the great mosque at Mecca where Muslims believe that Abraham built the first house for the worship of the one God; the focus of Islam to which all Muslims turn when praying, circumambulation of which is the climax of the **Hajj**.

Khalwatiya Sufi order based in Cairo whose influence spread through Africa in the 19th century. *Khalwat* means "retreat into prayer."

khan Turkish title, originally the ruler of a state; also a hostel for traveling merchants.

khoja Title given to sufi leaders in Central Asia who were descended from the Prophet and achieved political power from the 16th century. It is also the name given to the followers of the Agha Khan.

Kufic Script used for many early Qurans and monumental inscriptions. Named for the early center of learning at Kufa, Iraq, it is distinguished by the static form of its letters, which are often highly decorated.

kursi Lectern holding the Quran in a mosque.

madrasa School for the teaching of theology and law, Arabic grammar and literature, the *Hadiths,* and Quran commentary. Establishment for the training of *ulama* in the Islamic sciences.

Maghrib Literally "the west," the term was applied generally to the area now covered by modern Libya. Tunisia, Algeria, and Morocco.

Mahdi Title ("the guided one") assumed by Muhammad Ahmad in 1881 who captured Khartoum in 1885 and established a Mahdist state in the Sudan.

maidan Term used to describe an open space or square in a town.

Maliki one of the four **Sunni** schools of law, founded by Malik Ibn Anas (died 796). Influential throughout Muslim Africa, it usually looked to Cairo.

Mamluk Technically a slave (literally "owned"), later a member of an elite cavalry corps which controlled Egypt from 1260 to 1517.

mansabdar Holder of a civil and/or military appointment, graded according to a decimal ranking system, within the Mughal imperial service.

marabout Term commonly given to sufis in Morocco; it is a French corruption of Arabic and means a man "tied" to God.

Maratha In the general sense, an inhabitant of Maharashtra in western India. From the mid- 17th century Maratha Hindu warriors continually raided the Mughal empire.

masjid Place of prostration, mosque.

mawlid Ceremony to celebrate the Prophet's birthday, 12 Rabj al-Awwal.

mihrab Niche in a place of prayer that indicates the direction of Mecca. The niche itself (unlike the direction it indicates) is not sacred, but it is the central feature of any mosque.

millet Separate community in which religious minorities, or **dhimmis**, were allowed by the Ottomans to live under their own laws.

minbar Pulpit from which the **imam** delivers his Friday sermon. He does so from one of the lower steps: only the Prophet preached from the top.

muezzin Official at a mosque charged with giving the call to prayer five times a day.

mufti Learned exponent of the **Sharia** who issues **fatwas** when consulted.

mujtahid One who exercises **ijtihad** to inquire into and clarify the intent of the law.

mullah Religious leader, member of the **ulama**, especially in Shia Iran.

Muslim Brotherhood Militant movement for the reassertion of Islamic values which was founded in Egypt and has spread elsewhere in the Arab world. Its attempted assassination of Nasser in 1954 failed; a similar attempt on Sadat by an associated organization in 1981 succeeded.

Naqshbandiya Sufi order which played the major role in the 18th- and 19th-century movement for reform and revival in Asia.

Padri movement Movement for reform in early 19th-century Sumatra.

pishtaq Monumental gateway, usually decorated with colored tiles, a feature of Central Asian madrasas.

qadi Judge appointed to interpret the **Sharia**.

Qari Cantor who recites the Quran.

qiyas Argument by analogy, used to supplement the **Sharia**.

rakat Sequence of movements or "bowings" prescribed for prayer.

Shafii One of the four **Sunni** schools of law, founded by Imam al-Shafii (died 820). Preeminent in southeast Asia, Egypt, Syria, and the Hijaz.

shahada Basic statement of Muslim belief: "There is no god but God and Muhammad is the Prophet of God."

shaikh Literally "old man"; the chief of a tribe; any religious leader; in particular an independent sufi "master" in a position to guide disciples in his sufi way.

Shaikh al-Islam The **mufti** of Istanbul and supreme religious authority in the Ottoman state.

Sharia The law of Islam, based on the Quran and the *Hadiths*.

sharif Title (meaning "highborn" or "noble") which came to be applied to descendants of the Prophet.

Shia Group (or "party") of Muslims who, against the orthodox (**Sunni**) view, insist on the recognition of Ali as the legitimate successor (or **caliph**) to Muhammad. Initially most powerful in Iraq, their particular association with Iran was sealed by the triumph of the Safavids in the 16th century.

silsila Chain of spiritual descent, a sufi lineage.

sipahi Ottoman cavalryman, usually holding a *timar*.

sufism Islamic mysticism. A distinct strand of Muslim devotion, which cultivates the inner attitude with which the believer performs his outward obligations, sufism was an important vehicle for the dissemination of the faith.

sultan The reigning source of authority which came to be the normal Muslim term for sovereign.

Sunni "Orthodox" Islam, basing its teachings on the Quran, the *Hadiths*, and the four schools of law: the **Hanafi**, **Hanbali**, **Maliki**, and **Shafii**.

sura Chapter of the Quran.

tariqat A sufi's "way" of approaching God.

timar Grant of land in exchange for government service in the Ottoman empire.

Turkoman People who had ruled much of Anatolia after the decline of the Seljuqs. They continue to live in Iraq, Syria, and in the lands east of the Caspian.

ulama See alim.

Ummah The Islamic community as a whole.

vilayat Administrative unit of land.

vizier Anglicized form of *wazir*, an officer to whom a ruler delegated the administration of his realm; head of the imperial administrative council in the Ottoman empire.

Wahhabi Follower of Muhammad Abd al-Wahhab, who in the mid-18th century led a campaign for spiritual renewal in Arabia. The Wahhabis retained power in the Najd for much of the 19th century and played an important part in founding the Saudi Arabian state.

wayang Javanese shadow theater, based on traditional Hindu cycles of plays, but including one cycle (*wayang golek*) about the Prophet's uncle, Amir Hamza.

zakat Giving of alms.

zawiya Sufi lodge; also *ribat* in Arabic, *khanqah* in Persian, and *tekke* in Turkish.

Further Reading

General Reference

Ansary, Mir Tamim, *Destiny Disrupted: A History of the World Through Islamic Eyes.* New York: PublicAffairs, 2009.

Aslan, Reza, *No God but God: The Origins, Evolution, and Future of Islam.* New York: Random House Trade Paperbacks, 2006.

Calvert, John, Dr., *Islamism: A Documentary and Reference Guide.* Westport, CT: Greenwood Press, 2008.

Esposito, John L. (ed.), *The Oxford Encyclopedia of the Islamic World.* Oxford: Oxford University Press, 2009.

Fyzee, Asaf Ali Asghar, *A Modern Approach to Islam.* New Delhi: Oxford University Press, 2008.

Grieve, Paul. *A Brief Guide to Islam: History, Faith and Politics: The Complete Introduction.* New York: Carroll and Graf Publishers, 2006.

Lane, Jan-Erik. *Religion and Politics: Islam and Muslim Civilization.* Burlington, VT: Ashgate Pub. Company, 2009.

Martin, Richard C. (ed.), *Encyclopedia of Islam and the Muslim World.* New York: Macmillan Reference USA: Thomson/Gale, 2004.

Nagy, Luqman. *The Book of Islamic Dynasties: A Celebration of Islamic History and Culture.* London: Ta-Ha Publishers, 2008.

Ruthven, Malise, *Islam in the World.* Oxford: Oxford University Press, 2006.

Shepard, William E., *Introducing Islam.* New York: Routledge, 2009.

Turner, C., *Islam: The Basics.* New York: Routledge, 2006.

Ünal, Ali. *An Introduction to Islamic Faith and Thought.* Somerset, NJ: Tughra Books, 2009.

Western Attitudes to Islam

Drummond, Richard Henry. *Islam for the Western Mind: Understanding Muhammad and the Koran.* Charlottesville, VA: Hampton Roads Pub. Co., 2005.

McCullar, Michael D. *A Christian's Guide to Islam.* Macon, GA: Smyth & Helwys Pub., 2008.

Tyler, Aaron. *Islam, the West, and Tolerance: Conceiving Coexistence.* New York: Palgrave Macmillan, 2008.

Young, Mitchell (ed.), *Islam.* Farmington Hills, MI: Greenhaven Press/Thomson Gale, 2006.

Part Two: Revelation and Muslim History

The First Nine Centuries

Bravmann, M. M. *The Spiritual Background of Early Islam: Studies in Ancient Arab Concepts.* Boston: Brill, 2008.

Crone, Patricia, *From Arabian Tribes to Islamic Empire: Army, State and Society in the Near East 600–850.* Burlington, VT: Ashgate, 2008.

Gordon, Matthew. *The Rise of Islam.* Indianapolis, ID: Hackett Pub. Co., 2008.

Hazleton, Lesley, *After the Prophet: The Epic Story of the Shia–Sunni Split in Islam.* New York: Doubleday, 2009.

January, Brendan, *Arab Conquests of the Middle East.* Minneapolis, MN: Twenty-First Century Books, 2009.

Kennedy, Hugh. *The Prophet and the Age of the Caliphates: The Islamic Near East from the Sixth to the Eleventh Century.* London: Longman, 1986.

Khan, Ruqayya Yasmine. *Self and Secrecy in Early Islam.* Columbia, SC: University of South Carolina Press, 2008.

Lewis, David Levering, *God's Crucible: Islam and the Making of Europe, 570 to 1215.* New York: W.W. Norton, 2008.

Ohlig, Karl-Heinz and Gerd-R. Puin, *The Hidden Origins of Islam: New Research into its Early History.* Amherst, NY: Prometheus Books, 2008.

Powers, David Stephan. *Muhammad Is Not the Father of Any of Your Men: The Making of the Last Prophet.* Philadelphia: University of Pennsylvania Press, 2009.

Walker, Paul E., *Fatimid History and Ismaili Doctrine.* Burlington, VT: Variorum, 2008.

The 16th and 17th Centuries

Abisaab, Rula Jurdi. *Converting Persia: Religion and Power in the Safavid Empire.* New York: I. B. Tauris, 2004.

Babaie, Susan, *Slaves of the Shah: New Elites of Safavid Iran.* New York: I. B. Tauris, 2004.

Casale, Giancarlo. *The Ottoman Age of Exploration.* New York: Oxford University Press, 2010.

Floor, Willem M. *The Economy of Safavid Persia.* Wiesbaden: Reichert, 2000.

Floor, Willem M. *The Persian Gulf: A Political and Economic History of Five Port Cities, 1500–1730.* Washington, DC: Mage Publishers, 2006.

Gruendler, Beatrice and Louise Marlow (eds), *Writers and Rulers: Perspectives on Their Relationship from Abbasid to Safavid Times.* Wiesbaden: Reichert, 2004.

Haider, A. F., *The Administrative Structure of the Safavid Empire.* Patna: Khuda Bakhsh Oriental Public Library, 2000.

Kafescioglu, Çigdem. *Constantinopolis/ Istanbul: Cultural Encounter, Imperial Vision, and the Construction of the Ottoman Capital.* University Park, PA: Pennsylvania State University Press, 2009.

Massarrat Abid, *Cultural Heritage of the Mughals.* Lahore: Pakistan Study Centre, University of the Punjab, 2005.

Matthee, Rudolph P. *The Politics of Trade in Safavid Iran: Silk for Silver, 1600–1730.* Cambridge: Cambridge University Press, 1999.

Meserve, Margaret. *Empires of Islam in Renaissance Historical Thought.* Cambridge, MA: Harvard University Press, 2008.

Moczar, Diane. *Islam at the Gates: How Christendom defeated the Ottoman Turks.* Manchester, NH: Sophia Institute Press, 2008.

Mukhia, Harbans. *The Mughals of India.* Oxford: Blackwell Pub., 2004.

Newman, Andrew J., *Society and Culture in the Early Modern Middle East: Studies on Iran in the Safavid Period.* Boston: Brill, 2003.

Schimmel, Annemarie. *The Empire of the Great Mughals: History, Art, and Culture.* New Delhi: Oxford University Press, 2005.

Sharma, Gauri. *Prime Ministers Under the Mughals, 1526–1707.* New Delhi: Kanishka Publishers, 2006.

Smith, Richard L. *Ahmad al-Mansur: Islamic Visionary.* New York: Pearson Longman, 2006.

Wheatcroft, Andrew. *The Enemy at the Gate: Habsburgs, Ottomans, and the Battle for Europe.* New York: Basic Books, 2009.

Further Islamic Lands

Chinyong Liow, Joseph, and Nadirsyah Hosen (eds), *Islam in Southeast Asia.* New York: Routledge, 2009

Cribb, Joe, and Georgina Herrmann (eds). *After Alexander: Central Asia Before Islam.* New York: Published for The British Academy by Oxford University Press, 2007.

Gordon, Alijah, *The Propagation of Islam in the Indonesian-Malay Archipelago.* Kuala Lumpur: Malaysian Sociological Research Institute, 2001.

Israeli, Raphael. *Islam in China: Religion, Ethnicity, Culture, and Politics.* Lanham, MD: Lexington Books, 2002.

Jinju, Muhammadu Hambali, *Islam in Africa: Historico-Philosophical Perspectives and Current Problems.* Zaria: Bello University Press, 2001.

Malay Muslims: *The History and Challenge of Resurgent Islam in Southeast Asia.* Grand Rapids, MI: W. B. Eerdmans Pub., 2002.

Marcovitz, Hal, *Islam in Africa.* Philadelphia: Mason Crest Publishers, 2007

McAmis, Robert Day, Ludmila Polonskaya, and Alexei Malashenko (eds), *Islam in Central Asia.* Reading: Ithaca Press, 1994.

Radu, Michael. *Islam in Europe.* Broomall, PA: Mason Crest Publishers, 2006.

Tomohiko, Uyama (ed), *Empire, Islam, and Politics in Central Eurasia.* Sapporo: Slavic Research Center, Hokkaido University, 2007.

Decline, Reform, and Revival

Bowen, Wayne H., *The History of Saudi Arabia.* Westport, CT: Greenwood Press, 2008.

Gershoni, Israel, Hakan Erdem, and Ursula Woköck (eds), *Histories of the Modern Middle East: New Directions.* Boulder, CO: Lynne Rienner Publishers, 2002.

Khattak, Shahin Kuli Khan. *Islam and the Victorians: Nineteenth-Century Perceptions of Muslim Practices and Beliefs.* New York: Tauris Academic Studies, 2008.

Kramer, Martin S. *Arab Awakening and Islamic revival: The Politics of Ideas in the Middle East.* Piscataway, NJ: Transaction Publishers, 2008.

Part Three: Religious Life

Caner, Emir Fethi. *More than a Prophet: An Insider's Response to Muslim Beliefs about Jesus and Christianity.* Grand Rapids: Kregel Publications, 2003.

Caner, Ergun Mehmet. *Unveiling Islam: An Insider's Look at Muslim Life and Beliefs.* Grand Rapids, MI: Kregel Publications, 2002.

Farah, Caesar E., *Islam: Beliefs and Observances.* Hauppauge, NY: Barron's, 2003.

Gordon, Matthew. *Understanding Islam: Origins, Beliefs, Practices, Holy Texts, Sacred.* London: Duncan Baird, 2002.

Gulevich, Tanya. *Understanding Islam and Muslim Traditions: An Introduction to the Religious Practices, Celebrations, Festivals, Observances, Beliefs, Folklore, Customs, and Calendar System of the World's Muslim Communities, Including an Overview of Islamic History and Geography.* Detroit, MI: Omnigraphics, 2004.

Kabbani, Muhammad Hisham. *Encyclopedia of Islamic Doctrine.* Mountainview, CA: As-Sunna Foundation of America, 1998.

Marranci, Gabriele. *The Anthropology of Islam.* Oxford: Berg, 2008.

Marshall, Paul A., *Islam at the Crossroads: Understanding its Beliefs, History, and Conflicts.* Grand Rapids, MI: Baker Books, 2002.

Paas, Steven, *Beliefs and Practices of Muslims: The Religion of Our Neighbours.* Zomba, Malawi: Good Messenger Publications, 2006.

Ramadan, Tariq. *The Messenger: The Meanings of the Life of Muhammad.* London: Penguin Books, 2008.

Rippin, Andrew, *Muslims: Their Religious Beliefs and Practices.* New York: Routledge, 2005.

Schwartz, Stephen, *The Other Islam: Sufism and the Road to Global Harmony.* New York: Doubleday, 2008.

Part Four: Arts of Islam

Behrens-Abouseif, Doris, and Stephen Vernoit, *Islamic Art in the 19th Century: Tradition, Innovation, and Eclecticism.* Boston: Brill, 2006.

Blair, Sheila, and Jonathan Bloom, *Rivers of Paradise: Water in Islamic Art and Culture.* New Haven, NJ: Yale University Press, 2009.

Broug, Eric. *Islamic Geometric Patterns.* London: Thames & Hudson, 2008.

Burckhardt, Titus. *Art of Islam: Language and Meaning.* Bloomington, IN. World Wisdom, 2009.

Curatola, Giovanni, *The Art and Architecture of Persia.* New York: Abbeville Press, 2007.

Grabar, Oleg. *Islamic Visual Culture, 1100–1800.* Burlington, VT: Ashgate, 2006.

Grabar, Oleg. *Masterpieces of Islamic Art: The Decorated Page from the 8th to the 17th Century.* New York: Prestel Pub., 2009.

Husain, Salma. *The Emperor's Table: The Art of Mughal Cuisine.* New Delhi: Lustre Press, 2008.

Jones, Owen, *Ornament and Design of the Alhambra.* Mineola, NY: Dover Publications, 2008.

Kellner-Heinkele, Barbara, Joachim Gierlichs, and Brigitte Heuer (eds),

Islamic Art and Architecture in the European Periphery: Crimea, Caucasus, and the Volga-Ural Region. Wiesbaden: Harrassowitz, 2008.

Khalili, Nasser D. *Visions of Splendour in Islamic Art and Culture.* London: Worth Press, 2008.

Michell, George. *The Majesty of Mughal Decoration: The Art and Architecture of Islamic India.* London: Thames and Hudson, 2007.

O'Kane, Bernard, *The Treasures of Islamic Art in the Museums of Cairo.* New York: The American University in Cairo Press, 2006.

Rogers, J. M. *The Arts of Islam: Treasures from the Nasser D. Khalili Collection.* Sydney: Art Gallery of New South Wales, 2007.

Ruggles, D. Fairchild. *Islamic Gardens and Landscapes.* Philadelphia: University of Pennsylvania Press, 2008.

Welzbacher, Christian, *Euro Islam Architecture: New Mosques in the West.* Amsterdam: SUN, 2008.

Original Bibliography

The bibliography compiled for the original edition of this book remains a comprehensive summary of Islamic research in the 20th century.

Basic works of reference are *The Encyclopaedia of Islam* 2nd ed (Leiden 1954–), which is now just over halfway through the alphabet, and *The Shorter Encyclopaedia of Islam* (ed. H.A.R. Gibb and J.H. Kramers; Leiden 1953), which brings up to date selected articles from *The Encyclopaedia of Islam* 1st edn (Leiden 1913–38). Taken together the editions of the *Encyclopaedia* form the basic work of reference for any subject to do with Islam or Islamic civilization, particularly in premodern times. All entries have substantial bibliographies. Further bibliographical guidance may be gained from J.D. Pearson (ed.), *Index Islamicus 1906–55*, which continues to issue supplements, Jean Sauvaget, *Introduction to the History of the Muslim East* (Berkeley, Calif. 1965), and P. M. Holt, A. K. S. Lambton and B. Lewis (eds.) *The Cambridge History of Islam* (2 vols.; Cambridge 1970). Marshall G.S. Hodgson, *The Venture of Islam: Conscience and History in a World Civilization* (3 vols.; Chicago, Ill. 1974) remains a remarkable achievement and the most satisfying treatment of Islamic history as a whole. Those who wish to acquaint themselves with recent research and opinion at a general level should consult: *The Middle East Journal* (1946–), published by the Middle East Institute, Washington, D.C., and *The Muslim World* (1911–), published by the Hartford Seminary Foundation, Hartford, Conn., primarily designed for Christian missionaries. *The Islamic Quarterly* (1954–), published by the Islamic Cultural Centre, London, is edited by Muslim missionaries.

Western Attitudes to Islam

Trail-breaking work in this field has been done by Norman Daniel, in *Islam and the West: the Making of an Image* (Edinburgh 1960) and *Islam, Europe and Empire* (Edinburgh 1966). Richard W. Southern's *Western Views of Islam in the Middle Ages* (Cambridge, Mass. 1962) offers a first-class summary of what its title announces. A recent overview is also valuable, Maxime Rodinson, "The Western Image and Western Studies of Islam" in Joseph Schacht and C. E. Bosworth (eds.), *The Legacy of Islam* (Oxford 1974). The whole subject, however, has come to be dominated in recent years by a book of pugnacity and passion: Edward W. Said, *Orientalism* (London 1978), which asserts that Western studies of Islam tell us more about the West than about Islam. Most scholars, while admitting that Said has a point, find his conclusions immoderate. Another approach is through art and here Philippe Julian, *The Orientalists* (Oxford 1977), reveals in illustration the discovery of the East by 19th-century painters.

Part I: Revelation and Muslim History

The First Nine Centuries from 622 to 1500

There are several brief and excellent treatments of Islam in general: H. A. R. Gibb, *Islam* (2nd edn; Oxford 1975); Fazlur Rahman, *Islam* (2nd edn; Chicago, Ill. 1979); A. Guillaume, *Islam* (2nd edn; Harmondsworth 1976); Kenneth Cragg, *The House of Islam* (2nd edn; Encino, Calif. 1975). Kenneth Cragg's *House of Islam* is designed to accompany the first-class anthology he has compiled with Marston Speight, *Islam from Within* (Wadsworth, Calif. 1980).

The following offer useful treatments of part or all of the first nine centuries of Islamic history: Bernard Lewis, *The Arabs in History* (4th edn; London 1966); F. Gabrieli (trans. V. Luling and R. Linell), *Muhammad and the Conquests of Islam* (London 1968); John J. Saunders, *A History of Medieval Islam* (London 1965); G. von Grunebaum (trans. K. Watson), *Classical Islam: History 600-1258* (London 1970). The outstanding coverage by one man remains the first two volumes of Marshall G. S. Flodgson, *Venture of Islam*. Several recent treatments of the life of Muhammad should be noticed: William M. Watt, *Muhammad at Mecca* (Oxford 1953) and *Muhammad at Medina* (Oxford 1956), and the treatment by the French scholar Maxime Rodinson (trans. A. Carter), *Mohammed* (London 1971). Anthologies and translations of documents and literature abound; of excellent value is Bernard Lewis (ed.), *Islam: from the Prophet Muhammad to the Capture of Constantinople* (London and New York 1974). But strongly recommended as well as two of the masterworks of the period: Ibn Battuta's *Travels in Asia and Africa 1325–54* (translated and abridged by H. A. ft. Gibb; 3 vols.; Cambridge 1971), the introduction to Ibn Khaldun's world history (trans. Franz Rosenthal), *The Muqaddimah: An Introduction to History* (3 vols.; New York 1958). Two excellent illustrated surveys are: Michael Rogers, *The Spread of Islam* (Oxford 1976), and Bernard Lewis (ed.), *The World of Islam: Faith, People, Culture* (London and New York 1976), to which a team of scholars contributes.

Molding forces of Islamic civilization: Many feel that the best translation of the Quran for overall effect is A. J. Arberry, *The Koran Interpreted* (London 1980). Notable for its precision is that of Muhammad Ali of Lahore, The Holy Quran (6th edn; Lahore 1973). the version used with one exception throughout this book. Ignaz Goldziher, *Muhammedanische Studien* vol. two (Halle 1890; edited and trans. by C. R. Barber and S. M. Stern as *Muslim Studies* vol. two, Chicago, Ill. 1966, London 1971), is the classic study of the growth of the *Hadith*. A popular anthology of Hadiths from the six major compilations has been translated and is readily available: Al-Haj Maulana Fazlul Harim (trans.), *Al-Hadis: an English Translation and Commentary of Mishkat-ul-Masabih* (4 vols.; Lahore 1938). On Islamic law, Noel J. Coulson, *A History of Islamic Law* (Edinburgh 1964), offers an excellent brief introduction to the Sharia. The following works should also be noted: Joseph Schacht, *The Origins of Muhammadan Jurisprudence* (Oxford 1950; reprint 1979) and *An Introduction to Islamic Law* (Oxford 1964). On sufism useful brief introductions are: R. A. Nicholson, *The Mystics of Islam* (London 1914; reprint London 1963), and Arthur J. Arberry, *Sufism, an Account of the Mystics of Islam* (London 1950). However, a more substantial work is Annemarie Schimmel, *The Mystical Dimensions of Islam* (Chapel Hill, N.C. 1975). There is a readily accessible biography of al-Ghazzali: William M. Watt, *Muslim Intellectual: a Study of al-Ghazali* (Edinburgh 1963). The most recent study of Rumi's thought is Annemarie Schimmel, *The Triumphal Sun* (Boulder, Cola. 1978). Rumi's works are easily found in translation: R. A. Nicholson (ed. and trans.), *The Mathnawi of Jalaluddin Rumi* (London 1926); R. A. Nicholson (ed. and trans.), *Selected Poems from the Divan Shamsi Tabriz* (Cambridge 1898); while for the newcomer to Islam, in prose and extremely approachable, is A. J. Arberry (ed. and trans.), *Discourses of Rumi* (London 1961). As for Ibn al-Arabi, A. E. Affifi, *The Mystical Philosophy of Muhyid Din-ibnul Arabi* (Cambridge 1939), offers an attempt to reduce Ibo al-Arabi's writings to an orderly system. There is also Henry Corbin (trans. Ralph Manheim), *Creative Imagination in the Sufism of Ibn Arabi* (Princeton, N.J. 1969; London 1970). Ibn al-Arabi's summary of his life's work has translated: Ibn al-Arabi (ed., trans. and introduction by Ralph W. J. Austin), *The Bezels of Wisdom* (London 1980).

The processes of transmission: Scholarly work in this field is still in its infancy; for example, A.L. Tibawi, *Islamic Education: its Traditions and Modernization into the Arab National Systems* (London 1972). The most trenchant exposition of how teachers should be venerated can be found in a fascinating Arabic document of the 13th century: Burham al-Din, al-Zarnuji (trans. G.E. von Grunebaum), *Ta'lim al-Muta'allim at-ta'allum (Instruction of the Student; Method of Learning)* (New York 1947; Oxford 1948). Further work which illuminates the process of transmission is: Francis Robinson, "The Veneration of Teachers in Islam by the Pupils: its Modern Significance", *History Today* (London; March 1980) and Francis Robinson, "The Ulama of Firangi Mahal and their Adab" in B. Metcalf (ed.), *Moral Conduct and Authority: The Place of Adab in South Asian Islam* (Berkeley, Calif., forthcoming). S. Trimingham, *The Sufi Orders in Islam* (Oxford 1971), is the pioneering work, and further evidence can be gleaned from Annemarie Schimmel's *The Mystical Dimensions of Islam*. For a history of one of the major orders see John K. Birge, *The Bektashi Order of Dervishes* (London 1937). Richard M. Eaton, *Sufis of Bijapur 1300–1700: Social Roles of Sufis in Medieval India* (Princeton, N.J. 1978), is a fascinating study of the functions performed by sufis in one region over 400 years.

The Empires of the Heartlands in the 16th and 17th Centuries

Safavids: One book serves excellently as a starting point for further reading on Safavid Iran, R.M. Savory, *Iran under the Safavids* (Cambridge 1980). It is good on the changing relationship between Shiism and the Safavid state. Several good works exist on aspects of Safavid painting: L. Binyon, J. V. S. Wilkinson and B. Gray, *Persian Miniature Painting* (London 1931); B. Gray, *Persian Painting* (London 1930); S. C. Welch, *A King's Book of Kings* (London and New York 1972) and his *Royal Persian Manuscripts* (London 1976). Arthur Upham Pope (ed.), *A Survey of Persian Art* (6 vols.; Oxford 1938-58), is majestic in its range and places Safavid art in the context of the overall development of Iranian art. Anthony Welch, *Shah Abbas and the Arts of Isfahan* (New York 1973), focuses on the artistic flowering under that great monarch; Wilfrid Blunt and Wim Swann, *Isfahan: Pearl of Persia* (London 1966), provide a colorful introduction to the city of Isfahan.

Mughals: There is no effective up-to-date general history of the Mughal empire. The best point at which to begin is the appropriate chapters in *The Cambridge History of Islam* vol. two. M. Mujeeb, *The Indian Muslims* (London 1967), is also useful, and I. Habib, *The Agrarian System of Mughal India, 1556–1707* (Bombay 1963), is an important revisionist study. There are several superb contemporary works in translation: Babur (trans. A. S. Beveridge), *The Babur–Namah in English* (2 vols.; London 1922); Abul Fazl (trans. H. Beveridge), *The Akbarnama* (3 vols.; Calcutta 1907, 1912, 1939), and the same author's description of state and society (trans. H. Blockmann and H. S. Jarrett) *The Ain-i-Akbari* (2 vols.; Calcutta 1872 and 1874), offer a full description by Akbar's close friend; Jahangir (trans. A. Rogers, ed. H. Beveridge), *Tuzuk- i-Jahangir or Memoirs of Jahangir* (2 vols.; London 1909 and 1914), enables us to witness Mughal life through the eyes of this gifted emperor and art connoisseur. There are also two good illustrated books: Bamber Gascoigne, *The Great Moghuls* (London 1971), and Gavin Hambly, *Cities of Mughal India: Delhi, Agra and Fatehpur Sikri* (London 1968).

Ottomans: There are two up-to-date general accounts of Ottoman history: Haul Inalcik, *The Ottoman Empire: The Classical Age 1300-1600* (London 1973), and N. Itzkowitz, *Ottoman Empire and Islamic Tradition* (New York 1972). For Ottoman institutions see H. A. R. Gibb and H. Bowen, *Islamic Society and the West* vol. one, parts one and two (Oxford 1950 and 1957), Bernard Lewis, *Istanbul and the Civilization of the Ottoman Empire* (Norman, Okla. 1963), and for a striking first-hand account of the court of Sulaiman the Magnificent and the empire, see Ogier Ghiselin de Busbecq (trans. B. S. Foster), *Turkish Letters* (Oxford 1967). Elias J. W. Gibb, *A History of Ottoman Poetry* (6 vols.; London 1900–09), offers insight into the whole of Ottoman cultural life. A remarkable novel by Ivo Andric, winner of the Nobel prize for literature, evokes the nature of Ottoman rule in the Balkans over 400 years, *The Bridge on the Drina* (trans. L. F. Edwards; London 1959). Michael Levey has most lucidly surveyed Ottoman art in general, *The World of Ottoman Art* (London 1975), a subject O. Aslanapa treats in greater detail, *Turkish Art and Architecture* (London 1971). Geoffrey Goodwin's *A History of Ottoman Architecture* (London 1971) is first class. Arthur Stratton has written a biography of the greatest Ottoman architect and archetypal Ottoman figure, *Sinan* (London 1972).

The Further Islamic Lands from 1500 to the 18th Century

This introduces the problem of Islamization which can be followed in two trail-blazing books: Geertz, *Islam Observed: Religious Development in Morocco and Indonesia* (New Haven, Conn. 1968), the work of a cultural anthropologist who has been influential in breaking down old academic stereotypes of Islam, and Nehemia Levtzion (ed.), *Conversion to Islam* (London 1979), which brings together studies of Islamization from many areas of the Islamic world and is an important step towards the comparative study of the subject.

Southeast Asia: The best introduction to this period is H. de Graaf, "South-East Asian Islam in the Eighteenth Century" in *The Cambridge History of Islam* vol. two. Unfortunately most other work is locked away in journal articles (see the excellent bibliographies in Nehemia Levtzion's *Conversion to Islam*), of which those by S. M. al-Attas, G. W. J. Drewes and A. H. Johns should be noted in particular. Two important books by S. M. al-Attas deal with aspects of sufism in Aceh, *The Mysticism of Hamza al-Fansuri* (Kuala Lumpur 1970) and *Raniri and the Wujudiyah* (Kuala Lumpur 1966).

Africa: The study of Islam in Africa, particularly West Africa, has seen an explosion of activity over the last 20 years. The most useful starting points are syntheses of recent scholarship to be found in *The Cambridge History of Islam* vol. two; J. F. A. Ajayi and M. Crowder, *A History of West Africa* vol. one (London 1971); R. Oliver (ed.) *The Cambridge History of Africa* vol. three, c.1050–c.1600 (Cambridge 1977), and R. Gray (ed.), *The Cambridge History of Africa* vol. four, c.1600–c.1870 (Cambridge 1975). Thomas Hodgkin (ed.), *Nigerian Perspectives: an Historical Anthology* (2nd edn; London 1975), offers a lively collection of documents. Islamic art in Africa is so far poorly served. R A. Bravmann, *Islam and Tribal Art in West Africa* (London 1974), makes a brave start; for architecture one must turn to the brief survey in George Michell (ed.), *Architecture of the Islamic World: its History and Social Meaning* (London 1978). Turning to Morocco, Jamil M. Abun-Nasr provides an outstanding introduction in *A History of the Maghreb* (2nd edn; Cambridge 1975). Anthony Hurt offers a pleasant introduction to Moroccan architecture in the context of that of North Africa generally in *North Africa: Islamic Architecture* (London 1977), which can be followed in greater detail in Derek Hill and L. Golvin, *Islamic Architecture in North Africa* (London 1976).

Central Asia and China: Most work on Islam in Central Asia is in Russian. B. Spuler, "Central Asia from the Sixteenth Century to the Russian Conquests," *The Cambridge History of Islam* vol. one, and G. Hambly (ed.), *Central Asia* (London 1978), present the most accessible introductions. Coverage of Islamic architecture in the region after 1500 can be found in: M. Hrbas and F. Knobloch (trans. R. Finlayson-Samsour), *The Art of Central Asia* (London 1965), K. Gink and K. Gombos, *The Pearls of Uzbekistan* (Budapest 1976). Muslims in China are even more poorly served than those in Central Asia, and for this period R. Israeli, *Muslims in China: a Study of Cultural Confrontation* (London 1980), stands alone.

Decline, Reform, and Revival in the 18th and 19th Centuries

The ebbing of Muslim power: This is usually presaged in the works which deal with the great empires at their height. To those for Iran should be added two works by Laurence Lockhart, *Nadir Shah* (London 1938) and *The Fall of the Safavi Dynasty and the Afghan Occupation of Persia* (Cambridge 1958); for the decline of the Mughal empire, "Symposium: Decline of the Mughal Empire," *Journal of Asian Studies*, February 1976, is a good starting point; to the works on the Ottoman empire might be added the short essay by Bernard Lewis, "Ottoman Observers of Ottoman Decline," in Bernard Lewis, *Islam in History: Ideas, Men and Events in the Middle East* (London 1973).

Reform and Revival: There is no overall treatment of this process at the moment. Fazlur Rahman offers a brief introduction in *Islam* (London 1966). Suggestive articles are: J. Joll, "Muhammad Hayya alSindi and Muhammad Ibn Abd al-Wahhab: an Analysis of an Intellectual Group in Eighteenth-Century Medina," *Bulletin of the School of Oriental and African Studies*, part one, 1975, which examines the major school of *Hadiths* at Medina and those who studied at it; Hamid Algar, "The Naqshbandi Order: a Preliminary Survey of its History and Significance," *Studia Islamica*, vol. 44, and A. Hourani, "Shaikh Khalid and the Naqshbandi Order" in Samuel M. Stern, A. Hourani and V. Brown (eds.), *Islamic Philosophy and the Classical Tradition* (Columbia, S.C. 1973), which both illustrate the international connections of the Naqshbandiya and their significance for the revival; and B. G. Martin, "A Short History of the Khalwati Order of Dervishes" in N. R. Keddie, *Scholars, Saints and Sufis: Muslim Religious Institutions in the Middle East since 1500* (Los Angeles, Calif. 1972). The story of the rise of the first Saudi–Wahhabi empire is told succinctly by G. Rentz, "Wahhabism and Saudi Arabia" in D. Hopwood (ed.), *The Arabian Peninsula* (London 1972). W. R. Roff, "South-East Asian Islam in the Nineteenth Century," *The Cambridge History of Islam* vol. two, describes the three movements of holy war; Peter Carey, *Babab Dipanagara* (Kuala Lumpur 1981), offers the first detailed treatment in English of any of these movements. For a brief discussion of the revivalist movements in India see Peter Hardy, *The Muslims of British India* (Cambridge 1972).

For the movement in the Caucasus see Lesley Blanch's romantic study of Imam Shamil, *The Sabres of Paradise* (London 1960; reissued 1978). For a Russian view see Tolstoy's study of Shamil's deputy "Hadji Murad" in Leo Tolstoy, *The Death of Ivan Ilych and Other Stories* (London 1935). For the movement in China see Israeli, *Muslims in China*, and the very early Marshall Broomhall, *Islam in China: a Neglected Problem* (London 1910). For the movement in Africa, in addition to the chapters in the general histories recommended for "The Further Islamic Lands," there is a valuable series of studies in Bradford G. Martin, *Muslim Brotherhoods in Nineteenth-Century Africa* (Cambridge 1976); Martin is concerned to emphasize the interconnections of the movements. In addition, there are three excellent monographs: P. M. Holt, *The Mahdist State in the Sudan 1881–1898: a Study of its Origins, Development and Overthrow* (2nd edn; Oxford 1970); E. E. EvansPritchard, *The Sanusi of Cyrenaica* (Oxford 1949); M. Hiskett, *The Sword of Truth: the Life and Times of the Shehu Usuman dan Fodio* (New York 1973).

The Rise of Europe and the Response of Islam until the mid-20th Century

M. G. S. Hodgson, "The Islamic Heritage in the Modern World," book six of his *Venture of Islam* vol. three, provides an introduction to the period full of ideas. Bernard Lewis, *The Emergence of Modern Turkey* (2nd edn; London 1968), remains the best study of the transition from Ottoman empire to modern Turkey. For the Ataturk period it is usefully supplemented by a popular biography, Lord Kinross, *Ataturk: the Rebirth of a Nation* (London 1964). P. J. Vatikiotis, *The History of Egypt* (2nd edn; London 1980), achieves for Egypt what Lewis has for Turkey. But see also R. P. Mitchell, *The Society of the Muslim Brothers* (London 1969). Two autobiographies offer fascinating insights into Egyptian society and the stresses of modernization: Ahmad Amin (trans. I. J. Boullata), *My Life* (Leiden 1978), and the three volumes of the autobiography of Taha Hussein, a blind man who became Egypt's minister of education, *An Egyptian Childhood* (trans. F. H. Paxton; London 1981), *The Stream of Days, a Student at the Azhar* (trans. H. Wayment; 2nd edn, London 1948), and *A Passage to France* (trans. K. Cragg; Leiden 1976). A. H. Hourani, in *Arabic Thought in the Liberal Age 1798–1939* (London 1962), has written the authoritative account of the emergence of Arab nationalist thought, and for the later period Sylvia G. Haim, *Arab Nationalism; an Anthology* (Berkeley, Calif. 1962), should also be consulted. For the emergence

of Saudi Arabia see H. St J. Philby, *Saudi Arabia* (London 1955); J. S. Habib, *Ibn Saud's Warriors of Islam: the Ikhwan of Najd and their Role in the Creation of the Saudi Kingdom, 1910–1930* (Leiden 1978), is a valuable study of the militant religious organization which helped to bring Abd al-Azis Ibn Saud to power. Robert Lacey, *The Kingdom* (London 1981), is an accessible overview. Iran is well served with surveys of its recent history. There is A. K. S. Lambton, "Persia: the Breakdown of Society," and R. M. Savory, "Modern Persia," in *The Cambridge History of Islam* vol. two; moreover, N. R. Keddie, the leading scholar of modern Iran, has recently published *Roots of Revolution: an Interpretive History of Modern Iran* (New Haven, Conn. 1981). Nevertheless, the classic work on the first Iranian revolution should not be missed: Edward G. Browne, *The Persian Revolution of 1905–1909* (Cambridge 1910). For south Asia, P Hardy, *The Muslims of British India* (Cambridge 1972), is the established general history of the 19th and 20th centuries, as is Aziz Ahmad, *Islamic Modernism in India and Pakistan 1 857–1964* (London 1967), for the development of Islamic thought. For different aspects of Muslim responses to British rule see: C. W. Troll, *Sayyid Ahmad Khan: a Reinterpretation of Muslim Theology* (New Delhi 1978); D. Lelyveld, *Aligarh's First Generation: Muslim Solidarity in British India* (Princeton, N.J. 1978); F. Robinson, *Separatism Among Indian Muslims: the Politics of the United Provinces' Muslims 1860–1923* (Cambridge 1974). The best introductions to 19th- and 20th-century Islam in southeast Asia remain: W. R. Roff, "South-East Asian Islam in the Nineteenth Century" and H. J. Benda, "South-East Asian Islam in the Twentieth Century" in *The Cambridge History of Islam* vol. two. D. Noer, *The Modernist Muslim Movement in Indonesia 1900–42* (Singapore 1973), studies the progress of the movement. M Ricklefs, *A History of Modern Indonesia* (London 1981), is the most recent overview. There is relatively little work on Islam in Africa south of the Sahara in recent times: under colonial rule leadership fell into the hands of Christians and pagans. See J. S. Trimingham, *The Influence of Islam upon Africa* (London 1968); two surveys of specific societies, P. M. Holt, *A Modern History of the Sudan* (3rd edn; London 1967), and I. M. Lewis, *The Modern History of Somaliland from Nation to State* (London 1965); also Donal Cruise O'Brien's, *The Mounds of Senegal: The Political and Economic Organization of an Islamic Brotherhood* (Oxford 1971), which reveals how a sufi order found a major role to play in economic modernization. For North Africa, see again J. M. Abun-Nasr, *A History of the Maghrib*. Scholars have begun to study in detail the responses of *ulama* and sufis to the rise of European rule and the modern state. A few works must serve as guides: N. R. Keddie (ed.), *Scholars, Saints and Sufis*, and *An Islamic Response to Imperialism: Political and Religious Writings of Sayyzd Jamal ad-Din "al-Afghani"* (Berkeley, Calif. 1968), S Akhavi, *Religion and Politics in Contemporary Iran: Clergy State Relations in the Pahlavi Period* (Albany, N.Y. 1980), D. Green, *The Tunisian Ulama* (Leiden nd.). For brief introductions to the position of Islam and the *Sharia* in the modern state see: Erwin I. J. Rosenthal, *Islam in the Modern National State* (Cambridge 1965), and N J. Coulson. *A History of Islamic Law*. H. A. R. Gibb's lectures, *Modern Trends in Islam* (Chicago, Ill. 1947), remain stimulating.

Part II: To Be a Muslim

Religious Life

The best way to understand the Islamic life, the joy it can bring as well as the constant tensions between human desire and right conduct, lies in reading novels and biographies. Cragg and Speight's anthology, *Islam from Within*, is revealing, so is Constance Padwick's remarkable collection of Muslim prayers from throughout the world, *Muslim Devotions: a Study of Prayer-Manuals in Common Use* (London 1961), and so is Martin Lings, *A Sufi Saint of the Twentieth Century* (2nd edn; London 1971). Anthropologists have done much to reveal the activities and functions of sufi orders, for example, Ernest Gellner, *Saints of the Atlas* (Chicago, Ill. and London 1969), and Michael Gilsenan, *Saint and SuJI in Modern Egypt* (Oxford 1973). V. Crapanzano, *The Hamadsha: a Study in Moroccan Ethnopsychiatry* (Berkeley, Calif. 1973), examines the possession cults which are so often associated with sufi shrines. Muslim rites and festivals are explained simply by Riadh el-Droubie and Edward Hulmes, *Islam* (London 1980); G. E. von Grunebaum, *Muhammadan Festivals* (London 1976), studies them in greater detail. The pilgrimage, as befits the highpoint of religious life, has attracted most specific attention. C. Snouck Hurgronje, the Dutch scholar–administrator, who visited Mecca in disguise in the early 1880s, wrote a classic study (trans. J. H. Monahan), *Mekka in the Latter Part of the 19th Century* (Leiden and London 1931). It is not an infrequent practice to keep a journal of one's pilgrimage and these offer valuable insights:

H.H. Nawab Sultan Jahan Begum (trans. Mrs Willoughby-Osborne), *The Story of a Pilgrimage to Hijaz* (Calcutta 1909); H. T. Norris (trans. and ed.), *The Pilgrimage of Ahmad ... an Account of a 19thCentury Pilgrimage from Mauritania to Mecca* (Warminster 1977). Malcolm X, with the assistance of Alex Haley, *The Autobiography of Malcolm X* (New York 1965, London 1966), tells how the experience transformed his racial outlook. Modern illustrated books can project moving images of the spectacle of the pilgrimage and the spiritual intensity it generates; see Emel Esin, *Mecca the Blessed, Madinah the Radiant* (London 1963), and E. Guellouz and A. Frikha, *Mecca: the Muslim Pilgrimage* (London 1977). Serious study of the pilgrimage as the greatest annual international meeting in the world over 14 centuries has also begun; see D. E. Long. *The Hajj Today: a Survey of the Contemporary Makkah Pilgrimage* (Albany, N.Y. 1979), and Umar al-Naqar, *The Pilgrimage Tradition in West Africa* (Khartoum 1972). Finally, there is the autobiography of a German Jew who, as a newspaper correspondent in Arabia in the 1920s, slowly absorbed the Muslim vision of life; it is the moving self-analysis of a perceptive and intelligent European as he journeys into a Muslim consciousness: Muhammad Asad, *The Road to Mecca* (London 1954).

Arts of Islam

Titus Burckhardt's *Art of Islam* offers a sensitive introduction to the relationship between Islam and Islamic art forms. The most comprehensive introduction to calligraphy is Y. H. Safadi, *Islamic Calligraphy* (London 1978), which can be supplemented by Annemarie Schimmel, *Islamic Calligraphy* (Leiden 1970), which carries this fine scholar's especial sufistic angle of vision. For much Moroccan calligraphy, which is not widely known, and for many very beautiful plates, see A. Khatibi and M. Sijelmassi (trans. J. Hughes), *The Splendour of Islamic Calligraphy* (New York 1977). Few works have been devoted to ceramics alone. David Talbot Rice, *Islamic Art* (London 1965), offers a very simple introduction to the context of Islamic art in general. There is also Arthur Lane, *Later Islamic Pottery* (London 1957). Some of the achievement in Iran can be gleaned from Arthur U. Pope's *Survey of Persian Art*, and some of that in Turkey from O. Aslanapa, *Turkish Art*, and Tahsin Oz, *Turkish Ceramics* (Ankara 1957). Books on carpets and rugs, on the other hand, are legion. K. H. Turkhan offers a brief introduction from

his long experience in the trade, *Islamic Rugs* (London 1968). Useful wide-ranging treatments are: Jurt Erdmann (trans. C. G. Ellis), *Oriental Carpets, an Account of their History* (London 1961), and R. de Calatchi (trans. V. Howard), *Oriental Carpets* (2nd edn; Rutland, Vt. 1970). On tribal rugs, Jenny Housego, *Tribal Rugs: an Introduction to the Weaving of the Tribes of Iran* (London 1978), is excellent.

Society and the Modern World

Studies of nomadic tribes are plentiful. Important recent studies include: Fredrik Barth, *Nomads of South Persia: the Basseri Tribe of the Khamseh Confederacy* (Oslo 1961, New York 1965), Daniel G. Bates, *Nomads and Farmers: a Study of the Yoruk of Southeastern Turkey* (Ann Arbor, Mich. 1973), T. Asad, *The Kababish Arabs: Power, Authority and Consent in a Nomadic Tribe* (London 1970), D. P. Cole, *Nomads of the Nomads: the Al Murrah Bedouin of the Empty Quarter* (Chicago, Ill. 1975), and C. Nelson (ed.), *The Desert and the Sown: Nomads in Wider Society* (Berkeley, Calif. 1973). Isaaq Diqs, *A Bedouin Boyhood* (Oxford 1969), gives a first-hand account of growing up Bedouin in Jordan. John S. Habib, *Ibn Saud's Warriors* (Leiden 1978). and E. E. Evans-Pritchard, *The Sanusi of Cyrenaica* (Oxford 1949), illustrate the role nomads could play in making modern states. M. E. Meeker, *Literature and Violence in North Arabia* (Cambridge 1979), is an important recent book on pastoral nomadism and states. Moving to the village world, Joe E. Pierce, *Life in a Turkish Village* (New York 1964), is a straightforward account of growing up in a village; Hamed M. Ammar, *Growing up in an Egyptian Village: Silwa, Province of Aswan* (London 1954), is a classic. Village life can be savored in Z. S. Eglar, A *Punjabi Village in Pakistan* (New York 1960), and Robert A. Fernea, *Shaykh and Effendi: Changing Patterns of Authority among the El Shabana of Southern Iraq* (Cambridge, Mass. 1970). Literature also provides a way in to village life; see the novels of Yashar Kemal, for instance *Memed my Hawk* (London 1961), and V. M. Basheer (trans. R. E. Asher and A. C. Chandersekaran), *Me Grandad 'ad an Elephant!* (Edinburgh 1980). Regarding the Muslim town, an influential essay has been G. E. von Grunebaum's "The Structure of the Muslim Town" in his *Islam: Essays in the Nature and Growth of a Cultural Tradition* (Chicago, Ill, and London 1955). Three important collections of essays have appeared in recent years: A. H. Hourani and S. M. Stern (eds.), *The Islamic City* (Oxford 1970), I. M. Lapidus (ed.), *Middle Eastern Studies*

(Berkeley, Calif. 1969), and L. Carl Brown (ed.), *From Madina to Metropolis* (Princeton, N.J. 1973). J. L. Abu-Lughud, *Cairo: 1001 Years of the City Victorious* (Princeton, N.J. 1971), and F. 1. Khuri, *From Village to Suburb: Order and Change in Greater Beirut* (Chicago, 111. 1975), are important new studies. Again, novels can tell us much about life itself: Najib Mahfuz (trans. T. Le Gassick), *Midaq Alley* (London 1975), is based in Cairo, and Ahmed Ali, *Twilight in Delhi* (2nd edn; Bombay 1966), takes place in the old Mughal city. A. H. Sharar (trans. E. S. Harcourt and F. Hussain), *Lucknow: the Last Phase of an Oriental Culture* (London 1975), is a marvelous description of the persianate urban culture of this north Indian city. For houses, Guy T. Petherbridge. "Vernacular Architecture: the House and Society" in George Michell (ed.), *Architecture of the Islamic World: its History and Social Meaning* (London 1978), is a good introduction with a useful bibliography. See also James S. Kirkman (ed.), *City of Sanaa: Exhibition Catalogue* (London 1976). There is an outline of the traditional position of women in Islam in Reuben Levy, *The Social Structure of Islam* (Cambridge 1957). Charis Waddy, *Women in Muslim History* (London 1980), offers a survey of the power and achievement of Muslim women. C. Nelson, "Public and Private Politics: Women in the Middle Eastern World," *American Ethnologist*, August 1974, reviews the handling of women as a subject in ethnographic accounts. E. W. Fernea and B. Q. Bezirgan (eds.). *Middle Eastern Muslim Women Speak* (Austin, Texas 1977), and C. Beck and N. Keddie (eds.) *Women in the Muslim World* (Cambridge, Mass. 1978), are two outstanding recent surveys. The case for the position of women in Islam as traditionally understood is argued in B. Aisha Lemu and Fatima Heeren, *Woman in Islam* (London 1976). The argument that Muslim family mores and assumptions are fundamentally opposed to the equality of women is put forward with great passion by Fatima Mernissi. *Beyond the Veil: Male–Female Dynamics in a Modern Muslim Society* (New York 1975). Two books reveal the horrors Muslim women can suffer: L. P. Sanderson. *Against the Mutilation of Women* (London 1981), which deals with female circumcision, and Ian Young, *The Private Life of Islam* (London 1974), which is set in an Algerian obstetric hospital, and is definitely not reading for the squeamish. It is instructive to read the autobiographical works of women who have "beaten" the system: H. H. Nawab Sultan Jahan Begum, *An Account of my Life* (vol. one trans. C. H. Payne, London 1910; vol. two trans. A. S. Khan, Bombay 1922); Halide Edib, *Memoirs* (London 1926); Begum Ikramullah, *From Purdah to Parliament* (London 1963). Literature is again valuable. Some of the work of Assia Djeber, the prominent Algerian woman novelist, can be found in L. Ortzen (ed. and trans.), *North African Writing* (London 1970). The novel by Attia Hosain, first woman graduate from a north Indian *taluqdari* or landowning family, *Sunlight on a Broken Column* (London 1961), which depicts the stresses of changing values for an educated woman against the background of the Indian independence movement, is excellent.

Index